A
Vast Army
of Women:

Maine's Uncounted Forces
in the American Civil War

Lynda L. Sudlow

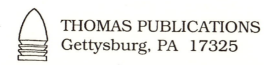

THOMAS PUBLICATIONS
Gettysburg, PA 17325

Copyright © 2000 Lynda L. Sudlow

Printed and bound in the United States of America

Published by THOMAS PUBLICATIONS
P.O. Box 3031
Gettysburg, Pa. 17325

Cover design by Ryan C. Stouch.

Cataloging-in-Publication Data:

Sudlow, Lynda L.
A Vast army of women: Maine's uncounted forces in the American Civil War/Lynda L. Sudlow.
272 p.   15.25 x 22.9 cm.
Includes bibliographical references and index.
ISBN-1-57747-049-4
1. United States—History—Civil War, 1861-1865—Women.   2. Maine—History—Civil War, 1861-1865—Women.   I. Title.
973.78—dc20

For all the noble women of the war and Spruce,
who encouraged and assisted me throughout.

Contents

Acknowledgments

There were many friends and associates whose information and research helped to complete this project. I would especially like to thank Spruce Whited who supported me every step of the way and shared the adventure of searching for the clues which uncovered information related to the contributions of Maine women to the war effort.

I would also like to thank historian and author Tom Desjardin; Bill Barry, Stephanie Philbrick and Nick Noyes of the Maine Historical Society Library; the staff of the Maine State Archives, (especially Sylvia Sherman); Paul D'Alessandro and Kathy Berry at the Portland Public Library; Eric Jorgensen of the Pejepscot Historical Society; SueAnn Gaitings and Bruce Moore of the Bangor Historical Society; the families of Mary Cotton, Emeline Rose, Addie Jackson, Mehitable Young, Isabella Fogg, Amanda Kimball, and Elizabeth Piper Cooper Bent; Charles Coleman, who shared letters sent by Harriet Wright to his soldier-ancestor; Faye Greenleaf of the Lynn Historical Society; Jack Chisholm of the McArthur Library; researchers and reenactors Cyndi and Pete Dalton, Lee Dionne, Kathy Kleiman, Judy Bielecki, and Ron Waddell; and the staff of the United States Army Military History Institute Library (especially the photographic department).

Others who helped uncover information were Noah and Athena Myers; the staff at the Evergreen Cemetery office (especially Beverly Pelletier); historian and author William Jordan who provided me with many leads over the course of my research; Ronald DiNinni; and my mother, who critiqued the manuscript in its early stages.

I am extremely grateful to all who encouraged me and provided me with clues, references to newspaper and journal articles, rumors, and more, which all added to the end product.

Sally Thomas and Jim Thomas also provided invaluable suggestions and assistance in bringing this project to its final form.

My sincerest thanks,
Lyn Sudlow

Preface

The idea for this book grew from my realization that very little has been written about the lives of the women who were involved in the American Civil War. Certainly there were exceptions such as Dorothea Dix, Clara Barton, Elizabeth Blackwell, and a few others, but there is next to nothing about thousands of other American women who also took an active role in the war.

My initial research revealed that there were a great number of women who had been forgotten in the last century, including women from my own adopted state of Maine. Both Linus Brockett's *Woman's Work in the Civil War* and Frank Moore's *Women of the War* included the names of many Maine women. The *Maine Adjutant General's Report* also mentioned several women. Other names appeared in newspapers from the wartime years; friends and other researchers gave me leads when they ran across information or names of women while doing their own research. Descendants contacted me and asked if I knew about their great-aunt or grandmother, and some names I stumbled across purely by accident. Thus began my list of names—names of Maine women who left home, risked life and limb, and took an active role in the war effort.

I included many women who might justifiably be claimed by other states, but all had some concrete Maine connection. Discovering more women's names to add to the list was not hard. Locating information about the lives of these women was much more difficult. I searched through town histories, records at the Maine Historical Society, the Maine State Archives, and the National Archives. I scoured many reels of microfilm containing images of newspapers from the 1860s and beyond, census records, vital statistics, and many other sources. In some cases little can be found; in others we may never find more than a mention that the woman even existed. Unfortunately, the record will never be complete.

Although we will never know the full extent of the tremendous effort put forth by 19th century women during the war, I hope that the combination of photos, firsthand accounts, and background information will give readers a better grasp of this oft-neglected aspect of the war.

Longer passages quoted from primary sources are indented and set in smaller a type size. Spelling and punctuation within quotes were copied as originally written. If I added words to the text of such quotes to clarify statements, I enclosed them in brackets[ ].

We cannot allow these women or their work to be forgotten. Nor can we allow our students to forget that the events of the American Civil War affected all the citizens of our land—male and female, black and white, whether they fought in battles or not. Fortunately, today more research is being done concerning women's activities during the war. I hope this book will be a worthy addition.

Lynda L. Sudlow
1999

Photo credit abbreviations used in this book:

MHPC	Maine Historic Preservation Commission, Augusta, Maine.
Maine Hist. Soc.	Maine Historical Society, Portland, Maine.
NY Pub. Lib.	U.S. Sanitary Commission Collection. Manuscripts and Archives, New York Public Library.
USAMHI	Massachusetts Commandery Military Order of the Loyal Legion and the U.S. Army Military History Institute, Carlisle, Pennsylvania.

THE
UNION
IS
DISSOLVED!

Passed unanimously at 1.15 o'clock, P. M., December 20th, 1860.

AN ORDINANCE

To dissolve the Union between the State of South Carolina and other States united with her under the compact entitled " The Constitution of the United States of America."

We, the People of the State of South Carolina, in Convention assembled, do declare and ordain, and it is hereby declared and ordained,

That the Ordinance adopted by us in Convention, on the twenty-third day of May, in the year of our Lord one thousand seven hundred and eighty-eight, whereby the Constitution of the United States of America was ratified, and also, all Acts and parts of Acts of the General Assembly of this State, ratifying amendments of the said Constitution, are hereby repealed; and that the union now subsisting between South Carolina and other States, under the name of " The United States of America," is hereby dissolved.

CHARLESTON
MERCURY
EXTRA

The Union is Dissolved! Front page from the Charleston Mercury Extra.

Chapter 1

The Union is Dissolved!

> The people are thoroughly aroused, and the war spirit pre-
> vails extensively. There is a great call for American flags, and
> numerous buildings are ornamented with the stars and
> stripes... Gov. Washburn is daily receiving offers of men and
> money, and the indications are that the ranks will be immedi-
> ately filled. Two companies from Portland, and two from
> Eastport, have already been promised, and from Biddeford,
> Gardiner, Ellsworth, Belfast and many other places, letters have
> been received showing the action of the Legislature is only re-
> quired to secure large enlistments.[1]

The response of Maine citizens to news that war had erupted
between the northern and the southern states of America was immediate and electric. The Confederate firing upon the federally held
Fort Sumter in the harbor of Charleston, South Carolina, on April
12, 1861, caused President Lincoln to call for 75,000 troops to defend
the Union. The news quickly reached every Maine town and in a
matter of days large and stirring patriotic rallies were held throughout the state pledging to crush the rebellion.

In Rockland, Maine, the response was recorded by historian
and author Cyrus Eaton who wrote, "...when April 17th, news arrived of the attack and capture of that fortress and the nation's flag
desecrated by the infatuated rebels of Charleston, S.C., one burst of
indignation arose from the whole population of the city."[2]

The *Lewiston Daily Evening Journal* reported an "Immense
Union Meeting! — Thousands of our Citizens in Council! — A
United Voice!":

> Central Hall was the scene of a most enthusiastic gather-
> ing on Saturday evening last, to take into consideration the ex-
> isting affairs of the nation. Every available spot in the Hall was
> filled, and the interest felt in the proceedings surpassed any-
> thing we ever witnessed....[3]

In Portland the display of the Stars and Stripes increased to
such a degree that manufacturers could not keep pace with the de-

mand. Several prominent businessmen of the area raised large flags above their establishments. "Mr. H. H. Hay also threw a beautiful flag across Middle street from his druggist shop at the junction of Middle and Free streets, which Lieut. Fessenden, with a detachment of the Light Guard, saluted with 34 guns." A flag staff 90 feet high was erected at the foot of High Street by Portland merchants who "are now animated by one common sentiment and love of country. The ladies have prepared a flag, and this afternoon at 3 o'clock it will be spread to the winds, amid a salute and music by the Portland Band."[4] The following day the *Eastern Argus* reported:

> Our city is alive with enthusiasm. Never before has such a time been known. Citizens of all classes and occupations are aroused to the importance of the crisis and businesses and every thing else gives way to the feelings inspired. Nothing else is talked of in streets or in families but the war and the latest intelligence is looked for with the utmost anxiety.[5]

That spring the people had more cause for anxiety than they could possibly imagine. Even though the previous December the *Charleston Mercury* of Charleston, South Carolina, had proclaimed in grand headlines, "The Union is Dissolved!" most felt the conflict would soon be resolved and the Union reunited.

Just four months previous, the *Brunswick Telegraph* responded to South Carolina's secession with the following ho-hum comment buried on page three:

> South Carolina has just voted itself out of the Union on Thursday the 20th, and then appointed a Commission of three to proceed to Washington and treat with the U.S. government in regard to the separation... The Senate and House Committees are at work, attempting to compromise the troubles between the South and the North, but no progress has as yet been made in either Committee... The only change is there is less excitement at Washington and elsewhere, and the money market is improving at the North. So much for Secession.[6]

By April 1861, however, six more southern states had seceded. A peaceful solution seemed far less likely. The troublesome issues of slavery and secession could no longer be solved through negotiations and compromise. The bombardment of Fort Sumter was a turning point which set off a war that would last four long years. Methods of warfare, medical treatment, transportation, and communication all changed drastically in those same four years. More Americans would lose their lives in this civil war than in all other American wars combined. The tragedy and horror of that time still fascinates and haunts the nation and was a pivotal event in our history.

In a fictional story, Samuel Langhorne Clemens (Mark Twain) commented, "Eight years are not many in the life of a nation or the history of a state but they may be years of destiny that shall fix the current of the century following. Such years were those that followed the double-shotted demand for the surrender of Fort Sumter."[7] His words about this war which still fascinates and haunts the nation were prophetic. The war would bring immense changes to the political and social structure of both the North and the South, regardless of the outcome.

But for most Northerners in early 1861 the thought was only to put down the rebellion and preserve the Union. Few believed the "war" would last more than a few months. There was little to

(Maine Hist. Soc.)

dampen the patriotic zeal so pervasive that spring. Even the state of Maine, as far away from the center of conflict as it was, found itself caught up in the emotional fervor. From the first news of the attack on Fort Sumter, Mainers threw themselves into the patriotic frenzy.

Eager to put down the rebellion, men immediately formed military companies. On April 25, 1861, the *Lewiston Daily Evening Journal* reported that the "Lewiston Zouave Riflemen looked admirable in their drill work;" the "Milo Piscataquis Artillery Co." was preparing for duty; and a recruiting office had opened to recruit for the "Lewiston Light Guards." They also printed a list of members of the "Lewiston Pioneers" who had volunteered, and a list of the men in the "Auburn Artillery." Similar reports appeared in papers throughout the state.

In Auburn, a document was drawn up which stated, "We the undersigned old patriots of Auburn freely offer our services in the cause of the Union, and respectfully offer our services as a volunteer company." The first signature was that of Amos Kyle, 69 years old and a veteran of the War of 1812.[8]

Women, too, rushed to volunteer their services. That same Lewiston paper which listed the formation of so many companies also reported, "The following noble and patriotic daughters of Maine, have tendered their services to the Governor, to serve as nurses to the Regiments from this State. Their names should be treasured by the brave:– Charlotte Z. McKay, Auburn; Hattie C. Weymouth, Lewiston; Lavina Lenfest, do [ditto]; Anna R. Works, do."

The paper went on to note the "Philanthropy and patriotism of the Ladies of Auburn" who were now holding meetings with the objective of providing, "as far as was in their power to do, for the comfort of the soldiers who are about leaving us to participate in the impending conflict." Their dedication was repeated in towns throughout Maine.

When Dr. Alonzo Garcelon, who had just been appointed Surgeon General of the Maine Volunteer Militia, asked for nurses to serve with the 1st Maine Regiment, the response was: "Prompt to the minute, fifty ladies residing in this place [Lewiston] offered their services, and great disappointment was expressed by those who were not fortunate to be selected to make up the twenty [needed], that they would be obliged to remain behind."[9]

Many Maine women sought to serve their country on the homefront or as nurses and laundresses with the troops. Despite the desperate need for such services, women met with a great deal of resistance. The accepted role for 19th century women was caretaker of home and family. Few ventured out to earn money. Because the concept of a female nurse was practically unheard of before the war, nursing positions were hard to obtain, even for volunteers. But the precedent had been set by an English woman named Florence Nightingale. Her service during the Crimean War had been invaluable and her book, *Notes on Nursing* was commonly read by women throughout the United States. Her example gave women the courage and the inspiration to follow the troops to the battlefields.

A few women managed to attach themselves to some of the early regimental units serving as field nurses like the 20 women from Lewiston. Isabella Fogg and Amy Bradley are two who managed that feat. Both later transferred into other services. Many women tried in vain to find out about positions in the army hospitals. Rebecca Usher only found out about a position at the hospital in Chester, Pennsylvania, because a friend had contacted her. She was lucky. Some women traveled all the way to Washington to apply for a nursing position with Dorothea Dix, Superintendent of Army Nurses, only to be rejected because they were too young or not plain enough to suit Superintendent Dix's standards.

As the war progressed, two large civilian organizations, the United States Sanitary Commission and the United States Christian Commission, were created. Women could apply to those organizations for positions as nurses and relief agents. State officials, too, began to recognize the great need to care for its citizen-soldiers and began advertising for female nurses to serve with the state agencies.

A Mrs. VanHorne responded on October 5, 1862, to Governor Washburn's call: "I have been informed on good authority that you have decided to appoint assistant female nurses in our camp hospitals." She described in full how very qualified she was. "[I] have healthy nerves, strong back, never fainted in all my life, never had a fever, & am not subject to them, can endure a great deal of fatigue without complaint, have studied medicine & am called a good nurse by those who ought to be judges, & more than all your excellency my whole heart & soul & life is in this work."[10] Despite her excellent qualifications there is no record to indicate Mrs. VanHorne actually received an appointment.

Mary Abigail Dodge, using her pen-name of Gail Hamilton, urged women to get involved in a less direct manner. She wrote in the *Atlantic Monthly,* "Urge them [the men] to the offering," she wrote, "fill them with sacred fury; fire them with irresistible desire; strengthen them to heroic will."[11] Many had already done so. When one woman learned her husband had enlisted with the Lewiston Light Artillery, she wrote to him, "Dear Elijah-Yesterday was the 9th anniversary of our wedding day. I thank God for the happy years we have spent together. Go! and may God's blessing go with you as do mine. Trust in the God of Battles, and be a true Christian soldier. Good bye; and may God speed the right!"[12]

Leaving home and family to care for complete strangers was a radical move for 19th century women, but there were those who stepped much farther beyond conventional boundaries. Some women managed to fight for the Union cause as soldiers.

For men, enlistment in the Union army was easy. Physical examinations were so perfunctory that many who should never have been accepted were freely mustered into service. Frederick Law Olmsted, executive director of the United States Sanitary Commission, was forced to plead with the various state governors (including the governor of Maine) to provide more thorough examinations. On August 17, 1861 he wrote:

> To his Excellency,
> Israel Washburn, Governor of the State of Maine.
> The attention of your Excellency is most respectfully called to the importance of a thorough physical examination of men offering to volunteer. It is quite impossible for any but perfectly sound, tough, and strong men to endure the privations, fatigue and exposure to which soldiers under our present Army Regulations, must be subject, without great suffering to themselves, and loss to the nation. It is not doubted that if our army had been entirely composed of such men, the result of the late disastrous battle at Bull's Run, would have been wholly different. That the inspection of recruits has been, hitherto, very inadequate, there is, unfortunately, too much evidence. For instance, twenty-two men have been discharged since the battle, on account of Hernia, from a single regiment....[13]

Slipshod exams allowed many women to disguise themselves as men and pass without their gender being detected. Nationally, over 400 cases of women serving as soldiers are known. Undoubtedly there were many more undocumented cases. Rumors have surfaced about such Maine women soldiers. Abner Small, adjutant of the 16th Maine Infantry, wrote in his history of that regiment:

The members of the Sixteenth were not all of the masculine persuasion. Company I boasted of the presence of one of the gentler sex in the ranks, who did good service at Fredericksburgh.

He further relates the story of Mary Jane Johnson which appeared, he says, in the *Richmond Whig*. The story was picked up and repeated in several papers. She was supposedly captured at Fredericksburg (December 13, 1862) and sent to Belle Isle Prison where she revealed her identity and was exchanged.[14]

In another instance, although unlikely that this woman actually went to the front, the *Portland Transcript* made the following note on July 25, 1863:

> A lady was drafted in Lewiston! Her name was given to the enrolling officer, at her boarding house, as Frank Parker (her Christian name being Frances) and she was accordingly enrolled, and happened to be drawn.[15]

Mrs. VanHorne asserted in her letter to Governor Washburn dated October 5, 1862, that if she could not get an appointment as a nurse, "I will go with the help of Heaven if I deny my sex by adopting your dress & begging my way to the sick & wounded & dying of our brave volunteers, God help me!"[16]

Ira Gardner, who wrote his memoirs including his time with the 14th Maine Infantry Regiment, said:

> One of the recruits who enlisted at New Orleans proved to be a woman and did duty until about the close of the war. She was small and slightly built and for that reason was excused from some heavy fatigue duty. She was very plain looking and had informed me that she had worked at tailoring; and she used to do mending for me very nicely. She enlisted in New Orleans with her lover and was with him until discharged from the service. I did not learn of her sex till the close of the war. If I had been anything but a boy I should probably have seen from her form that she was a female.[17]

Although Ira excuses his oversight due to his being a mere boy, he was probably 21 at the time. Far more likely is Lauren Burgess' explanation that the men were simply not expecting to see a woman in soldier's clothing and therefore did not.[18]

One other woman who may have disguised herself as a soldier was Mary Brown of Brownfield, Maine. She said, "I carried a musket—a 16 shooter, and a sword and a dirk, too, to fight my way through like the rest of them."[19] Although she did not say she was disguised, General Grant did not allow women at the front during the siege of Petersburg, Virginia, and that is exactly where she was with her unit.

Throughout the war, hundreds of Maine women served the Union cause with distinction in a variety of ways. Scores risked their lives through contact with disease and infection and sometimes from enemy fire. Thousands more worked at home and within their communities to support the troops. No draft was ever needed to enlist their support throughout the four long years.

By the end of the war, 72,000 men had served with Maine regiments in the Union army. The population of Maine in 1860 was 628,279; thus more than one in nine of the entire population

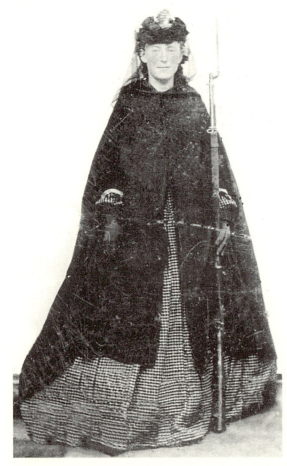

Photo of an unknown woman holding a musket to show support for the Union.
(Bangor Hist. Soc.)

(men, women, and children) of the state enlisted. Of the men who served, 9,398 died and many more suffered from wounds for the rest of their lives.

Accurate statistics on women's participation in the war effort are impossible. Many were unpaid volunteers. Few records were kept, even of those who were paid for their services. The names of the regimental field nurses do not appear on muster rolls. Contract nurses and agents for the commissions often went without recognition for their efforts. Over 20,000 cards in the National Archives in Washington record the services of nurses and matrons during the American Civil War. Each card lists only a name (sometimes misspelled or incomplete), the date the roll was taken, and the hospital. Exactly how many Maine women responded to the crisis and left their homes and families to help cannot be known. The number is most likely many hundreds, with many thousands more laboring at home to do what they could.

Between 1861 and 1865 nationwide, over three million soldiers fought in more than 10,000 engagements. Approximately 600,000 died of wounds or disease. The war touched everyone in the land. Women, Maine's included, could not and would not let their boys die of neglect, nor let the Union be dissolved without a fight.

Chapter 2

On the Homefront

As the guns of the American Civil War continued to blaze, women realized that the chances of losing a husband, son, neighbor, or friend to wounds, disease, or simply neglect were great. Many took it upon themselves to do whatever they could to relieve the agony of the suffering soldiers. In towns all over the North this often took the form of gathering and preparing needed supplies to be sent to the front. Women organized aid societies to systematize their efforts.

> If it were possible, the women of Bangor were more excited than the men. Their husbands, fathers, brothers and lovers were enlisting and making active preparation to leave for the South. While they shed many tears in secret, they were all courage in public, and rendered much assistance. Many articles of clothing were needed, which neither the State nor the United States could furnish at that time, and the patriotic women worked with willing hands to furnish them.[1]

"Think of it!" wrote the authors of *Eastern Maine in the Rebellion*, "Delicate women sat there day after day, gradually forming from the shapeless mass of cloth, garments for loved ones; garments soon to be rent by the bullet or the bayonet and drenched, may be, with the life current of him so dear to the maker. No wonder the men of the land were fighters! How could they be otherwise when the women set them such an example of heroism?"[2]

Short articles such as the following, which appeared in the *Baltimore American* on June 29, 1861, could frequently be found in papers of the day:

> THE FEAST OF DOUGHNUTS.—The ladies of Augusta, Me., some time ago distributed over fifty bushels of doughnuts to the Third Volunteer Regiment of Maine. A procession of ladies, headed by music, passed between double lines of troops, who presented arms, and were afterwards drawn up in a hollow square to receive the welcome doughnation.
>
> Never before was seen such an aggregate of doughnuts since the world began. The circumambient air was redolent of

doughnuts. Every breeze sighed doughnuts—everybody talked of doughnuts. The display of doughnuts beggared description. There was the molasses doughnut and the sugar doughnut—the long doughnut and the short doughnut—the round doughnut and the square doughnut—the rectangular doughnut and the triangular doughnut—the single twisted doughnut and the double twisted doughnut—the "light riz" doughnut and the hard-kneaded doughnut—the straight solid doughnut and the circular doughnut, with a hole in the center. There were doughnuts of all imaginary kinds, qualities, shapes, and dimensions. It was emphatically a feast of doughnuts, if not a flow of soul.[3]

A similar scene was enacted at Fort Preble at what is now South Portland when the ladies of Biddeford and Stroudwater presented the 5th Maine Infantry Regiment with doughnuts and oranges. The *Biddeford Union and Journal*, June 21, 1861, stated, "If the soldiers are as valorous in attacking the rebels as they were in the attack upon the doughnuts, they will prove themselves courageous soldiers."

The Kennebunk Soldiers Aid Society was organized soon after. In her report, secretary Elizabeth W. Hatch states:

> The first efforts put forth in this town on behalf of the sick and disabled soldiers of the United States Army, originated with Mrs. William F. Lord, in July 1861. She communicated her views to a few friends who at once became interested in them, and several young ladies were sent out to collect money for the purchase of materials. In so small a degree were the needs of the soldiers realized, but the small sum of twenty five cents only, was solicited. Forty eight dollars, fifty one cents were collected, expended in materials and made as expeditiously as possible into various articles for hospital use. Meetings for this purpose were held in the First Parish Hall, where matrons of seventy years and little girls of seven joined with those of intermediate ages in working for our suffering soldiers. In addition to the money subscribed, many articles of clothing and bedding were contributed. These supplies, valued one hundred fourteen dollars, ten cents ($114.10) filled two boxes and were transmitted to the United States Sanitary Commission. This was the first offering from this state to the Commission.[4]

Other towns were not to be outdone. According to Biddeford's *Union and Journal*: "The ladies of Alfred have been busily engaged of late in sewing and knitting for the soldiers.

They meet daily at the Grand Jury room and seem determined not to be excelled in devotion to the cause by any of their sisters in the neighboring towns. A gentleman who lives at the "mills" fears that unless their patriotic ardor is somewhat subdued before the cold weather sets in, the Home Guard will be obliged to go barefoot".[5] The *Union and Journal* also printed the following on March 27, 1863:

Soldiers Aid Society, Saco

The Secretary of the Soldiers' Aid Society of Saco, presents the following statement of the transactions of the past quarter, ending Jan. 10th 1863:

Twelve meetings have been held for work.

Cash on hand at commencement of quarter	$24,18
Avails of Fruit Festival	72,00
Avails of Old Folks Concert Dec. 21	91,12
Collection at meetings	24,67
From ladies of N. Kennebunkport	3,00
From other sources	5,25
	220,22
Expenditures for the quarter	162,69
Leaving balance in treasury	$57,53

Three boxes have been forwarded through Mr. Temple, to the New England Women's Auxiliary Association, Boston, Containing the following articles viz: 20 pairs cotton drawers, 27 pairs woollen drawers, 125 cotton shirts, 82 woolen shirts, 20 pairs slippers, 94 pairs woollen socks, 5 pairs mittens, 11 vests, 8 pairs pants, 5 coats, 5 bed sacks, 1 blanket, 7 quilts and comforters, sheets, pillow cases, lint, soap, sugar, dried apples, books, pamphlets, newspapers and dressing gowns. Each box has been promptly acknowledged.

Respectfully submitted,
P.A. Goodale,
Sec. and Treas.
Saco, March 10th 1863.[6]

The work meetings were not the only times women spent on the effort. During the war women seldom went anywhere without their knitting close at hand: "Mrs. Dominicus Lord, the widow of a Revolutionary soldier, in the ninety-sixth year of her age, sent us a pair of excellent socks the work of her own hands... Mrs. James Dorrance, also blind and upwards of seventy years of age, has knitted for us during the war fifty three pairs of socks."[7]

Another newspaper reported that, "A lady in Somerset County, aged seventy-two years, who during the past year has spun three hundred and fifty skeins of woolen yarn, on a hand-wheel, wove two hundred yards of woolen cloth, made two patchwork quilts and six dozen fine shirts, besides a large quantity of other sewing and knitting."[8]

From Rockland came numerous boxes of supplies. In writing about the ladies of that city it was said, "Their hands have been untiring, and their exertions almost uninterrupted... [in] addition to three boxes containing 624 garments sent on to the Sanitary Commission, they, in July, 1862, transmitted four large boxes of hospital clothing, bedding, soap, sponges, spices, corn starch, farina, &c.; with two boxes of wines and jellies, to the State Relief Society. The city was at the same time canvassed in the several wards and $500 contributed to aid the Sanitary Commission."[9]

William Howell Reed wrote: "Almost every home in the north was thus made tributary of the streams of charity which flowed onward to the stores of the Sanitary Commission. The women had enlisted for the war and there was nothing intermittent or spasmodic in their labors."[10]

Frequent letters from soldiers, nurses in the field, stories printed in the papers, and circulars from the United States Sanitary Commission kept them informed about what was most needed:

Advertisement for play to raise money for the Sanitary Commission.
(Maine Hist. Soc.)

#617

Amateur Dramatic Entertainments

FOR THE

BENEFIT

.... OF ....

The Sanitary Commission.

On Tuesday Evening, April 7th, 1863,
Will be enacted the Comedy of

STILL WATERS RUN DEEP.

JOHN MILDMAY,	MR. NOYES.
CAPT. HAWKSLEY,	MR. GRAY.
MR. POTTER,	MR. THOMAS.
DUNBILK,	MR. PATTEN.
LANGFORD,	MR. RAND.
MARKHAM,	MR. SHERWOOD.
GIMLET,	MR. FERNALD.
JESSOP,	MR. CRAM.
MRS. MILDMAY,	MISS S. WARE.
MRS. HECTOR STERNHOLD,	MISS FURBISH.

SONG, ... By Mr. THOMAS.

To conclude with the Farce of the

TWO BUZZARDS.

MR. BUZZARD,	MR. NOYES.
MR. GLIMMER,	MR. SHERWOOD.
JOHN SMALL,	MR. PATTEN.
MISS BUZZARD,	MISS VARNUM.
SALLY,	MISS S. WARE.

ORCHESTRAL MUSIC,
BY THE
BAND OF THE 17TH UNITED STATES INFANTRY,
Generously furnished for this occasion, by Col. GREENE.

ADMISSION 25 CENTS. - - - RESERVED SEATS, 50 CENTS.
DOORS OPEN AT 7 O'CLOCK. - - PERFORMANCE TO COMMENCE AT 8.

Tickets and reserved seats can be secured at the store of Edmund Dana, Jr., Deering Block.

Stephen Berry, Printer, 177 Fore Street, Portland, Me.

In answer to the appeal of the Surgeon-general for aid in mitigating the sufferings of the wounded in the battles which so mournfully closed the month of August, 1862, the ladies, misses, and children of this city [Rockland] set themselves promptly at work preparing lint and bandages, gathering every evening at various places, whilst the members of the Universalist Sewing Circle and the children of Miss Eaton's school devoted their Wednesday afternoon to the same purpose; so that on the evening of that day, Sept. 3d, two large dry-goods boxes were forwarded, and the work still went on. Mrs. C. N. Germaine of this city, associate manager of the Commission, herself, alone, from the time the 4th Regiment left Rockland till July, 1863, cut, rolled, and put up in packages for hospital use, 3824 yards of bandages.[11]

Rebecca Usher wrote from the hospital in Chester, Pennsylvania, that, "We are very much in need of stockings here, and somewhat in need of flannel shirts, but have plenty of bedding and everything else I believe.   Should we have a new arrival of wounded then we should need bandages, old cotton and many other things. I am afraid all our soldiers must suffer for stockings this winter. Too great an effort cannot be made to supply them."[12]

On February 14, 1863, the *Portland Transcript* published this letter from Harriet Eaton, an agent for the Maine Camp Hospital Association:

> Near Falmouth, Virginia
> Jan. 28th, 1863
>
> Miss Fox:
>
> Some 2 or 3 weeks since a letter was received from you, giving information that a barrel of Hospital supplies had been forwarded to us through you, as Secretary of the Maine Camp Hospital Association. It is now about a week since its contents were unpacked, and it gives me pleasure to inform you that the articles were in excellent condition, nothing broken or injured.
>
> The contents were just such articles as we needed, and I have no doubt they will prove a blessing to many a poor soldier. You may think me dilatory in my reply, and I acknowledge that more time has elapsed than seems desirable, but with us, time is exceedingly precious, every moment is occupied; we had some ten boxes and four barrels that arrived at the same time, and a large number of letters have been required, acknowledging their reception. Just now, we do not even have our evenings, as an officer of the Maine 20th is here, and occupies the room where we have our fire. He is very sick, and in

Free Street Baptist Church where the Maine Camp Hospital Association had its roots.
(Portland Press Herald)

the evening other officers of the Regiment call to see him; but I know you understand my position and will excuse the delay.

You inquire what articles are most needed for the relief of the sick and wounded soldiers. We feel that thus far the supply most lacking has been butter; we have also been unfortunate in losing nearly all the pickles that have been sent by the breaking of the glass bottles in which they were sent. It would be better to pack them in stone jars. So.t crackers, we can never be too largely supplied with, also canned chicken. Send us tea in small packages, suitable to give to the men in their tents, as we carry it to them when we visit the "quarters." Black pepper, cayenne, ginger, farina, maizena, &c. barley, dried apples, bottled cider, cranberry preserves with other preserves or jellies, handkerchiefs always needed in large quantities, made from old dresses, better colored than white, towels, stockings, woolen under clothing. This perhaps will do for a list, at present, but in this cause, no apology is needed. I love to beg for our suffering men who give up everything for our country. With other writing pressing on my immediate attention, I must

Maine Camp Hospital Association.

It having been represented during the latter part of 1862, that there was much suffering among the soldiers of the Potomac army, not reached by any other organization then at work, and as there were at that time ten Maine Regiments in that Department, it was resolved by a few gentlemen and ladies at the residence of our late Hon. JEDEDIAH JEWETT, on the evening of Nov. 17, to form a Society to labor more particularly among the Maine Regiments, and to be called the MAINE CAMP HOSPITAL ASSOCIATION.

Two ladies then on the field, were asked to distribute such stores as we might be able to forward to them, which they kindly consented to do; the first barrel was sent Jan. 4th, 1862. From that time until Jan. 4th, 1863, there was collected and forwarded to our nurses, supplies amounting in value to $5857, much of which was purchased by money donated. The ladies of the Free Street Baptist Society, have also contributed to the Association $1130 during the year.

Our stores are transported free by Mr. Geo. R. Davis, Maine State Agent for transportation, and we desire to thank him for his faithfulness to his trust. Not a box or barrel has failed of its destination,—"not one has failed from an acknowledgment from the nurses."

We have at present but one nurse upon the field, Mrs. Ruth S. Mayhew, of Rockland, a lady in every respect most favorably known, and admirably fitted for her work. Mrs. Mayhew labors without remuneration, as did Mrs. Eaton and Mrs. Fogg.

It has always been the custom of our nurses in visiting regiments, to call first at the Surgeon's tent, and to visit and administer to the sick under his direction. They have been ever welcomed, and as occasion required, have prepared gruels, broths, and whatever the sick needed, presented by themselves, or have seen that the articles furnished were properly prepared.

Their labors at Chancellorsville are already history; the only nurses or agents on the ground with supplies when the battle opened, they received and administered to the first company of wounded sent back from the front; were shelled once from their position, but continued their heroic work until the army retreated. And afterwards when our soldiers were brought from the rebel lines, our nurses were requested to join the Surgeons, which they did with liberal supplies, and remained with a detail of twenty men to act under their direction in ministering to the sufferers as they came. Thus they labored for five days, until the last man was brought over, giving nourishment, bathing wounds, bestowing comforts, nothing of which they could have received until after a further ride of fifteen miles. It will be remembered that these sick and wounded had been in rebel hands a fortnight, with only hard tack and water, and wounds undressed.

Although it is intended that our nurses should labor particularly among the Maine Regiments on the Potomac, they are instructed to administer to all whom they can give relief, of whatever nationalities, States, grades or colors; whenever a soldier is found sick or wounded, to give him help. They have, in the course of their labors, given aid to one Michigan Regiment, two Massachusetts, one Pennsylvania, and to four very sick officers of a New York Regiment, who were left suffering without aid, and to many soldiers from other States.

A lady who has been with the army ever since the first Bull Run battle, is so well satisfied with the labors of the Association, that she wrote to New Jersey and Pennsylvania, telling them that "Maine is not only taking care of her own soldiers but many of theirs." She immediately received an invoice from New Jersey, consisting in part of 120 pairs of drawers, 160 flannel shirts, and large quantities of other stores, and was soon to receive supplies from Pennsylvania. Thus has it ever been with those who become acquainted with the broad, prompt, humane and tender workings of the Maine Camp Hospital Association.

We receive constant assurance of confidence in our labors, for which we are profoundly grateful, and ever hold ourselves in readiness to forward with faithful care any thing which may be entrusted to us.

We received in the month of February, 25 blankets and 70 caps from Bridgton Centre; one quilt, 15 pairs stockings, 7 shirts from Union Falls, Buxton; 7 pairs stockings, 10 pairs mittens, 6 bottles of blueberries and ketchup, 1 keg of pickles from Hollis; five dollars from Hatty Bradley and Lizzie Day; and ninety-five dollars from various individuals.

Packages may be sent to Mrs. W. P. Preble, 397 Congress street; Mrs. Dr. Bacon, 70 Park street; Miss Harriet Fox, 59 Danforth street, or to the store of Mr. James E. Fernald, 87 Middle street.

The members of the Association are Rev. G. W. Bosworth, President; Mr. L. B. Smith, Secretary; Miss Harriet Fox, Corresponding Secretary; Mr. G. W. Woodman, Treasurer. Directors, Mr. Henry Fox, Mr. S. E. Chase, Mr. James Crie, Mr. T. R. Hayes, Mr. F. C. Moody, Mrs. Wm. W. Thomas, Mrs. J. E. Fernald, Mrs. Wm. P. Preble, Mrs. Elbridge Bacon, Miss Ann Sampson.

(Maine Hist. Soc.)

close this very hastily written letter. Continue earnest in the work. The daily blessing of the soldier rests upon the daughters of Maine, who with her sons, aid in this glorious cause.

Yours sincerely, Harriet Eaton[13]

The Sanitary Commission systematized the types and quality of clothing sent from the local organization by publishing monthly circulars which often gave fairly detailed instructions for making such things as drawers, hospital gowns, slippers, stockings, and other items needed by soldiers in the hospitals.

By fall 1863 it became apparent that scurvy was becoming a major problem and the Sanitary Commission made a special plea for potatoes, onions, turnips, cabbage, and apples.[14] But as hard as the ladies worked, there were grave doubts concerning whether supplies sent were actually getting to their intended destinations. Reports filtered back of gross misappropriation and confiscation of supplies meant for the sick and wounded by perfectly healthy officers, doctors, and those seeking to make some quick money. Mrs. Emma Manson, president of the Biddeford Soldiers' Aid Society wrote (using her own unconventional spelling style) to nurse Ellen Forbes:

> Miss Forbes enclosed you will find some articals for our sick soldiers, we have through various trials succeeded in gathering a few together and made your flannels, we hope they will do good, will you pleas send us a receipt also tell us where each artical goes. we hear so many stories about the Hospital that we sometimes get disheartened.
>
> I will now give you a list of articals there are 17 shirts, 17 pairs of drawers, 15 pairs stockings, 18 handkerchiefs, one bottle bacon rinds, two bottles currant jelly, also paper, I will close and trust this to the expressman,
>
> Yours, Mrs Emma Manson
> President of Soldier's Aid Society[15]

When asking for donations in Buxton and Hollis, Martha Osgood reported, "The chief opposition received was, the argument that the soldiers would never receive any of the articles sent. We were, however enabled to refute this objection, by numerous and grateful letters received from soldiers and for every barrel or box sent we received one or more letters, proving they were neither lost or misapplied."[16]

On January 1, 1862, George R. Davis was appointed by the state legislature as Maine Agent for the Sanitary Commission to counteract the complaints. He worked closely with both the Commission and aid societies in Maine to ensure that Maine soldiers received needed medical supplies.

In February 1862, Dr. Henry Bellows, President of the United States Sanitary Commission, spoke in Portland. He reported that Maine soldiers suffered more from sickness than soldiers from other states. "Where 50 out of 1,000 men were sick in Massachusetts regiments, 125 were sick in Maine regiments."[17] Such statistics gave extra impetus to local relief efforts.

The Maine Camp Hospital Association was formed in Portland for this purpose. An outgrowth of the Ladies Committee of the Free Street Baptist Society, the association had collected supplies and was searching for an efficient, reliable method of transportation and distribution. With the help of several prominent Portland men, between January 4, 1862, and January 4, 1863, according to their own calculations, they collected and forwarded supplies worth $5,857. Officially organized on November 17, 1862, this group was able to sponsor field agents to receive and distribute the supplies for them.

Beginning in October 1862, Mrs. Isabella Fogg, of Calais and Mrs. Harriet Eaton, of Portland became their first agents who traveled to locations very near the Army of the Potomac's front distributing supplies and tending to the sick and wounded of the various Maine regiments. They became well enough known and trusted that other Maine towns also contributed to their efforts.

Donations were acknowledged in a lengthy list printed in their "Semi-Annual Report" published in 1863. In addition to the 26 boxes sent by the Maine Camp Hospital Association in the previous year, the agents received boxes and barrels of supplies from Portland's Free Street Soldiers' Aid Society, societies in Gorham, Calais, Yarmouth, Brunswick, Windham, Peru, Turner, Monmouth, Bath, Otisfield, Bangor, and many other Maine communities.

Mr. George R. Davis, the state relief agent, arranged for free transportation of supplies and hospital goods. Most railroads gave free transportation for hospital supplies, anyway, as did other transportation companies. Adams Express was mentioned many times as delivering supplies for the relief agencies free of charge.

Mrs. Fogg and Mrs. Eaton followed the Army of the Potomac, moving from site to site, throughout the fall, winter, and spring of 1862 and 1863. Their letters to the Maine Camp Hospital Association were often published in the Portland papers and kept Maine women informed of their work.

In 1864, agents of the Maine Camp Hospital Association established headquarters at City Point, Virginia, near Petersburg. General Grant was laying siege to Petersburg and the army was not moving. Whenever they could, the women of the Maine Camp Hospital Association helped more than just Maine boys. On March 22, 1865, Rebecca Usher wrote in her diary:

> A boy from Michigan who was an orphan & had lost 3 brothers in the army came in with one of our Maine boys. He had lost his voice from the measles & was the only one of his family left. We gave him a comfort bag. It seemed a great comfort to him. He smiled & appeared as pleased as a child as he examined its contents. He found a letter in it from a Yarmouth girl, which pleased him more than all.[18]

Some men from other states, believing the Maine Agency would help only Maine boys, lied about their home town and named some Maine town in order to receive help. "Some amusing revelations of geographical knowledge would often take place when Mrs. Mayhew or Miss Dupee would question them about their homes in Maine."[19] But the agents had their instructions: "Although it is intended that our nurses should labor particularly among the Maine Regiments on the Potomac, they are instructed to administer to all whom they can give relief, of whatever nationalities, States, grades or colors; whenever a soldier is found sick or wounded, to give him help."[20] Few were turned away.

Mrs. Adelaide Smith worked at City Point, spending much time at the "Maine Agency" even though she was not from Maine. She related one incident which shows how the various agencies worked together, at least occasionally. For a while, she was in charge of cooking for the 2nd Corps convalescents—some 400 soldiers. Late one morning she found that supplies had not been delivered for dinner (the noontime meal). After a few moments' panic, Mrs. Smith ordered a large kettle be set to boil. "I took an orderly with a wheelbarrow and started on a forage among the agencies. At Maine I begged some fresh vegetables, Ohio gave some canned meat, Indiana onions, New Jersey more canned goods.... We got another barrow load from Pennsylvania, the Christian and the Sanitary Commissions." All was thrown in the pot to satisfy the 400 hungry soldiers.[21]

The Maine State Agency, although associated with the U.S. Sanitary Commission, was created by the state government, with offices in Washington which received supplies sent from the state. It was often confused with the Maine Camp Hospital Association. In fact, the two organizations, which had always cooperated, merged at City Point.

It is impossible to get any kind of accurate statistics on the value of goods sent by Maine women to the front. Some groups sent supplies directly to nurses they knew. Others supported national organizations like the U. S. Sanitary Commission or the Christian Commission. Still others supported organizations like the Maine State Agency and the Maine Camp Hospital Association. Many gave to more than one organization.

The Maine Adjutant General's Report for 1864/65, Vol. I, pp. 85-91, gives an approximation of the dollar value of the contributions of Maine women divided by town. That estimated total was $731,134.00 and George R. Davis, who compiled the figures, stated quite clearly in his report, "Many towns having failed to keep a record, whilst others have neglected to make a return, the following figures are given only as an approximate estimate."[22] The true amount must have been much higher, and in those times, a monthly wage might have been no more than $12.00. There is a listing of those Maine towns whose associations contributed to the United States Sanitary Commission in Appendix B.[23]

As the battles raged and Maine men were wounded, those who could travel were sometimes sent home. This created opportunities for Maine women to help the sick and wounded soldiers without leaving home. In Portland, a "Soldier's Home" was established by the local churches. Run by two sisters, Hannah and Mary Ann Kilbourn, it was a rest stop for penniless soldiers on their way home from hospitals in the South. In June 1863, the first installment of wounded arrived—450 men on their way to Augusta. More continued to arrive daily throughout the summer until the total who had stopped on their way through was around 3,500. During the remainder of the year another 10,000 were cared for. "The majority of this large number were from hospitals in the field and from Washington, Baltimore, Annapolis, Philadelphia, New York and Portsmouth Grove, most of them being turned loose from those hospitals without money or even rations, having only an order for transportation."[24]

The state government began to prepare for the return of the wounded in 1863 and built what were called "new and commodious buildings" for this purpose at Camp Keyes in Augusta. It was named Cony U.S. General Hospital and opened June 1, 1864. By the

time it was discontinued on November 30, 1865, over 2,000 patients
had been treated. Lists exist of the surgeons in charge, medical ca-
dets, hospital stewards, and of those who died there. The reports
also state that 33 matrons and female cooks worked at Cony, and
were paid from $8 to $18 per month. Fifty-two contract nurses were
also employed at various times, and received $24 per month. Their
names are not given. The Soldiers' Rest Hospital was also established in Bangor in May 1864. More than 5,500 soldiers were admitted during the time it was in existence.

The effects of the war were far-ranging for women, expanding
their horizons well beyond previous limits. Whereas mid-19th century women had been expected to stay home and care for their
homes and families, leaving everything else to the men, now the
survival of families, towns, and even the nation depended on rede-
fining those jobs that were acceptable for a woman to perform. Even
before the onset of the war, women for the first time began organizing themselves into effective agencies for change. Abolition, temperance, and suffrage were all causes women rallied around. With
the onset of the war rose another cause women could support: aiding the poor, suffering soldiers.

Some found new and exciting opportunities opening to them.
Elizabeth Akers worked as an assistant editor for the *Portland Advertiser* and later, the *Portland Transcript* before she went to Washington to be a war correspondent. Mrs. Caroline Cowan became
postmaster of Biddeford when her husband, Louis O. Cowan, who
had just been appointed to that post, left to become a captain in the

Cony Hospital in Augusta, the only Federal hospital set up in Maine.

(MHPC)

1st Maine Cavalry. She administered her office so well that even after her husband was killed in the war, she continued as postmaster and was reappointed under President Grant's administration several years later. Most women had no choice but to cope with the exigencies of war. With large numbers of men away from home, many found themselves forced to run farms and businesses.

Asa Dore, a private with the 1st Maine Heavy Artillery then at Fort Sumner, wrote back to his wife Elizabeth in Wellington, Maine: "I want you to manage the whole business at home the best you can for you can tell better than I can as I am a great ways from home and I want you to write me all about how you manage the farm."[25] In March of that same year, he wrote from Washington (after sending her $90), "you wanted me to write what I wanted you to do with it I shall leave it with you all together but I think if william dose not carry on the place that you had not better pay him more than the thirty four dollars and interest as you have got all your seed to b[u]y you can tell better than I can about it do what you think best."[26]

The meager amounts of money sent home were often not enough to keep their families going. Many women had to seek employment outside of the home to support their families. Jobs were now opening up for them, especially in the mills and factories.

One sail-making company in Rockland switched over during the war into making tents for the army. William S. Cochran employed between 100 and 200 workers. And as the reputation of his tents grew and orders increased, he expanded the company to 500 workers, mostly women and girls, which turned out 100 tents a day.[27]

Although raw cotton was scarce at the beginning of the war, supplies stabilized. The Pepperell Mills of Biddeford (whose workers were mainly women and children) reported that sales jumped from $670,000 in 1862 to $2,447,544 in 1863. Agent Francis Skinner had gone to New York and secured large contracts to make army cloth. By September 1862, Pepperell Mills was making duck for tents and wagon covers and heavy drills[28] and jeans for widespread army and navy use. In September 1862, they made over a million yards of cloth and a million and a half in October of that year. Since Biddeford sent at least half of its able-bodied men to the war, there were ample positions available for women. Their pay, however, was usually no more than $1.00 per week.[29]

Engraving of women at work making cartridges in a Federal arsenal.

(Harper's Weekly)

Other limited opportunities for women emerged. Catherine Clinton, in *The Other Civil War,* reported, "Women quickly replaced men as store clerks. Sales work meant long hours, sometimes in excess of one hundred hours per week, and poor pay (as little as $5 per week.) Even so, the tedious and tiring work in the stores compared favorably with factory labor."[30]

The lack of able-bodied men at home created other challenges for the women. On April 20, 1862, a major commercial block (the Union Block) burned down in the city of Biddeford. *Biddeford's Union and Journal* printed the following note a few days later: "Worthy of all praise are those valiant ladies who, at the late fire, in view of the ravages of the flames, nobly volunteered their services in working one of the fire engines, there being a lack of men to do the work."[31]

Maine women received some praise for their hard work. George R. Davis wrote, "The formation of the Soldiers' Aid Societies throughout our State was one of the most humane acts of the war."

Governor Cony, in an address delivered in January 1864, said:

> This war, fruitful as it has been in stimulating the inventive genius of our countrymen to devise new methods of defence and destruction, has also developed a spirit of hu-

manity strangely in contrast with the inevitable barbarities of war. The charities of our people, like everything else connected with the war, have been gigantic in their proportions. The cry that our soldiers are suffering, is the "open sesame" that unlocks all hearts, and at its call, no matter how oft repeated, affluence pours forth its abundance, and penury contributes its mite for their relief. The women of the country, in this, as in every labor of beneficence, the first to enter and the last to retire from the field, from city, village, and hamlet have sent forth a continuous stream of the fruits of their industry to make comfortable the frame of the suffering soldier, and to cheer his heart by these reminders, that though far away, he is still the object of their kind regards.[32]

Praise and recognition for their efforts must have been welcome to these women, but the real reasons for their labor lay much deeper and were varied. Some wished to come to the aid of their country, believing slavery wrong and the dissolution of the Union totally unacceptable. Others worked for money. Most commonly, however, the women heard the cry for help, not from the Army generals or even from the surgeons, but from the soldiers: their sons, husbands, friends, and neighbors in their sickness and pain. They did the only thing they could do—answering with hospital supplies, clothing, bedding, food, and more.

In the *Maine Adjutant General's Report*, Military Agent Henry Worcester so aptly wrote:

> If our State has won imperishable renown from the exploits of her sons on the battlefield, she had gained also a bright record for the noble, self-sacrificing spirit displayed by her daughters.[33]

LADIES' SANITARY FAIR,

NOROMBEGA HALL, BANGOR, MAINE.

Opening Day, December 20th, 1864.

The LADIES' SANITARY FAIR will embrace so many departments that nothing can possibly be sent amiss, and every article donated will have a place waiting to receive it.

We therefore beg to make to you personally, and through you to your friends, and all you can influence, our respectful but urgent appeal to forward in time for our Exhibition, all that a generous, patriotic heart may suggest, and willing hands prepare.

The Fair is for the purpose of raising money for the benefit of our sick and suffering Soldiers, by furnishing them with comforts and necessaries which cannot well be provided by the Government.

MRS. SAMUEL HARRIS,
MRS. HOLLIS BOWMAN,
MRS. G. K. JEWETT,
MRS. DR. BARKER,
MRS. S. P. STRICKLAND,
MRS. R. W. GRISWOLD,

G. K. JEWETT,
DAVID BUGBEE,
J. G. CLARK,
S. D. THURSTON,
SAM'L F. HERSEY,

Executive Committee.

NOTE.—All goods and packages, of whatever kind, should be distinctly marked with the name of the donor, and place from whence sent, and directed to "G. K. JEWETT, City Hall, Bangor, Me. (for L. S. Fair.)"

☞ Donations of Money are specially solicited, and should also be sent to "G. K. JEWETT, Treasurer of Ladies' Sanitary Fair."

☞ Packages by ADAMS' or EASTERN EXPRESS will come Free. ☜

(Maine Hist. Soc.)

Chapter 3

United Efforts

In the process of preserving the Union of 1776, while purging it of slavery, the Civil War also transformed it. Before 1861 the words United States were a plural noun: 'The United States are a large country.' Since 1865 United States has been a singular noun. The North went to war to preserve the Union; it ended by creating a nation."[1]

The mental and political shift to the concept of the union as one nation, undivided, with a centralized government from the former conglomerate of state governments working loosely together, was a second revolution for our nation. That same shift from independent units to a national identity and national cohesion was paralleled by the development of the civilian relief effort during the war.

When the war began in April 1861, neither North nor South was prepared for the massive effort that would be required to support a prolonged battle. Lincoln made the first call for 75,000 troops and soon after, another for 750,000 more. There was no mechanism in place to provide sustenance, shelter, and care for so many. Sanitation was neglected, nutrition was practically unknown, exposure and hardship common. There were no hospitals to respond to the resulting sickness.

In towns and cities throughout the nation, civilian organizations sprang up to aid the suffering soldiers. As Katherine Wormeley, one of the leading organizers, stated, "As men mustered for the battle-field, so the women mustered in churches, schoolhouses, and drawing-rooms,—working before they well knew at what they ought to work, and calling everywhere for instruction."[2]

Many sent their supplies and donations to people they knew to be in the field, to officers of their local volunteer regiments or to nurses who had written to them directly for aid. Such arrangements were often unsatisfactory. Regiments moved. Nurses too, became worn out, sick, went home, or transferred, and supplies often did not reach their intended destinations. Such piecemeal and haphazard efforts missed those soldiers who needed help the most.

One of the best organized of the early local efforts was the Woman's Central Association for Relief. The idea for a large relief effort was born during a meeting called by Dr. Elizabeth Blackwell, the first American woman doctor. She had invited some of the leading women of New York City to her New York Infirmary for Women. That group of 50 to 60 women called for a much larger meeting to be held at Cooper Union on April 25, 1861.[3] Nearly 3,000 women gathered to deliberate on "measures for the consolation and comfort of the gallant men who are about to risk their lives." Louisa Lee Schuyler was elected the first president and a board of 24 managers was chosen. Dr. Blackwell immediately began to train nurses.

Enlisting the support of Dr. Henry Bellows, the group sent a delegation to Washington to determine the greatest needs in the army and to work with the government to provide whatever help they could. According to some sources, Dr. Bellows, Dr. Elisha Harris, and other associates who went to Washington to meet with government officials may not have been totally enthusiastic about their mission at first. But as their attempts to arrange meetings and appointments with officials met with delays and postponements, they spent some free time visiting surrounding camps, and quickly realized the urgency of their mission. The appalling conditions were proof enough that a massive relief effort was of paramount impor-

Thousands of women met at the Cooper Union Hall in New York on April 25, 1861 to organize the Woman's Central Association for Relief. (Harper's Weekly)

tance. Dr. Bellows and the organizers of the Woman's Central Association for Relief pushed even harder for the creation of what became the United States Sanitary Commission.

President Lincoln feared that the creation of a vast civilian organization would be a "fifth wheel;" a hindrance to the army. The Medical Department, led by officers with no experience in handling the sickness and casualties of such a large army, saw no great need for civilian help. Dr. Bellows persisted, however, and eventually was rewarded with an official sanction—but little else.

On June 9, 1861, Secretary of War Simon Cameron issued an order appointing Dr. Bellows and others as commissioners of the United States Sanitary Commission. They were to serve without pay to inquire into the sanitary condition of the volunteer soldiers. A few days later, on June 16, the newly appointed commissioners called upon President Lincoln and Cameron to present the plan of organization. With only limited powers, the plan called for the Commission to investigate actual conditions of camps and hospitals in terms of diet, quarters, and clothing, and to give advice based on its conclusions. Those recommendations approved by the army's medical department were to be carried out by the officers and men.

Frederick Law Olmsted was chosen chief executive of the organization. They soon appointed 60 inspectors including surgeons, chemists, professors in medical schools, and physicians. Ordered to report on camp conditions, drainage, tents, ventilation, bedding, cooking, clothing, and water quality, they all returned with similar reports. Conditions were so unwholesome, and the peril to men's health so alarming, that pressure was brought on the government to adopt immediate reforms.

In December 1861 the Commission issued its first full length official report to the Secretary of War. One hundred and five pages long, it gave a detailed description of conditions in camps, complete with statistics on various diseases—and correlated them to living conditions. Major problems were noted and recommendations made. The report placed great emphasis on forcing volunteers to conform to military discipline and cleanliness. One segment of the report states:

> Of two hundred regiments, all were provided with pantaloons [pants]—one hundred and seventy-five sufficiently, eight indifferently, seventeen very poorly.
> Men have been frequently seen during the summer on duty and on parade in their drawers alone.[5]

Such deficiencies were blamed on the ignorance or negligence of the officers and contributed to a general lack of discipline and slovenliness which led, of course, to disease.

> The recommendation made to the Department, in August, that each soldier should be provided with a clothes brush, shoe brush, tooth brush, comb, and towel, adapted to be carried snugly in the knapsack, and for which he should be required to account weekly, is therefore, respectfully renewed.[6]

Unfortunately, few of the recommendations were adopted at that time. Even statistics showing the number of sick in the various regiments to be from 33 to 49 percent had no effect. No one expected the war to last more than a few months. Only after the first major battle at Bull Run in June 1861 came the realization that this war might not end soon.

Yet even after such a major fiasco as the rout of Union troops at Bull Run in Manassas, Virginia, the Medical Department could not be convinced of the need for change. Medical procedures had been in place for decades. They simply would not allow civilians to tell them how to run their department. It did not matter that procedures in place for an army of 15,000 fell apart for an army of 700,000. Every recommendation from the Commission met opposition from the Medical Department.

The struggle between the Commission and the Medical Department was in stalemate until the Commission appealed directly to Congress for reorganization of the Department. Congress abolished the Medical Department and set up an entirely new system under a new Surgeon General. This action was deemed the first great success of the United States Sanitary Commission.

The work for which the Sanitary Commission became best known was the collection and distribution of supplies. William Howell Reed, a Union army nurse, reported:

> At a period when arms and clothing could not be furnished the newly raised regiments, when the Quartermaster-General was forced, in the month of October, 1861, publicly to solicit donations of blankets for men in active service, it was not to be wondered at that, overtaxed as the government was at that time, articles of the first necessity were wanting in the hospitals and on battlefields. Hospital clothing there was none. Even the supply of the most common medicine was scanty and irregular, and no provision had been made for a hospital diet.[7]

Over 7,000 aid societies became tributaries to the Sanitary Commission. During the course of the war it is estimated that these organizations donated supplies valued at over $15 million. Of that amount, over $4 million was raised by holding great fairs which sold everything from donated food, farm goods, and fabrics to a draft of President Lincoln's Emancipation Proclamation. In addition, some $5 million more in cash was raised as well as another $5 million in donated services. Mr. Reed wrote, "The women had enlisted for the war, and there was nothing intermittent or spasmodic in their labors. As long as the need lasted they were ready for service."[8]

Another triumph of the Sanitary Commission was the initiation of the hospital transport service. The plan was to transport the sick and wounded away from battlefields on specially outfitted steamboats. First tried in Tennessee at Fort Donelson in February 1862, its success continued at Shiloh that April, then on a much broader scale in Virginia during McClellan's Peninsula Campaign in the summer of 1862.

The Army of the Potomac had been encamped for weeks in unhealthy conditions on the Virginia peninsula. Thousands took ill; the army could not care for them, or move them to where they could receive care. Meanwhile, skirmishes were fought and on June 25, the Seven Days' Battle began. In addition to thousands of fever-ridden soldiers, thousands of wounded soldiers lay helpless, scattered over the fields.

> The Sanitary Commission, undaunted by this mass of suffering, threw itself into the breach. A number of large passenger steamers that had been used by the government as transports were then lying idle at Fortress Monroe at a cost of $800-$1,000 a day each. The Commission secured all of them by an order of the Secretary of War, on an agreement to take charge of all the sick and wounded on the Peninsula, and land them in Washington. These vessels were bare of everything for hospital purposes, but they were promptly fitted up and supplied from the storehouses of the Commission and made ready for this beneficent service. An ample corps of surgeons and nurses was assigned to them, and fully fifteen thousand men, shattered and helpless, were gathered in and loaded on these boats as they came into our hands from these battlefields.[9]

Both Amy Morris Bradley from Vassalboro, Maine, and Isabella Fogg of Calais, Maine, worked aboard hospital transports during the Peninsula Campaign.

The Commission outfitted special railroad cars to transport sick and wounded soldiers, installing shock absorbers. It established soldier's homes and lodges in various locations for soldiers who were awaiting orders, in transit, or in need of assistance while detached from their units. These homes cared for up to 2,000 soldiers a day, and totalled more than one million during the war. The Commission maintained a hospital directory to help families locate their relatives, and it established distribution centers in needed areas. Furthermore, its agents could often be found just after a major battle, distributing supplies on the field. At Gettysburg, the Commission set up a supply depot near the railway station from which supplies were sent to the field hospitals. One witness said,

> [It] became the center of the busiest scene which I have ever witnessed in connection with the Commission. Car-load after carload of supplies were brought to this place, till shelves and counter and floor up to the ceiling were filled, till there was barely a passage-way between the piles of boxes and barrels.... Each morning the supply wagons of the division and corps hospitals were before the door, and each day they went away laden with such articles as were desired to meet their wants....[10]

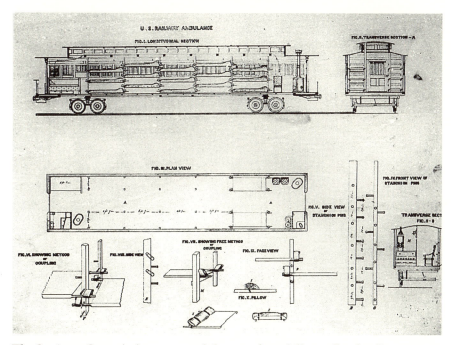

The Sanitary Commission promoted the use of specially outfitted railway cars to transport the wounded.   (NY Pub. Lib.)

The Commission also maintained a lodge near the railroad. It was built complete with a field kitchen staffed by ten cooks and thirty to forty attendants.

The Sanitary Commission's newsletter, published bi-monthly, plus the frequent letters it sent to newspapers all over the North, kept the homefront informed of its activities. Included in the newsletter were anecdotes, testimonials, and reports from its various tributaries. Also included were requests for food, supplies, and instructions for making such things as hospital clothing, mittens, special pillows, and bedding.

The Commission was not alone in its mission to provide support to the army and relief to soldiers on a national scale. In November 1861, representatives of various religious organizations, including the Young Men's Christian Association (YMCA), the American Bible Society, and the American Tract Association met to discuss the spiritual needs of soldiers. Those delegates formed the Christian Commission, whose mission was to promote soldiers' and sailors' spiritual and temporal welfare, collect and transmit civilian contributions, and hold services in the field. On December 11, 1861, a five-man executive committee was appointed with George H. Stuart of Philadelphia as the chair.

In May 1862, the Christian Commission sent its first agents into

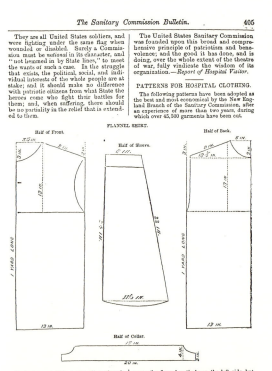

A page from a Sanitary Commission Bulletin with directions for making hospital clothing.

the field to hold religious services, work in hospitals, and bury the dead on the battlefields. They also set up diet kitchens. The superintendent of the diet kitchens was Mrs. Annie Wittenmyer of Iowa, who employed about 70 women to manage the kitchens and food storerooms that served the hospitalized soldiers.

Another great accomplishment was the creation of a loan library system which consisted of complete libraries containing 125 volumes each, carefully selected and shipped in special wooden cases and equipped with cards and methods of record-keeping. Over 200 of these libraries were placed in hospitals throughout the North, and exchanged on a regular basis. The Commission also distributed over 300,000 Bibles, 6,500,000 religious newspapers, and over 2,700,000 non-library books.

Although many soldiers used their newspapers for something far different than the intended purpose, many others were aided by the service. Mrs. Isabella Fogg, for instance, a relief worker from Maine, found where her wounded son, Hugh, had been taken through the Christian Commission. Later, "dismissed" by the Maine Camp Hospital Association, she continued her work helping wounded soldiers under the auspices of the Christian Commission.

The two major relief organizations experienced some rivalry, especially in the East where the Christian Commission was better organized. Yet in December 1864, when Mrs. Mary Ann Bickerdyke happened to be in Philadelphia on a fund-raising tour for the Sanitary Commission, she received a summons from General Sherman to go immediately to Savannah, Georgia. The Christian Commission filled a ship for her with supplies—clothing, crackers, butter, cheese, tea, sugar, milk, tapioca, lemons, an ambulance, and more.[11]

As the war progressed, and under pressure from civilian organizations and Congress, the army's Medical Department also became better organized and better prepared to handle vast numbers of sick and wounded. It learned to work with the Commissions, reorganized its ambulance service, and set up large hospitals where the sick and wounded could be taken. Nurses at these hospitals were under the direction of Dorothea Lynde Dix who, theoretically, appointed them to their positions. In reality, however, as Dix made her inspections, she frequently found nurses whom she had not appointed. Some had come to care for relatives and stayed, either of their own accord or by the urging of the surgeons. In most cases Dix did not, or perhaps could not, remove them. She must have realized, as the war dragged on, that every pair of hands was needed.

The *Soldier's Directory*, published in October 1862, lists 59 hospitals operating in the Washington, D.C. area. Many were buildings that had been converted from other purposes into hospitals. One such was the Union Hotel Hospital in Georgetown, where Hannah Ropes from New Gloucester, Maine, worked. Others were in churches, former schools, the Patent Office, and warehouses. The Sanitary Commission issued a report dated July 31, 1861, in which it states:

> Old buildings do not make good Hospitals. It is also fixed in the experience of those most able to judge, that large buildings are liable to grave objections. They form storehouses for morbid emanations, and are only comparatively safe when ventilated at great expense, by complicated artificial means. The scaly walls and cracked wood-work of old buildings present innumerable lurking places for foul air, and patients occupying

A listing of hospitals and other agencies in the Washington area.

(Maine Hist. Soc.)

such buildings are too frequently attacked by erysipelas,[12] or scourged by Hospital gangrene. Even when such maladies are absent, the almost constant presence of animal impurities imposes a weight upon the recuperative energies of the sick, which by inducing debilitating complications retards or prevents their recovery.[13]

By 1864 the War Department had perfected a design for a good general hospital. With advice from the Sanitary Commission for a new "pavilion style" hospital, Secretary of War Edwin Stanton issued detailed instructions on the construction of hospitals. These included site selection, layout of wards, ventilation, water supply, "sinks" [toilets], and more. Instructions were to "be deviated from only in cases of imperative necessity." Pavilion style hospitals were made up of wards, each ward consisting of a long, narrow, well-ventilated building with room for 60 beds. Separate buildings housed the administration, dining area, the kitchen, laundry, storehouse, guard house, chapel, operating room, dead house, stable, and quarters for female nurses. The wards, administration building, kitchens, dining rooms, and chapel were to be connected by covered walks.[14]

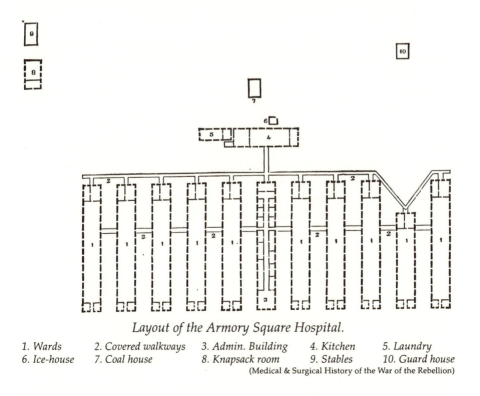

Layout of the Armory Square Hospital.

| 1. Wards | 2. Covered walkways | 3. Admin. Building | 4. Kitchen | 5. Laundry |
| 6. Ice-house | 7. Coal house | 8. Knapsack room | 9. Stables | 10. Guard house |

(Medical & Surgical History of the War of the Rebellion)

The Armory Square Hospital opened on August 15, 1862. Considered to be a model in efficiency and organization, it was the prototype for the new design. Built specifically as a hospital, with 14 wards and a capacity of 800 patients, the chief surgeon, Dr. D. Willard Bliss, made sure it ran smoothly. Visitors often remarked on the neatness and order of the wards and the comfort and care given to the patients. One visitor wrote, "All the people in charge of its affairs, under the guidance of Dr. Bliss, understand their duty and perform it successfully, and with credit to themselves and the institution."[15] President Lincoln often visited this hospital, chatting with the patients and staff. Most of the nurses were from New England, and many of those from Maine.

While some Maine women participated in local efforts, others participated in national ones. Maine agents, nurses, soldiers, and observers all agreed that a national effort was needed to coordinate the individual efforts made by local communities in Maine and elsewhere.

At the Naval School Hospital, Louise Titcomb of Portland, Maine, was horrified to learn that a comment of hers, printed in the papers back home, had been misinterpreted as criticism of the Sanitary Commission. "I never dreamed that the San. Com. had not done their full duty here: their work has been grand and glorious everywhere, and our Surgeon in charge has made enormous requisitions [which] have as readily been met.[16]

Hugh McLellan, a Maine state agent, wrote the governor, "No one ever need fear of doing wrong by giving to the Sanitary Commission. Even if a small amount should by chance go astray, it is my opinion, that there is still enough that does go right to bring a big helping on the whole situation."[17] Even President Lincoln, once hesitant to approve the creation of the U. S. Sanitary Commission, fearing it would be "a fifth wheel" to military operations, remarked on March 18, 1864, at the closing of the Sanitary Fair in Washington:

> In this extraordinary war, extraordinary developments have manifested themselves, such as have not been seen in former wars; and amongst these manifestations nothing has been more remarkable than these fairs for the relief of suffering soldiers and their families. And the chief agents in these fairs are the women of America.

I am not accustomed to the use of language of eulogy; I
have studied the art of paying compliments to women; but
I must say that if all that has been said by orators and poets
since the creation of the world in praise of women were applied to the women of America, it would not do them justice
for their conduct during the war. I will close by saying, God
bless the women of America.[18]

In one of the last official documents sent by the U.S. Sanitary
Commission to its branches and aid societies, the following tribute
from the officers of the Commission was included:

It is not too much to say, that the Army of women at
home has fully matched in patriotism and in sacrifices the
Army of men in the field. The mothers, sisters, wives and
daughters of America have been worthy of the sons, brothers, husbands, and fathers who were fighting their battles.[19]

Chapter 4

Notes on Nursing

It was just past midnight after the February 15, 1862, battle at Fort Donelson on the Cumberland River in Tennessee. An officer looked from his tent to see a faint light flitting here and there across the recent battlefield and he sent a man to find the cause. He discovered a woman who would become one of the best known nurses of the Civil War. Mary Ann Bickerdyke, searching with her lantern, was groping through the dead still left on the field. As Mary Livermore described it, "She could not rest while she thought any were overlooked who were yet living."[1] And this was reportedly after making five trips on the hospital boat from Fort Donelson to Cairo, Illinois, taking the wounded to hospitals up the river more than 100 miles away.

Conditions in field hospitals were often harsh. The last days of 1863 and the first of 1864 had found "Mother" Bickerdyke camped in the mountains of Tennessee with icy winds sweeping through the valleys, overturning hospital tents, and threatening to freeze her patients to death if the torrential rains did not drown them. All through the night she struggled to keep fires going to save the patients. When fuel gave out partway through the night, she called on men of the Pioneer Corps to tear down nearby abandoned wooden breastworks. Working without proper orders, the men obeyed, and kept the fires going. She also prepared cauldrons of hot coffee, and heated bricks to place around her patients.

In the early hours of the next morning a train of thirteen ambulances arrived, with more wounded men so frozen they were past complaining, slipping into the sleep that ends in death. She and the surgeons worked without rest, and they saved hundreds who would have otherwise died that night. For her efforts, she was arrested the next morning by a major who was upset that she demolished the breastworks without authorization. Mary Ann Bickerdyke had her supporters, however, and refusing to go to the guard-house (at least until the weather warmed), she continued her work.

The experiences of Mrs. Bickerdyke, Civil War nurse, were very different from the experiences of nurses today. In fact, her experiences were very different from anything any woman had known before that time, as well. Nursing, as a profession for women, did not exist prior to the American Civil War. Victorian sensibilities made the home and family the woman's "sphere of influence." Respectable women only nursed family members, and possibly neighbors and close friends.

That is not to say there were no women employed as "nurses' in Victorian times. In England, the common conception of such women was chillingly portrayed by Charles Dickens in his book *Martin Chuzzlewit*, published in 1844. The name of the nurse in the story, Sairey Gamp, came to be synonymous with an uncouth, illbred woman. The character was based on a person Dickens once met.

Other than nuns, the only women in this country who generally performed nursing duty outside the home were convicted prostitutes. Given the choice of prison or serving their sentences by working in a hospital, they chose the hospital. Consequently, the unsavory reputation of female nurses existed on both sides of the Atlantic.

When Florence Nightingale traveled to Kaiserwerth, Germany, to study nursing in 1851, her parents were so mortified that they forbade her to tell anyone where she was going. Kaiserwerth, however, was an exception to the dismal picture painted by Dickens. Begun in 1836 by Friederika and Theodor Fliedner, the institution trained women for hospital work, private duty, or district nursing, and was an early model for nursing instruction. The course of instruction consisted of three years training and work in cooking and housekeeping, laundry and linen, and pharmacology. In addition, there were rotating assignments in the associated hospital's wards. Florence Nightingale, apparently not completing the full course of study, spent three months at the school prior to taking a position as director of nurses at a hospital for "gentlewomen during illness." She left after a year to become the world's most famous "angel of mercy" during the Crimean War.[2]

The *London Times* sent the world's first war correspondent, William Howard Russell, to the Turkish front. After the Battle of Alma, he reported that the British army had made no provision for cooking equipment, medicine chests, bedding, hospital wagons, etc. for the survivors. Russell also noted that the hospital had no food, no buckets, no bandages, and few army surgeons. An outcry was heard throughout England; a call for supplies and nurses was made.

Florence Nightingale responded. She and 38 other women, mostly Roman Catholic and Anglican sisters, went to the Crimea. Upon arrival, they immediately set up kitchens, laundries, cleaned the barracks thoroughly, and gave the men clean bedding, hot soup, and hospital shirts. The death rate dropped dramatically.

Although she did not know about germ theory, Florence Nightingale demanded clean dressings, clean bedding, well-cooked food, proper sanitation, and fresh air. Good nursing meant ensuring that the sick and wounded received these simple necessities. She incorporated her thoughts and advice into a small book called *Notes on Nursing*, which she published in 1859. That same year she opened a school for nursing associated with the St. Thomas Hospital in London, England. The book became the textbook of her new school.

Notes on Nursing also traveled across the Atlantic and became widely available in America. Many women used it as a guide to nurse members of their own families. Not intended as a how-to manual, it nevertheless contained Nightingale's thoughts and opinions on such subjects as ventilation, warming, noise, food, bedding, cleanliness, and observation of the sick in order to restore health. She wrote, "[Nursing] has been limited to signify little more than the administration of medicines and the application of poultices. It ought to signify the proper use of fresh air, light, warmth, cleanliness, quiet, and the proper selection and administration of diet—all at the least expense of vital power to the patient."[3]

Other endeavors into the field of nursing also occurred at this time. In 1827 Mary Catherine McAuley,[4] who had inherited a fortune, built a large house in Dublin, Ireland, to serve as a school to train hundreds of poor women and girls. Two years later, in 1829, they were placed in charge of a cholera hospital. Unlike the usual treatment for the disease which consisted of "bleeding" the patient, followed by calomel and large doses of opium, the "sisters" used brandy, laudanum, and heat with some success. In 1831 the order became known as the Sisters of Mercy. When the Crimean War began in 1854, like Florence Nightingale, they traveled to the scene of battle to nurse the sick and wounded. Later, other sisters of their order would take a similar role in nursing the sick and wounded in our Civil War.

By the time the American Civil War began, the entire United States could boast of only 150 hospitals. The army itself had only 40 beds available. In the opening days of the war, Lincoln called for 75,000 men. Never before had so many men been brought together with so little planning for their health and welfare. The prewar army consisted of about 16,000 men, and the surgeon general had a staff of approximately 100 surgeons. Those surgeons cared for 30,000 cases in 1859 and 1860 and had only 138 deaths, mostly from tuberculosis or gunshot wounds during skirmishes with Indians. Within the first six months of the Civil War, over thirty percent of the troops, now ten times larger than before, were suffering from malaria, typhoid fever, smallpox, and dysentery. Admit it or not, the medical department was overwhelmed.

In its first report to the secretary of war in 1861, the Sanitary Commission outlined the extent of the problem. Of the 200 regiments inspected, almost 13,000 men were on the sick-list. The most prevalent disease reported was diarrhoea [sic], with "intermittent fever" the second most common. The report noted, "That men everywhere, throughout these wonderful multitudes, are daily suffering from the ignorance, neglect, mistakes, and impositions of their officers and of each other." The report contained suggestions for the improvement of sanitation, distribution of supplies, living accommodations and the construction of better hospitals.[5]

Despite improvements in organization, staffing, and hospital construction as the war went on, sanitation continued to be a problem. When neglected wounds became maggot infested, calomel or common elder was initially used to clean out the larvae. Realizing that the maggots were destroying only the unhealthy tissue, surgeons began using "maggot therapy," which had also been used in the Napoleonic Wars.

As strange as that sounds, allowing maggots to remain was actually a better medical practice than other common procedures. Since the relationship between lack of cleanliness and infection was not yet recognized, surgeons seldom cleaned their hands between operations. Neither did they clean their instruments until, perhaps, the end of the day. The result was that most wounds became infected and pus leaked from them. Because this was so common, surgeons believed it was a sign of healing and called it "laudable pus."

Surgery was primitive and entirely unsanitary. Ether was discovered in 1846, chloroform in 1847, but both were often unavailable. Surgeons preferred chloroform, since ether was flammable. Over the course of the war, it is estimated that Union surgeons used some form of anesthesia during surgery approximately 80,000 times. Seventy-five percent of those were performed with chloroform alone. The rest used ether or a combination of ether and chloroform. Only forty-three deaths from chloroform are known to have occurred. Opium pills and grains of morphine sprinkled on wounds, or mixed with whiskey to drink were common methods of reducing pain. Later in the war, morphine syringes became widely available. Quinine was the common treatment for various fevers, or in stubborn cases, arsenite of potassa (now known as an insecticide).

Doctors assigned to regiments were not well screened. Appointments were usually political rather than based on qualifications. The civilian doctors often balked at military protocol and regulations, making efficient operation even less likely. Screening of new recruits by doctors was also minimal. There are reports of one doctor who "examined" 90 recruits in one hour. Recruits paraded before another doctor, who passed them all "en masse." The unfit would later clog the hospitals, stymie military procedure, and use scarce resources earmarked for the wounded.

Although doctors had been appointed to provide treatment and surgery, no thought was given to who would care for the soldiers in their sick beds. After the chaos of the Battle of Bull Run, newly appointed Medical Director of the Army of the Potomac, Dr. Charles S. Tripler, began the task of organizing the Army Medical Corps. Under his direction, doctors were required to treat all soldiers (not just those in their regiment). Regimental musicians were trained as stretcher-bearers, and men were assigned to hospital service. Commanders often sent their least able men. Many male nurses were convalescents, usually feeble, sick, and unfit for duty. As nurses, they were totally unsuited. Into these dour conditions descended women, armed with Florence Nightingale's *Notes on Nursing*, ready to nurse the poor soldiers back to health, or at least, to make their last days more comfortable.

The exigencies of war allowed women freedom to enter this all-male world, to break the stereotypes created by Victorian society which confined them to domestic duties, and care for strangers outside their homes. Even so, the struggle for acceptance was extremely difficult. Arguments against female nurses ranged from the assumption that they would faint at the sight of blood and disturb hospital wards with their hysterics, to being constantly in the way of doctors and unable to help with demanding tasks such as lifting and moving patients. Propriety and modesty were also factors in the public debate. Despite these doubts, no one could stop the flood of women that poured into Washington to "enlist."

Dorothea Lynde Dix, already known for her humanitarian endeavors on behalf of the mentally ill, was named superintendent of women nurses in June 1861. Women she appointed to work in the army hospitals did not need to be trained—they needed to be plain, healthy, and over thirty years old. Many younger women managed to obtain nursing positions despite Miss Dix.

Dr. Elizabeth Blackwell, a graduate of Geneva Medical College in 1849, established the New York Infirmary for Women. Working with the Woman's Central Association for Relief in New York, she began to train nurses for duty. In the summer of 1861, that organization sent Dorothea Dix thirty-two trained women for duty in the hospitals around Washington. Friction developed between the Woman's Central Association and Miss Dix over the proper employment of these women, who expected to direct nursing activities in hospitals. Instead they were given menial tasks which did not take advantage of their training. The result was that the Woman's Central Association for Relief decided not to send any more women to Dix, but rather worked with the Sanitary Commission to find suitable employment for their trained nurses.

The United States Sanitary Commission employed dozens of women in 1862 to work aboard the hospital transports, moving the sick and wounded from battlefields of the Peninsula Campaign to hospitals further north. When Amy Bradley took over as matron of the *Knickerbocker*, her first order of business was to clean it from top to bottom. Once patients were aboard and comfortable, a strict routine was followed: breakfast of bread or toast with butter and tea or coffee at 7 a.m.; dinner of beef soup or stew with hominy, bread or crackers at 1:15 p.m., and at 7 p.m. tea, a repeat of breakfast. Nurses had the same with the possible addition, at the surgeons' advice, of a drink of quinine-laced whiskey to ward off swamp fever. Their time was divided into "watches," taking turns caring for their passengers. Their instructions read, "two or more nurses are to be constantly on duty in each ward. They will perform any and all duties necessary in the care of the patients, under instructions from the surgeons received through the ward-masters." The women managed to prepare food and care for their passengers even in the tight spaces and the inadequate conditions offered by the ships. One surgeon wrote, "To get the proper food for all, decently cooked and distributed, has given me more concern than anything else. The ship servants are brutes, and our supply of utensils was cruelly short. Fortunately the Captain is a good-hearted and resolute man, and the ladies—God knows what we should have done without them!—have contrived to make some chafing-dishes with which the kitchen is pieced out wonderfully."[6] The hospital transports were in operation in Virginia from May 1 through July 1862.

Patients transported away from the front were taken to army hospitals. Typically, a larger hospital of 1,000 beds would be run by a steward with two or three assistants. There may have been twenty wards, each with a ward master, 40 to 100 male nurses to work in the wards, five or six cooks, eight to ten assistant cooks, ten to fifteen storeroom workers, three to four "dead house" attendants, and ten or so clerks in the administrative office and library. Only surgeons and stewards were permanently assigned to a hospital. Male nurses could be recalled to their units at any time. By the end of the war, as it became clear that convalescent soldiers did not make good nurses, there was approximately one female nurse for each four or five male nurses. At Gayosa Hospital in Memphis, Mary Ann Bickerdyke dismissed all male nurses and installed her own female nurses, often employing negro women, former slaves who had flocked behind Union lines. At Armory Square Hospital, the model for other hospitals, each ward had a ward master, a surgeon, a female nurse, an orderly, a cadet surgeon, three attendants, and two night watchers.

Amanda Akin, a nurse at Armory Square Hospital, described her duties clearly. Each morning she started by dispensing medicines prescribed by the surgeon. Then she supervised the distribution of breakfast. After her own breakfast, she met with the surgeon to discuss prescriptions for medicines and diet for each patient. Instructions were written on cards that hung on each bed. She then wrote the orders for medicines to be requested from the dispensary and for special diets from the kitchen. Medicines were kept under her lock and key in a medicine chest. She described other duties:

> Besides our regular morning duties there is the constant supervision and care of so many worn and suffering, and yet so grateful patients; letters to be written, etc. ...We again dispense

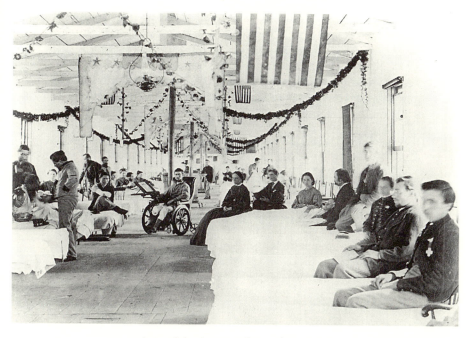

A ward in Armory Squard Hospital. (Library of Congress)

Armory Squard Hospital, an example of the new "pavillion" style design.

(Library of Congress)

the medicines, etc., before 12 M., the hour for the men's dinner.
As the hospital now is not crowded, the engagements of late
having been in the south, we get a few hours for rest or a walk
before 5 p.m., when we resume our duties at the medicine chest,
etc. We spend the evenings trying to entertain our men. At a
quarter to nine, when the night watchers come, we give our last
directions and retire.[7]

Not all nursing experiences by women were as ordered as that
described by Amanda Akin. Louisa May Alcott wrote of her nursing experience at the Union Hotel Hospital in Georgetown:

> My three days' experience had begun with a death, and,
> owing to the defalcation of another nurse, a somewhat abrupt
> plunge into the superintendence of a ward containing forty
> beds, where I spent my shining hours washing faces, serving
> rations, giving medicine, and sitting in a very hard chair, with
> pneumonia on one side, diphtheria on the other, five typhoids
> on the opposite, and a dozen dilapidated patriots hopping, ly-
> ing, and lounging about, all staring more or less at the new
> "nuss," who suffered untold agonies...and blundered through
> her trying labors with a Spartan firmness....[8]

Sophronia Bucklin wrote,

> Our duties here [at the Judiciary Square Hospital] were to
> distribute food to the patients, when brought up from the
> kitchen; wash the faces and hands, and comb the heads of the
> wounded; see that their bedding and clothing was kept clean
> and whole, bring pocket handkerchiefs, prepare and give the
> various drinks and stimulants at such times as they were or-
> dered by the surgeon.[9]

Women also worked as "special diet supervisors," doing their
best to make the hospital food prescribed by the doctor as palatable
as possible. They supplemented army allotments with delicacies
sent from home or acquired from the Commissions, and vegetables
grown on hospital grounds. They also made purchases with the
"fund" that many hospitals started as the need for supplementary
food grew obvious.

Mrs. Annie Wittenmeyer, appointed state sanitary agent by
the Iowa state legislature, visited many camps and hospitals
housing soldiers from Iowa. She determined that soldiers in the
hospitals were not getting the proper food needed to recover.
Joining forces with the Christian Commission and getting en-
dorsements from both President Lincoln and Surgeon General

Joseph K. Barnes, Mrs. Wittenmeyer established a system of "diet kitchens," adopted throughout the North by 1864. By the end of the war, over 100 of these diet kitchens were established, all under the direction of U.S. Army surgeons, supplied by hospital commissaries, with supplements from the Christian Commission and others. The kitchens were managed by experienced and competent women selected by the Christian Commission and approved by Mrs. Wittenmeyer.

Surgeons prescribed "low diet," "half diet," or "full diet" depending on the patient's condition. A standard "low diet" usually consisted of coffee or tea, bread or toast and butter served for both breakfast and supper. Dinner would be something like farina gruel (hot cereal) and bread. For the "half diet," breakfast and supper were the same with the exception that milk could be added to the tea, but dinner might be mutton soup or some kind of meat, boiled potatoes, and bread. Those on "full diet" could enjoy meat with breakfast and such things as pork and beans and bread pudding for dinner. Supper was the same tea, bread and butter. Unfortunately, patients were often kept on "low diet," until they showed some sign of recovery when, in many instances, a better diet might have hastened recovery or saved lives.

The diet kitchen managers received specially prepared books with instructions on duties, deportment, suggested recipes, and selections from Florence Nightingale's *Notes on Nursing*. In addition, the women were encouraged to visit patients whenever possible, and in accordance with hospital regulations. Cheerful visitors who read to the men, wrote letters, or sang, were regarded as beneficial to recovery.

Women as a rule did not assist with surgery, but it was known to happen. Amy Morris Bradley of Vassalborough, Maine, was called upon to help while she worked aboard the steamship *Louisiana*. Working with Dr. McRuer, she assisted with several amputations. She wrote that she was glad they had the chloroform to help the patients through, and, although she normally abhorred liquor, she found that her "snifters" of milk punch helped weaker patients. Milk punch was generally made by mixing milk with eggs beaten until light (one egg per pint of milk) and then adding brandy, sugar, and nutmeg.

Similar stories abound about women who followed the troops and acted as field nurses. Sarah Sampson, Isabella Fogg, Harriet Eaton, and Charlotte McKay, among others from Maine, all experienced the horrors of war from a perspective the hospital nurses never had. Often all they could do was provide a refreshing drink or a cup of soup to soldiers passing on the march.

During the war, an ability to create order out of chaos was as important as the actual care of the patients. Women were often put in charge of distributing hospital supplies. A well-run hospital was usually due to the excellent managerial skills of the hospital "matrons." Procurement of supplies was often a major role of nurses. This could range from visiting the nearest Sanitary Commission storehouse for needed items, to the much more demanding effort of traveling long distances, as did Abba Goddard each week, from Harpers Ferry to Baltimore to get the week's supplies, or scavenging throughout the countryside as did Isabella Fogg after the battle of Gettysburg. Probably the most amazing procurement was made by Mary Ann Bickerdyke when she left the hospitals of Cairo, Illinois, and Memphis, Tennessee, to go back to Chicago for supplies. She returned with a hundred cows and a thousand chickens so her patients could enjoy fresh milk and eggs.

Amy Bradley, Special Relief Agent of the Sanitary Commission, developed such an efficient method of distribution at Camp Convalescent in Alexandria, members of the rival Christian Commission left her with their contributions to distribute as she saw fit.

As untrained and ill-accustomed to such nursing as they were, women achieved a great deal of success in their endeavors to help suffering soldiers during the war. Certainly problems arose. Protocol was not always followed, or, in some instances, not applicable. Clearly there was a great deal of confusion as to who would do what and by what authority. Women nurses were confronted with prejudice, ignorance, and incompetence, and in some cases, they aggravated their own problems with an unwillingness to abide by military regulations and follow orders. Some women gave up in the face of such barriers. Others fought back and used the system to cause the dismissal of incompetent and unethical surgeons who opposed their "meddling" in hospital affairs.

At Gayosa Hospital, Mrs. Bickerdyke once found that patients still had not been served breakfast by eleven o'clock. The negligence, it was determined, was due to the fact that the assistant surgeon in charge had been out drinking the previous night, had slept very late, and had not yet made out the diet list. When he finally arrived, this spunky lady spoke some very angry words to him. According to some accounts she said, "Here these men, any one of them worth a thousand of you, are suffered to starve and die, because you want to be off upon a drunk! Pull off your shoulder straps, for you shall not stay in the army a week longer." Within a few days he found himself discharged from the army. The poor doctor went to General Sherman and asked to be reinstated. Sherman asked who had procured his discharge. "Why," said the surgeon, "I suppose it was that woman, that Mrs. Bickerdyke." "Oh!" responded Sherman, who knew very well that Mary Ann Bickerdyke claimed her authority came from God, "Well, if it was her, I can do nothing for you. She ranks me."[10] In fact, Mary Ann Bickerdyke was well known to both Generals Sherman and Grant, and usually received their full support for all her endeavors. Sherman specifically asked for her to accompany his army on its march across the South.

By the end of the war, women were generally accepted as nurses and their work was gratefully acknowledged. Their efforts paved the way for the creation of organized schools of nursing. Many hospitals developed nursing programs just after the war. The American Nurses' Association was organized in 1896. Within two years it had 2,000 members, all trained nurses, graduates of professional nursing schools. From their ranks came numerous applications to serve as nurses during the Spanish American War in 1898. This time they were readily accepted. The Army Nurse Corps and the Navy Nurse Corps were both formed in 1901, and women have been serving as nurses in the American military establishment ever since.

Chapter 5

Heroines All!

Introduction

Despite the extremely poor records kept on the activities of 19th century women, the names of over 100 Maine women who took an active role in the American Civil War have been uncovered. Some, like Harriet Beecher Stowe and Dorothea Lynde Dix, are still remembered today for their contributions. Others, like Isabella Fogg, Amy Bradley, and Sarah Sampson were fondly remembered for a time but then sank into relative obscurity. Still others such as Adaline Walker and Hannah Ropes gave their lives to save Union soldiers and were scarcely mentioned, even in their own time.

Why are some remembered and others not? This phenomenon seems to be simply a function of whether or not they or someone else took the time to write about their experiences and whether those written documents were published.

A visit to the Antietam battlefield gives any visitor the impression that Clara Barton was the only nurse there ministering to the wounded. In truth, she was only one of several at that battlefield and one of thousands of women who labored throughout the war for the sick and wounded. She is so well remembered today only because in her later life she participated in the organization of the American Red Cross and therefore kept herself in the public view.

Unfortunately, many history books are so selective in the information they convey to their readers that much is lost. All too often the picture painted is vague and incomplete. Very few history books mention the thousands of women like Clara Barton who risked their lives for their country during the Civil War. They were all heroines and should all be remembered by history students and scholars; by descendants, and historical societies; by anyone interested in an accurate portrayal of the participation of the citizenry in the war.

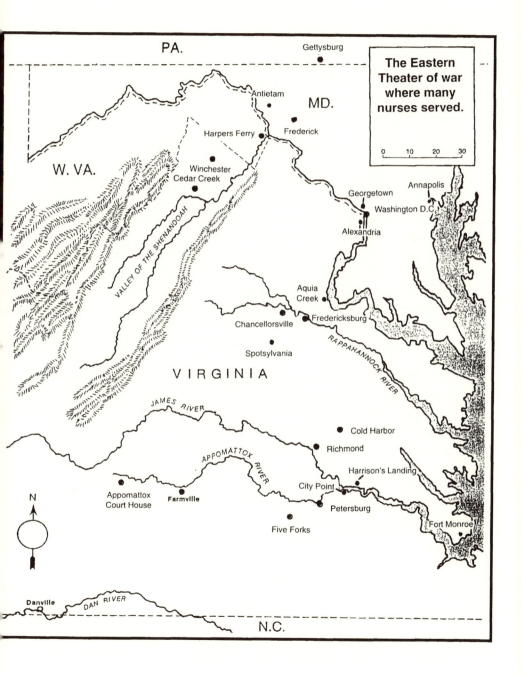

The Eastern Theater of war where many nurses served.

The list of Maine women who should be remembered as heroines of the Civil War is long. Some of the names of those who took an active role in the war were easy to discover—others far more difficult. The list will never be complete. The stories will never be completely told. Documents have disappeared, records have been lost, families have scattered and carried away letters and diaries to be sold to collectors or hidden away in unknown attics. Some women never wrote of their experiences. Newspapers often ignored their achievements. Despite these obstacles, it is still possible to uncover information about some of the most remarkable women in the history of Maine, living in a time that was crucial to our nation's history.

The biographical sketches focus on the contributions these women made to the war effort. They are arranged alphabetically by the name the woman used at the time of the war. Within quotations, anything added by the author is included in brackets [ ]. For the most part, spelling and punctuation were left as originally written.

Included is a secondary list of Maine women who were reportedly active in the war, but almost nothing is known of their lives or activities. Perhaps someday more information will be available about these women. They are mentioned to encourage further research.

All of these women had strong ties to Maine. They were either born in Maine or lived in Maine during a portion of their lives. Because people move, many could easily be claimed by other states as well. Wherever they were from, they were all heroines under difficult and often harrowing conditions, doing what they could to save lives and their country.

Sketches

Zylpha Adams
(1835–April 21, 1913)

Zylpha Adams' worst fears were realized when she received the news that her husband had been wounded at the Battle of Gettysburg. Without delay she set out on an anxious and arduous journey from her home in Skowhegan, Maine, to find him. Her husband, John B. Adams, in Company C of the 19th Maine Volunteer Infantry, was one of thousands wounded in that battle, but one of the few whose wife came to care for him.[1]

Born in Canada, Zylpha Bouillette married John Adams on May 17, 1855, and lived most of her married life in Skowhegan. The devoted couple had three children: Nathan, George, and Phoebe— but when the war broke out, John, like many other patriotic men, left his home and family and enlisted.

The 19th Maine was involved in two major battles, Fredericksburg and Chancellorsville, before it advanced on Gettysburg. At Gettysburg John was shot three times, once through the body and twice in the leg.[2] Few ever recovered from wounds such as his and it is unlikely he would have survived had it not been for Zylpha's special attention.

She found him at the newly formed Letterman Hospital just outside of Gettysburg, and remained to nurse him back to health. Zylpha also took care of as many other wounded soldiers as she could while she was there. Because of the severity of her husband's wounds she was there for several months before he could travel and be mustered out.[3]

Elizabeth Akers
(October 9, 1832–August 7, 1911)

> Backward, turn backward, O Time, in your flight,
> Make me a child again just for to-night!
> Mother, come back from the echoless shore,
> Take me again to your heart as of yore;
> Kiss from my forehead the furrows of care,
> Smooth the few silver threads out of my hair;
> Over my slumbers your loving watch keep;—
> Rock me to sleep, mother,—rock me to sleep![4]

Thus runs the first stanza of what became Elizabeth Akers Allen's most enduring poem. Written during the war, it was set to music 38 times with different melodies and sung by soldiers around their campfires as they undoubtedly yearned for home. Elizabeth received only $5.00 in payment for the poem, which first appeared in the *Saturday Evening Post*. When it appeared elsewhere under another name, she took the plagiarist to court and eventually won, but not financially. Her obituary states:

> While *Rock Me to Sleep* was unquestionably of high poetic merit, Mrs. Allen afterward wrote many poems which were

equally good, and not a few that were, in her own estimation and the estimation of discriminating literary critics, on an even higher plane of excellence; but none of them happened to touch the popular heart quite so deeply and so tenderly. During the Civil War it was sung at every camp fire North and South, and printed on leaflets, was treasured by many a soldier of the army of the Potomac, among which body of men it had a wide circulation.[5]

Elizabeth was born to Thomas and Mercy Barton Chase in Strong, Maine. Her mother died while she was still young and her father, a Methodist preacher, moved the family to Farmington. An unhappy child, when her father remarried she felt isolated from her mother's family. At age fourteen she gained her independence working at a bookbindery and later became a teacher for $1.25 per week. "Lizzie" began writing verses, however, almost as soon as she could read. In 1885 she wrote, "From my childhood I had been accustomed to writing—for publication, for various newspaper waste-baskets, or for the private benefit of the kitchen stove, as my own whim or that of some bigoted and prejudiced editor might dictate." Her literary career began at the age of fifteen when she received $2.00 from the publication, *The Olive Branch* for a piece she had written. Besides being a poet, Elizabeth was a pioneer in journalism for women. By 1855 she was working as an assistant editor of the *Portland Transcript*, a position she held for six years.[6] Writing under the name of Florence Percy, her columns and poems frequently graced the pages of that newspaper. It was said "while engaged on this publication she manifested a surprising versatility, as there was no department of the paper on which she did not perform more or less work. Her range was wide even in that early time, and she wrote stories, poems and leaders with equal facility and success."[7]

Elizabeth was married three times. Her first marriage was to Marshall S. M. Taylor of Vermont in 1851. Upon the birth of their daughter, he left for California, never to be seen again. In 1856, after demanding $50 payment from the *San Francisco Chronicle* for letters she sent for publication, she was told that her "husband" had already collected it. Since they were still married, he had the legal right to all her earnings. She promptly procured a divorce saying, "I was forced to do it or starve." The sculptor, Benjamin Paul Akers, was her second husband. After a tumultuous courtship and extended travel in Europe, they married in 1860. He died less than a

One version of Elizabeth Akers-Allen's "Rock Me to Sleep" which appeared in Godey's Lady's Book. (Vol. LXVII-10, 1863)

year later at age 36 of tuberculosis, leaving his brother Charles executor of his estate, and Elizabeth once again penniless. She left Portland and her position at the *Transcript* in 1863 to live in Washington, D.C.[8]

Washington held particular fascination for a journalist during the war, but journalism alone could not support her. She obtained an appointment on February 24, 1863, as a copyist in the Quartermaster General's Department for the rather generous salary of $600 a year. During her free time she tended the sick in the local hospitals and continued to write special columns for the *Transcript* back in Portland. On July 4, 1863 she wrote:

Dear Transcript—Out of the midst of wars and rumors of wars—out of the depths of stir and soldiering, patriotism and perplexity, confusion and cavalry, I write. Washington just now is not in the least danger of stagnation. In fact, at present, this city and sister Baltimore are extremely lively little places. Rumor waits, voluble, at the street corners, pouring out in the ears of all who will listen, such startling stories as have the singular effect of increasing immediately the size and prominence of people's eyes. I have been waiting until something reliable should be evolved from this chaos of reports, to write you, but one might as well wait for the Potomac to run by, so that he might pass over dry shod....

Coming up the avenue the other day, I saw a remarkable sight. The Black Regiment - not yet quite full, I believe, but composing a greater number of negroes than I ever saw before—marching grimly along, armed and equipped for war. Handsome, dark-looking men, whom the most hopeless victims of color-phobia could not accuse of the least "white-livered" appearance,—they proceeded with an evident sense of their own dignity, and their importance in the great question of the hour.

Seriously, it was a remarkable scene, and full of marvelous significance. Do you suppose John Brown, standing on the scaffold, under the dangling rope, saw any vision stranger than this? A regiment of armed negroes marching along in the shadow of the Capitol, within arrow-flight of which not three years since, their brethren and sisters changed owners like sheep! "Gods mills grind" not so "slow," now-a-days, methinks.[9]

Elizabeth possessed a knack for stringing words together to deftly describe the events of her time. In a worn volume of her poetry published in 1866, next to the poem "Return of the Regiment," which reportedly describes the return of the 10th Maine Volunteer Infantry to Maine, a former owner of the book wrote "Grand!"

The Return of the Regiment.

> The bells boom out to the cloudy sky,
>   The deep drums beat tumultuously,
>   And the martial music's crash and cry
>   Make all the city dumb;
> There are tender eyes at every pane,
> And, spite of wind and sifting rain,
> From square and alley, street and lane,
>   The eager people come.
>
> What do they come to seek and see?
> Why do they gaze so earnestly?

What may the strange attraction be?
    A handful of haggard men!
Men who have stepped in crimson stains
    Warmly flowing from traitorous veins,—
Soldiers from red Antietam's plains,
    Heroes of battles ten.

Ah, it is only a little while
Since in unbroken rank and file,
Cheered by many a nod and smile
    From thousands as they passed by,
Fresh in their unstained uniform,
Eyes all hopeful and hearts all warm,
They went to meet the Southern storm,
    To triumph - or to die.

Haggard with toil, fatigue, and pain,
Soiled and smoky with battle-stain,
Back they come to their homes again,
    Changed as by many years;
But leaning out from the gazing bands
Many a woman silent stands,
Who longs to grasp their hard, brown hands,
    And wash them white with tears!

Their banner wide in the wind unrolls,
Tattered and ragged with bullet-holes;
Think of the strong, heroic souls
    Who hailed it as their pride;
And with their faint and anguished eyes,
Lifted in deathful agonies,
Saw it between them and the skies,
    Blessed it, and blessing died!

Many a cheek at the memory pales;
The jubilant music faints and fails,
Dying in low and mournful wails
    For those whose graves are green;
The crowd grows still with a conscious dread,
So still that you almost hear the tread,
The ghostly tread, of the gallant dead
Who walk in the ranks unseen.

Crippled and mangled in trunk and limb
Are these, whose souls have passed the brim
Of that wide sea which, strange and dim,
    Knows no returning flow;
Solemn and still, in strange array,

Pallid with illness, and gaunt and gray,—
The ghosts of those who went away
But fourteen months ago!

The eyes of women and lips of men
Welcome the soldiers of battles ten,
Coming back to their homes again,
Sobered, but not dismayed.
Uncover your head and hold your breath;
This boon not every lifetime hath,—
To look on men who have walked with death,
And have not been afraid![10]

Elijah M. Allen of New York became her third husband in 1865. They met in Washington and he wooed her with charm and expensive gifts. Again, she met with financial disaster. He moved his mother and half-sister in with them and squandered all her earnings on worthless investments. By 1874, Elizabeth was back in Portland, this time working for the *Portland Daily Advertiser*. After eight more years as a journalist, she retired to devote herself to her poetry.[11]

Joining other women to push for the right to vote and to own their own property, she corresponded with Mary Livermore (another woman who attained national attention for her work during the war) in the 1890s. Mary wrote, "I shall not live to see the reform triumphant. But then I did not expect to live to see it as victorious as it is today." Mary Livermore died in 1905. Neither Mary nor Elizabeth lived to see women gain the right to vote.[12]

During her lifetime, besides her frequent contributions to newspapers and periodicals including the *Atlantic Monthly*, *Harpers*, and *Scribners*, Elizabeth Akers Allen published five books and numerous booklets. She was an active member in the Society for the Prevention of Cruelty to Animals and of the Sorosis Club[13] of New York. Her obituary, published in the *Maine Sunday Telegram* on September 3, 1911, stated:

> Elizabeth Akers Allen, who recently passed away at her home in Tuckahoe, N.Y., was one of the most noteworthy poets to which this Country has ever given birth, and was the author of at least one poem that is perhaps oftener on the lips of men and women than is any other in the wide range of American literature; a poem that has made the tour of the world, been translated into every modern tongue, and set to music by a hundred composers.[14]

Nancy M. Atwood

(1834–September 11, 1904)

Nancy Atwood, daughter of John Verplast, a farmer in Montville, Maine, was a seamstress living in Bangor, a widow with one child, when the war broke out. She enlisted as a field nurse under Colonel Abner Knowles of the 6th Maine Infantry Regiment in May 1861. She said, "I felt it my duty to do what I could to help the Union cause by ministering to the sick and wounded." She and Mrs. Mary MacDonald, also from Maine, went first to Augusta and from there to Washington, D.C. They arrived in time to hear the cannons firing at the first battle of Bull Run.[15] In her own words she described her service:

> We were in Hancock's Corps, and went into camp at Chain Bridge, Va. There I remained until after the first battle of Bull Run. During this time we were in close proximity to the rebels' line. Times without number the camp was thrown into confusion by skirmishes, and we were driven into the swamps. The weather was severe, and my tent was often flooded or blown away. There was much sickness in the regiment. The measles broke out, and I was continually employed among the afflicted.
>
> At the first battle of Bull Run I had my first experience with wounded men. My brother [Sherman Verplast] was injured, and I was transferred to his regiment, the 2d Maine, and entered the field hospital at Fort Cochrane, on Gen. Robert Lee's farm, on Arlington Heights. Here great hardships were endured, many of the wounded from the battle of Bull Run having been brought there; and I worked almost day and night to lessen their sufferings. Mrs. Hartsun Crowell, of Bangor, Me. was the only nurse besides myself in the hospital.[16]

Nancy M. Atwood Gross
(Our Army Nurses)

With her care, her brother recovered. In addition to her duties as nurse, she put to use her skills as a seamstress and repaired or "made-over" hundreds of overcoats and blankets for the men. She spent the winter of 1861/62 at Hall's Hill, Virginia, with the 2nd Maine Infantry. She wrote:

> But bad as the scenes were at Fort Corcoran they could not begin to compare with the awful scenes at Halls Hill where our regiment was sent. Oh, it was terrible. I saw many a poor man die through the shock of the amputation of an arm or a leg who might have lived and have had all his limbs saved, had there been but a chance to give them proper attention.... We were washed out by the rain many times at Halls Hill and several times our tents were blown away. Many a time I had to make the gruel or attend to some poor sufferer as best I could in a pelting rain, with not a dry garment for myself or the poor men who were sick and wounded.[17]

On March 14, 1862, she transferred to the Seminary Hospital at Georgetown where she remained until her health began to fail. She was honorably discharged and went home to Maine. By 1864, she was once again nursing soldiers, this time in the hospital set up in a Bangor gymnasium. After the war she married former patient, Stover P. Gross, a sergeant with the 2nd Maine Infantry, who was wounded at the battle of Malvern Hill. The couple settled in Bucksport, Maine.

In 1890, U.S. Representative from Maine, Seth Milliken, introduced a bill to grant a pension to Nancy M. Gross. Supporting evidence of her dedication and need was so overwhelming that the bill passed without opposition. Affidavits came from Lincoln's former vice president, Hannibal Hamlin, H. P. Crowell of the 2nd Maine Infantry Regiment, and Dr. William A. Hammond, surgeon general of the U.S. Army during the war. One such affidavit came from Louis P. Abbott of the 6th Maine Infantry:

> I would most respectfully call your attention to the fact that Mrs. Nancy M. Atwood-Gross went out with the Sixth Maine Regiment Volunteers as a nurse, and served in that capacity in the field and hospital, caring for our sick and wounded with untiring zeal, and participating in our long and weary marches by day and night, through the dark days of the Rebellion; often standing by the side of some dying comrade who gave his life for the country we so much love, blending her tears and prayers that those comrades be enrolled in the great army of which God is the supreme commander. Believing that this

good woman's health was impaired by this arduous duty, and untiring energy and zeal to render assistance to her country in those days of bloodshed and hardship, we ask that the Government, now in the zenith of its prosperity, render her a compensation for her services from 1861-1863, believing her most deserving.[18]

She died September 11, 1904, in Bucksport, Maine. Funeral services arranged by the Grand Army of the Republic and the Women's Relief Corps were held in her home on Franklin Street in Bucksport. For some unknown reason, she and her husband apparently tried to change their name from Gross to LaGross. Her obituary appears under the name of Mrs. Nancy M. LaGross. She is buried in Silver Lake Cemetery in Bucksport.[19]

Hannah Babb
(1808-July 20, 1897)

Hannah Thurlow Babb had lost four children and her husband, Bailey Babb, by the time the war began. Answering an ad in the paper, she journeyed to Washington and enlisted as a nurse, serving from June 1, 1862 until August 1865. Dr. Albion Cobb, a surgeon at the Harewood Hospital in Washington, said she was one of the best nurses there until she became ill from her duties.

She told Dr. Charles O. Hunt (formerly of the 5th Maine Light Artillery and wounded at Gettysburg) that her troubles originated on January 1, 1865, when she slipped and fell on the doorstep of Harewood Hospital, fracturing several ribs. It was over a month before she was well enough to resume her duties as a nurse. Many years later Dr. Hunt treated her at the Maine General Hospital (now Maine Medical Center) for cystocele (a hernia of the urinary bladder into the vagina).

Dr. James M. Bates, a surgeon for the 13th Maine Regiment, wrote, "I have known Mrs. Hannah Babb, now Mrs. Hutchins for several years past, and at one time attended her professionally for an extensive humor in her hands, wrists, and arms, which she supposed to be the result of blood poisoning, which she received while performing the duties of hospital nurse during the war."

Scores of people attested to her efficiency as a nurse. Twenty-five people of Chelsea, Massachusetts wrote on her behalf for a pension, "We knew her before the war as a worthy woman, and during the war some of us were in constant correspondence with her, forwarded her supplies from the Soldiers' Aid Society and from individuals. Her services and sacrifices seem to entitle her to recognition by the Government, and we earnestly commend her to the favor of the Congress."

She married Solomon L. Hutchins of Pownal, Maine, on November 15, 1866. He died December 19, 1880. Without means of support, she was granted a pension of $12 per month by act of Congress on July 14, 1886, which was increased to $25 per month in 1888.[20]

Hannah bought a stately cape-style house on Main Street in Freeport in 1885. She shared it with another couple until 1894, when she sold it to them, but continued living there until her death in 1897.[21] She is buried with her first husband, Bailey Babb and three of their four children in the Woodlawn Cemetery in Westbrook, Maine.[22]

Elizabeth Ann Bent

> Madam [wrote the representative from the Bureau of Pensions to Mrs. Cooper in 1894]; You are again advised that to give title to pension under the Act of August 5, 1892, the law requires that you must have served at least six months as nurse, matron, or superintendent of diet kitchen. The records of the War Department fail to show that you rendered services in any hospital in any capacity."[23]

Elizabeth Bent-Cooper spent years trying to convince the government that she deserved a pension for her work as a nurse during the war. She could easily prove that she did the work, for her letters and affidavits fill a large folder in the pension records at the National Archives. Due to a mere technicality, she never received the pension. In August 1896, she wrote to plead her case with President Cleveland:

> Our loved President I write you to get your aid. I was a nurse in the first hospital organized at Fort. Monroe. In June 1861 I commenced nursing a patient from the Big Bethel engagement. I think the first that required a nurse at the Hygeia Hospital... I have sent good proof from parties who know I served in the Hygeia hospital more than the six months which is required to get a pension. I am old and feeble and need help will you please assist me as it is very little for you to do and a world to me. I would not ask it if it did not belong to me... sincerely your humble servant Mrs. E A Bent Cooper.[24]

Elizabeth Bent-Cooper could prove she worked as a nurse at Fort Monroe, but the government still did not grant her a pension.

(Battles & Leaders II)

Apparently, the president did not respond because two months later she wrote again to the Pension office:

> ...I hope to convince the parties of my right. You say that Dr. Kimball was not authorized to employ nurses. Dr. Gilman Kimball organized and had charge of the Hygeia Hospital by order of General BF Butler gave employment to eight women nurses. I took care and prepared food for our poor fellows who were dreadfully wounded at the Big Bethel fight. In one statement from Dan Caverly a soldier of the 7th Massachusetts Battery was detailed to work in the Hygeia hospital he says he was there the day I got there and saw me every day for nearly a year and so many more proofs of my time as Nurse it took time that the Bureau does not look at my case with the spirit of kindness or justice of all. If the Pension had not been...given I should have been perfectly satisfied but now it belongs to me and I expect to get it justly and honestly I hope I will be able to give this administration the honor of doing me the just reward of my valor.[25]

Her proofs included letters from Sarah Winsley, who served with her at the Hygeia Hospital; Charles Gallagher, a sutler at the post in 1862-1863; William L. James, former quartermaster at Fort Monroe; a hospital steward; a sergeant of the 7th Massachusetts Light Artillery; and Daniel D. Caverly, who wrote on November 30,

1894, that he was detached from his company in June 1861 to do some repairs on the hospital under command of Dr. Kimball. He said:

> I often saw Mrs. Bent now, Cooper, at work there as nurse and saw her often until the company was changed to the Battery and left there in the spring of 62. I think General Ward took command at the Fort after Gen Butler. The Hospital Dr. Kimball had charge of was outside of the Fort in what was called Higea Hotel. How long she remained there after the Battery left I could not say.[26]

On November 3, 1899, former sutler Charles Gallagher wrote a second time that he was at Fortress Monroe in 1862 at the time that General McClellan landed there and, as sutler, erected his tent adjoining the Hospital and there met Mrs. Elizabeth Bent and her son, Samuel, who sold newspapers. He wrote:

> I know that Mrs. Elizabeth Bent (now Cooper) was there in the capacity of nurse under Gen. B.F. Butler who was there in command at Fortress Monroe. Further, I met Mrs. Elizabeth Bent at Fortress Monroe and her son Samuel, and that she was a nurse for the Federal Soldiers at said Fort, and up to the time of the retreat of Gen. McClellan from Harrison's Landing after the seven days fight. I did not meet Mrs. Bent after this time until 1863 at the said Fortress Monroe, and I then understood that she was still employed as a nurse there. I met her with several ladies who were coming to Yorktown as nurses for Federal troops here, under the command of Brig. General Wister [Isaac Jones Wistar] commanding the troops at Yorktown and Gloucester Point, Va and Fort McGruder, Va. Later I rec'd the appointment as post sutler at Yorktown, Va. in December of 1863 from BF Butler. And I certify that the above are facts. That I am not in any way interested or connected in the matter, and that Mrs. Elizabeth Cooper (then Bent) is in a very destitute condition and hope that her petition may be granted. Charles Gallagher.[27]

Mr. Gallagher was in a position to know Elizabeth Ann Bent-Cooper's plight because she had moved permanently to Yorktown, Virginia, after the war, as had Charles Gallagher.

Despite all her "proofs," the Surgeon General's Office of the War Department finally declared that Dr. Gilman Kimball was only an acting assistant surgeon and therefore not the medical officer in charge of that hospital. "Under the Act of Congress approved August 3, 1861, only the medical officer in charge (and the Surgeon

General) possessed authority to employ female nurses." Since Dr. Kimball was not authorized to employ Mrs. Bent, her request for the pension, so desperately needed, was denied.

Information about her life before the war is sketchy. According to unconfirmed family records, Elizabeth Ann was born in Newfield, Maine, to Nathaniel and Hatty Ann Varney Piper. Her first husband, Samuel Bent, died before the war began in Lowell, Massachusetts, where they were then living. One child also died and the other, named Samuel after his father, enlisted. After the war she married William A. Cooper and the couple ran a hotel in Yorktown, Virginia.

Amy Morris Bradley
(September 12, 1823–January 15, 1904)

Mary Livermore, Director of the Northwest Sanitary Commission, visited Washington, D.C. in November 1862. While there, she and other associates toured the hospitals and camps in the area. One place she visited in Alexandria was officially known as Camp Convalescent. The soldiers called it Camp Misery.

In the large encampment at Alexandria were included four camps. One was for "new recruits awaiting orders to join regiments in the field." Another was for paroled prisoners waiting exchange. Another for stragglers and deserters, captured and soon to be forwarded to their regiments. And the fourth was for convalescents from the Washington and Maryland hospitals. The first two were in anything but a good condition, there being great destitution of everything needful and convenient. The stragglers' camp was neglected and disorderly, as might be expected; but the convalescent camp was a perfect Golgotha. The four camps were located on a hillside, bare of grass, whose soil was so porous that a heavy shower saturated the whole like a sponge. The convalescents were camped at the foot of the slope, where it was forever damp, even in dry weather, from the drainage of the camps above. Here, ranged in streets named from the states to which they belonged, were fifteen thousand feeble men, all of them unfit for duty, and sent here to recover. "Recover!"— this was the governmental fiction which glossed over the worst condition of things I had ever beheld.

Most of the men were poorly clad, without blankets, straw, or money, though many had seven or eight months' pay due them. They were lodged, in the depth of a very severe winter, in wedge and Sibley tents of the smallest pattern, five or six to a tent, without floors or fires, or means of making any, amid deep mud or frozen clods. They were obliged to cook their own food and obtain their own fuel; and, as all the timber in the neighborhood had been cut, it was necessary for them to go a mile for even green wood.

They slept on the bare ground, or, when it rained, as it did while we were there, in the mud. Their food was the uninviting rations of the healthy men. There were but three surgeons for the four camps; and if the boys needed medicine, they must go to one of them. The surgeons only visited the hospital of the camp, which was full and running over, so that many were refused admission who were seriously sick, and who remained in their fireless and bedless tents. Such destitution, squalor, and helplessness I had never beheld. Bowel diseases were very prevalent, throat and lung difficulties met us at every turn, and the incessant coughing made us all nervous.

In our party were representatives from most of the Northern states; and there was a simultaneous burst of indignation from the lips of all, as we saw the utter neglect of these invalids.... When, on our return to Washington, I read in a morning paper that half a dozen of these convalescents had frozen to death in their tents during the previous cold night, I was not surprised.

...All of us had been accustomed to hospitals from the beginning of the war, and were used to sad sights; but this convalescent camp,- where fifteen thousand brave men, who had lost health and heart in the service of the country, were huddled as no good farmer would pen up cattle,—outweighed in sadness anything we had previously seen. The apparent indifference of the authorities concerning them seemed almost brutal. An endless stream of protests had been sent to the Secretary of War and Sur-

Amy Bradley   (USAMHI)

geon-General, to whom the horrible condition of this camp was made known; and still it was not broken up, nor was any apparent attempt made at its improvement.[28]

The protests did make a difference, however. Changes were made. The camp was moved, a new commanding officer was put in charge, and the U.S. Sanitary Commission sent Miss Amy Bradley to help put matters in order.

Into this hellish place, Amy Bradley, a schoolteacher from East Vassalboro, Maine, went, to do what she could to improve conditions for men assigned there. It was a tremendous undertaking. Her previous experience was serving as a nurse with the 3rd and 5th Maine Regiments until sent back from the front. She then spent several months working for the U.S. Sanitary Commission on the hospital transports rescuing sick and wounded soldiers from the disasters of the Peninsula Campaign. Amy assisted with amputations and prisoner exchanges and as the Peninsula Campaign wound down, she was put in charge of the Soldier's Home at 374 N. Capitol Street in Washington. But all this paled in comparison to her work at Camp Convalescent. In a letter, Amy noted:

> I entered upon my duties as soon as the camp was moved to the present location, on the 17th of December 1862. The soldiers (2,000) were in tents; no barracks had been erected. Many I found sick, and stretched on the almost frozen ground of midwinter, with only a suit of ragged and fever-soiled clothes and

Amy Morris Bradley's home in North Vassalborough, Maine.

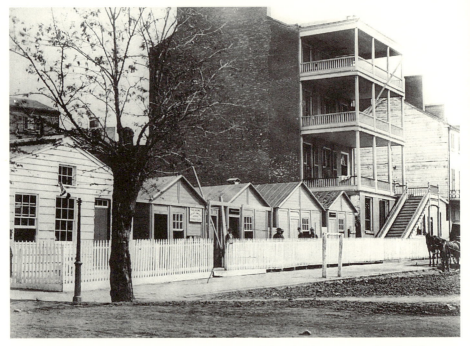

In the fall of 1862 Amy Bradley took charge of this Soldiers Home in Washington, DC.   (Library of Congress)

Amy standing outside of the Sanitary Commission headquarters at Camp Convalescent.   (Library of Congress)

one army blanket, with no nourishment that they could take, or that was suitable for sick men....

Making out a requisition form, I drew a quantity of woolen shirts, and on Sunday morning, at inspection, I went with the officer, and found in the line of men, on that damp and chilling day, on the banks of the Potomac in mid-winter, seventy-five with only thin cotton shirts. To these I gave warm flannels at once; and ever since the really needy have been supplied. Then I went through the sick tents, and immediately after sought an interview with the commanding officer, told him my plan, and asked for hospital tents. These were at once pitched and floored. Stoves were placed in them, and the sick collected and made as comfortable as possible. A squad of men was detailed to assist me, and every facility placed in my power.

Another wretched class I found, of those who had proved incapable of service on account of chronic ailments, or feeble constitutions, but who had not yet received honorable discharges, or their arrears of pay. Their papers had been lying for three or four weeks in the surgeon's office, while they were too weak or ill clad to go out in the cold and stand till their turn came. These I brought to my hospital; warmed, fed, and clothed them, applied for their papers; obtained their transportation orders, and sent them to Washington in my ambulance, to go to the stations where they could take the proper train, go home, and die among friends.[29]

Amy went on to devise such an efficient system for distributing clothing, blankets, and other needed items to the soldiers that even the rival Christian Commission would turn their supplies over to her. She wrote:

I have preserved, in a book kept for the purpose, the names, company, regiment, and state of nearly two thousand soldiers who have for the past seven months been thus aided by me. I took them first to the Lodge, No. 389 H Street, where they deposited their knapsacks for safe keeping; then to the paymaster-general's office; thence to their regimental pay-master's, when any doubt or difficulty arose. Finally, they went with me to the office of Major Taylor, the paymaster for discharged soldiers, where they settled their final account, and then I took them back to the Lodge, where they resumed their knapsacks, found lodging and meals free, and found tickets to return to their homes at reduced rates. Within the past two months I have obtained certificates for the arrears of pay for some one hundred and fifty soldiers, several of whose names were "dropped from the rolls." These I have had reinstated by proper authority, and they then drew their back pay...The sum total of the moneys thus paid in settlement to soldiers whose accounts were placed in my hands during the year, is between seven and eight thousand dollars.[30]

Like others, Amy Bradley experienced opposition to her methods and to her authority. Two assistant surgeons who tried to have her dismissed were themselves dismissed. The results of her work were testimony enough to carry any argument. In October 1863, Frederick Knapp, President of the U.S. Sanitary Commission, reported:

> The whole work is managed efficiently and with great success. She [Miss Bradley] has the confidence and co-operation of all the officers in charge of the camp, and daily she comes with ambulances into Washington, to the Paymaster's Office, and to the "Home" and railway station, bringing the sick and discharged men who have been receiving her care.
>
> Miss Bradley's report for the past nine months' labor in this camp of some five thousand men, shows what an amount of work can be done, relief afforded, influence exerted, by one individual thoroughly in earnest, and with resources at hand.[31]

In addition to her other duties at the Camp, Amy Bradley devised and carried out a plan to print a camp newspaper. It was called *The Soldiers' Journal* and made its debut on February 17, 1864. The subscription price was $2.00 a year or five cents an issue. After paying for the printing press, the proceeds went into a fund to help the orphans of soldiers who had died for the Union cause. The paper contained government office directories, instructions for securing pensions, instructions on applying for artificial limbs, information about the progress of the war, poetry, and anything else soldiers might find of interest. Copies can still be seen at the New York Public Library's Special Collections Department.

Amy became widely known as "the soldiers' friend." Officers, including Colonel McKelvey, who was in charge of the camp, Surgeon Sanford Hunt, and others, gave her a gold watch and chain in recognition of her work.

When Camp Convalescent was disbanded in 1864, Amy stayed on to work at the new Auger General Hospital, which took its place. In charge of the diet kitchen, she still managed to spend much time on the newspaper. She was proud that her subscribers included President Lincoln, General Grant, and Vice President Hannibal Hamlin.

The Soldiers' Journal covered Lee's surrender on April 9, 1865, and printed special black-bordered editions on April 19 and 26 to mourn President Lincoln's death. On April 17, Amy published a special "Mustering Out" edition which proved so popular that she had to print an additional 20,000 copies.

With the war over, Amy finally allowed her weary body to collapse. In September, 1865, she returned to Maine for a much needed rest.

She did not rest for long, however. In 1866, she set off on a new career in Wilmington, North Carolina, where she established a new educational program for the poor of that area. Despite initial opposition to a spirited, Northern, "carpetbagger," her methodology gained widespread acceptance. She became known as a pioneer educator, and her school was a stunning success. There is still a school named after her in Wilmington.[32]

She died in North Carolina at the age of 81, and was buried there. Several hundred people attended her funeral and flags flew at halfmast throughout the city of Wilmington in a final tribute she never received from her home state of Maine.[33]

Mary A. Brown
(June 30, 1840–March 15, 1936)

Forty-two year old Ivory Brown from Parsonsfield, Maine, had just returned from the war when he met pretty 21-year old Mary Ann Berry in Lewiston. Although he had already been married and widowed and was now a veteran, he must have been set on beginning life anew when he asked Mary to be his wife. They married in the fall of 1861 and settled in Brownfield, Maine.

But the effects of the war continued to be felt even in far off Brownfield. In October 1864, Ivory decided to reenlist and Mary made up her mind to go with him. Together they journeyed from Brownfield to the state capital to sign up. Ivory joined Company M of the 31st Maine Infantry Regiment. Not surprisingly, they refused to enlist Mary.[34]

Mary, however, was determined, and she made herself useful in Augusta, helping with the paperwork for new recruits and continuing to argue her case. The officers in charge were no match for her determination and soon allowed her to join her husband's regiment— most likely as a field nurse.

Mary Brown shows off her badges and medals 60 years after the war.
(Portland *Press Herald*, 1936)

There do not seem to be any records documenting Mary's service but her own testimony tells quite a story. In 1930, she was interviewed by a reporter from the *Portland Sunday Telegram*, and the article which ran on September 14, 1930 labeled her "Maine's only woman to shoulder a musket in the Civil War." She was 90 years old at the time of the interview and her memory may have been somewhat faulty. But the story as a whole rings true. Besides nursing the soldiers and sometimes cooking for them, she said that she participated in many battles and was not wounded once. She was standing right next to her brother-in-law when he was killed at Petersburg. Her husband, Ivory, was also injured while on march to Fort Davis near Petersburg, and she spent time caring for him and other soldiers both at the field hospital and later at Harewood Hospital in Washington until he was discharged in June 1865. Following the war, Mary and Ivory went home to Brownfield.

When asked, "Did you shoulder a musket and fight with the Union men?" Mary Brown replied sharply, "Yes, sir: I carried a musket—a 16 shooter [possibly a Henry Repeating Rifle], and a sword and a dirk, too, to fight my way through like the rest of them."

She also told the reporter, "We would have been slaves today, if it hadn't been for the Union men and women—it made a free Country for us and not a slave state. We thought slavery was an awful thing, and we were determined to fight it down—and we did fight it down!"[35]

Mary was one of seven children; five girls and two boys, born to William and Lydia Berry of Kent's Hill, Maine. During her early years, she said, her family "kept board from the school there" to make ends meet. Later, they moved to North Wayne and then again to Lewiston, where she was living when she met Ivory Brown. He had just returned from his first enlistment with the 1st Maine Volunteer Infantry Regiment, a three-month unit that saw action at the first Battle of Bull Run.

Throughout her life, Mary Brown suffered from health problems. She said that at age 11, "I had asthma so bad that I couldn't speak, and one day when the doctor came to see me he filled up a small pipe with some tobacco and told me to smoke it. My mother, I can see her now, objected to my smoking a great deal, but when the doctor asked her whether she would rather lose her daughter or have her smoke, she consented. The smoking made me terribly sick, but my lungs were relieved and I began to get better, although I still have asthma." She continued to smoke a pipe for the rest of her long life.

Another strange malady seems to have set in during her time with the Union army. In the 1930 interview, she complained of being in agony from what she thought were lizards in her digestive system. She explained:

> During the Civil War our canteens in which we carried our water often got empty quickly as we traveled miles over the battlefields, and it often became necessary for me and the other fighting soldiers to drop down on our hands and knees and drink water from a brook or small stream.... And it may have been one of those times when I did this that I drank something in the water. I don't know what it was that I drank, or how many kinds of living creatures went into my system, but whatever it was they undoubtedly have multiplied as the years have gone on, until today I am full of them and in this suffering condition.[36]

Whatever the reason for Mary Brown's strange condition, this spunky lady outlived her husband by 34 years. Ivory had been a Baptist minister and after his death in 1902, Mary moved to Portland and continued his work. Known in that city as a preacher, she often conducted meetings in various parts of Portland several times a week. She boasted that she had read the Bible all the way through fifty times.

A great-granddaughter recalled that her uncle went to Portland to visit Mary probably in the early 1930s. To his surprise he found her to be a guest of honor in a parade that day. It was the first and perhaps only time Mary rode in an automobile.

Sadly, at the end of her years, she was forced to depend on a small government pension of $50 a month. Mary lived alone in what is called a three-flatter apartment building in a rundown section of Portland, a building at the corner of Washington Avenue and Monroe Street which no longer exists. Although she was determined to live to be 100, by 1932 she had become so ill that friends placed her in the Farrington Hospital on Brighton Avenue in Portland. She died there on March 15, 1936—only four years from her goal of becoming a centenarian.[37]

The people of Brownfield still remember Mary Brown. When the town decorates the graves of their war heroes, Mary's is included. She is buried next to her husband, Ivory, in the Pine Grove Cemetery in Brownfield—finally at rest after an extremely long and memorable life.

Mary Carson
(October 18, 1832–?)

Mary Hunt Carson was one of those unlucky civilians who happened to be living in Gettysburg, Pennsylvania, during those fateful July days of 1863. For her brother, Lieutenant Charles O. Hunt of the 5th Maine Battery, however, her presence was life-saving.

Mary and Charles were both born in Gorham, Maine, to Charles and Mary (Fogg) Hunt. Mary met and married a banker from Philadelphia named T. Duncan Carson in 1856. They moved to Gettysburg where he worked at the Gettysburg National Bank on York Street. The couple lived in the adjoining bank residence.

On the morning of July 1, 1863, the 5th Maine Battery passed through the town of Gettysburg and right past the Carson house. As they went by, Lt. Hunt said to a fellow officer, "If ever I am to be wounded, it should be here for my sister lives over there," and he pointed out the bank residence.[38]

As the battle began, citizens of Gettysburg sought safety wherever they could find it. Many fled to basements and cellars to escape the bullets and shells that threatened their homes. Duncan was away at the time but Mary did not panic. One citizen reported, "Word was sent to the citizens to go to their cellars, as the enemy were driving our men and the fighting would probably be from house to house on our streets. Mrs. C[arson] proposed that we should go to the vault of the bank—which we did—nineteen women and children, two dogs, and a cat."[39]

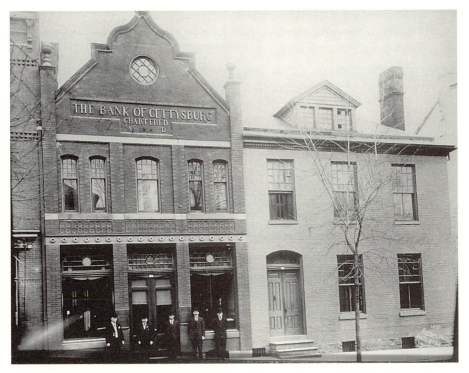

Mary Carson hid herself and neighbors in the bank vault.

(Adams County Historical Society)

York Street, Gettysburg. (Adams County Historical Society)

Late that afternoon, Lt. Hunt and his companions were caught in a fight on Seminary Ridge where he was severely wounded. Hunt was taken to his sister's home; she took him into the vault and placed him on a piano box. Dr. Robert Horner, a neighbor, extracted a bullet from his leg in full view of all the refugees. Charles remained with his sister, who cared for him until mid-July when he returned home to Maine.

Charles O. Hunt, Mary's brother.
(Maine Medical Center Library)

After the battle, like most women of Gettysburg, Mary nursed as many wounded soldiers as best she could, and even boarded women who came to Gettysburg to tend the wounded. One soldier, Lt. Charles Fuller of the 61st New York Infantry, described his care:

> I was taken to the house of Mr. Carson.... At this time every house in town was at the service of any wounded, or their friends. When I was deposited at his house, Mr. Carson was in Philadelphia to get and return the bank's property, but Mrs. Carson was there, and, if I had been a near relative, she could not have done more to make my stay tolerable....[40]

Lt. Charles O. Hunt got his medical degree from the University of Pennsylvania in 1868. He became the first superintendent of the Maine General Hospital, now known as Maine Medical Center in Portland and served on the faculty at Bowdoin College in Brunswick. He is buried in Portland's Evergreen Cemetery.[41]

Mary and her husband moved to Philadelphia in 1867 where he worked for the Fidelity Insurance Trust and Safe Deposit Company.

Mary E. Chamberlain

(May 5, 1839–November 18, 1893)

Mary E. Chamberlain was born in Brewer, Maine, in 1839. At the age of seven her family moved to Enfield, Maine, where she was living when the war commenced.

Mary immediately volunteered her services to the 11th Maine Volunteer Infantry and accompanied them to Washington, where she worked at the hospitals attached to their brigade. According to her own account she was on the rolls of the 11th Maine as nurse from November 1861 until February 1862 and was not paid. She did receive payment from April 14 to September 30, 1862. Her pension records state that she worked as a volunteer nurse from November 18, 1861 until April 1862 at Camp Carver Regimental Hospital and Warren Brigade Hospital in Meridian Hill, Washington. Her service with the 11th Maine was confirmed by an affidavit from the surgeon of that unit, Greenleaf A. Wilbur, who wrote from Skowhegan, Maine, in 1890, "that the only fault I could find with her services was that she worked too hard" and a few years later, "she was a very excellent nurse and remained with the Regt. under my charge until breaking camp at Meridian Hill on or about the 28th of Mar. 1862. We left her I think, at Newport News, Va." signed G.A. Wilbur, MD. (Late Surg. 11th Reg't. Me. Vols. Dated March 29, 1893.)[42]

When the Peninsula Campaign was launched, she assumed she would accompany the 11th Maine to Fort Monroe in March 1862. However, upon arrival, orders had been issued that no nurse be allowed at the front. Like many women did who were turned away, she sought work elsewhere. She worked at the Hygeia Hospital in Hampton, Vir-

Mary Chamberlain-Perkins.
(Our Army Nurses)

ginia, where she had to prove herself to Miss Dorothea Dix, Superintendent of Army Nurses. She was younger than Miss Dix wished to accept, but "upon the earnest solicitation of the surgeons and nurses, telling of her qualifications and zeal in the work, Miss Dix mustered her into the service." There she remained until the Peninsula Campaign ended.[43]

Thrice during this time she worked aboard the hospital transports and went to White House Landing in Virginia to receive and care for the wounded. In September 1862, the Hygeia was broken up. Mary was transferred to a temporary hospital near Fort Monroe until October, when she requested a discharge to return North to nurse her only brother who had been disabled in the service. She received her discharge and went home to Maine.[44]

In April 1865, she married Andrew F. Perkins and they moved to St. Cloud, Minnesota. Unfortunately, Mary's reminiscences about the war came many years later, when she desperately needed the money a pension would bring. In February 1893, she wrote to the pension office, "It has been so many years and from much sickness my memory has become so impaired I find it impossible to give exact dates but will as nearly as I can." The records at the National Archives help fill some of the gaps.

In June 1893, officials were still debating if Mary deserved a pension. Dr. Wilbur's testimony decided the case and on June 27, 1893, Mary was admitted to the pension rolls with a payment of $12 per month, commencing in August, 1893.[45] She died only a few months later of pneumonia at age 54.

Permelia Crowell
(1820–?)

Permelia Crowell from Bangor, Maine, was 30 years old, married to Hartsun P. Crowell, and had three children according to the 1850 census. When the war began, Hartsun Crowell enlisted as a private with the 2nd Maine Infantry, and then later a band member.[46]

Apparently, she accompanied him to the war because Nancy Atwood Gross mentions working with her after the first Battle of Bull Run. Mrs. Gross wrote:

> My brother was injured, and I was transferred to his regiment, the 2d Maine, and entered the field hospital at Fort Cochrane, on Gen. Robert Lee's farm, on Arlington Heights. Here great hardships were endured, many of the wounded

from the battle of Bull Run having been brought there; and I worked almost day and night to lessen their sufferings. Mrs. Hartsun Crowell, of Bangor, Me., was the only nurse besides myself in the hospital.[47]

Something happened between the Crowells during the war. When the 2nd Maine mustered out, he reenlisted with the 56th Massachusetts Infantry. Many years later he claimed on his pension application that he and Permelia had divorced before the war. His pension went to his second wife.

Emily W. Dana
(July 24, 1840–January 27, 1929)

Emily Dana was a high school teacher in Portland when the war began and continued teaching until several women from the area, including Louisa Titcomb, Susan Newhall, Almira Quinby, Adeline Walker, Mary E. Dupee, Mary Pearson, and Eunice D. Merrill, together decided to support the war effort closer to the front. They left Portland on August 20, 1863, to travel to Annapolis where they worked at the Naval School Hospital until April 4, 1864. Frank Moore wrote of that hospital:

Emily Dana.   (USAMHI)

The soldiers who came there were those whose constitutions had been shattered to the foundation by long sickness, fearful hardships, or deep and torturing wounds...during the last year of the war this hospital became the general rendezvous of the hundreds and thousands of starving prisoners just released from Belle Isle, Libby, Salisbury, and Andersonville. No language can be too graphic to depict the appearance of those miserable groups that every few days came in special trains from Washington, or in boats from Fortress Monroe, fresh from the long tortures of those infamous prison pens. Moving skeletons they were, or shrivelled mummies they seemed, half restored to the world of breathing, hopeful existence, the minds of many stupefied by the dreary and hopeless monotony of suffering through which they had passed.[48]

Emily Dana devoted herself to these thousands of patients under surgeon Dr. Vanderkieft and superintendents Miss Tyler and Miss Maria M.C. Hall. She wrote of her time there, "No matter, what the case or cause,—I rarely heard a word of repining or regret; so rarely, indeed, that such a word was noted, and the unfortunate complainant marked, and almost scorned, by those of stronger will." Her pension record states that she was attached to the hospital service on August 30, 1863 and was relieved on April 4, 1864.[49]

Although born in Kenosha, Wisconsin, her family was from the Portland area and summered in Falmouth, Maine. Her father, Oscar Fingal Dana, was an attorney and later chief of the Department of Internal Revenue in Washington. Her mother was Susan McLean. Both died in Falmouth.

Emily remained unmarried and spent most of her remaining years in the home she inherited from her parents on Waites Landing Road in Falmouth. John F. Dana, a prominent Portland lawyer, was her nephew. In 1905 he married Helen Hunt, daughter of Dr. Charles O. Hunt and niece of Mary Hunt Carson, another Maine woman who was caught up in the events of the Civil War.

Emily died January 27, 1925 of bronchial pneumonia and is buried in the Dana family plot in Portland's Evergreen Cemetery.[50]

Dorothea Lynde Dix
(April 4, 1802–July 17, 1887)

Much has been written about Dorothea Lynde Dix, one of the best remembered women of the Civil War. Appointed Superintendent of Female Army Nurses in 1861, as the first woman to hold an executive position in the federal government, she also became one of the most controversial women of the war.

Dorothea Dix was born in Hampden, Maine, to Joseph and Mary Bigelow Dix and lived a rather unhappy life with her parents until the age of ten, when she left to live with her grandmother in Boston. She prepared for a teaching career which she began at age fourteen in Worcester, Massachusetts. She continued in that profession for a number of years, establishing a school for young girls in Boston. Poor health forced her to give it up when she was only 33 years old. She was described as nervous, delicate, and overstrained with incipient lung trouble. In an attempt to regain her health, she journeyed to Europe–England in particular–visiting with friends. She returned to Boston in 1838, still in poor health. In 1841 she vis-

ited the jail of East Cambridge, finding conditions for inmates there appalling, especially for the insane prisoners. She visited other prisons in Massachusetts and concluded that all insane poor were treated similarly. Thus began her campaign to provide humane treatment for the insane. She gained the support of Dr. Samuel Gridley Howe, who later became an organizer of the Sanitary Commission, Charles Sumner, U.S. Senator from Massachusetts, and others. The bill to provide for relief of these conditions soon passed the state legislature.

Dorothea Dix.

(Library of Congress)

Dorothea Dix felt compelled to make sure similar legislation was passed throughout the country. She was successful in nine other states, two Canadian provinces, and even influenced care in foreign countries. She was still promoting her cause on behalf of the mentally ill in 1861 when the war began. She immediately traveled to Washington, and volunteered her services to the surgeon general. On June 10, 1861, Dix was appointed Superintendent of Female Nurses to select and assign women to general or permanent military hospitals.[51]

Why she was chosen to head such a potentially powerful organization remains a hotly debated question. Surely someone with a solid medical background like Dr. Elizabeth Blackwell, or someone with more extensive administrative experience like Louisa Schuyler, who helped organize the New York Central Association for Relief, would have been a better choice. Dorothea Dix was not an administrator, nor had she any medical background. Perhaps the military leaders felt threatened by the idea of women taking active roles in the war and therefore chose a woman with no medical or administrative training, who was bound to fail.

To compound the challenge she faced, Dix's authority was undermined by the very order which authorized her position. It specified that she was to oversee the nurses but "control and direction" were given to the "medical officer in charge." Yet the creation of the position appeared to give a sizable portion of the population what they wanted (care for the wounded) and still kept military control over that care. Regardless of the reason for her appointment, Dorothea Lynde Dix was well known by that time, having traveled extensively throughout the country, both North and South, pursuing justice for the less fortunate mentally ill.

The groundwork had been laid. Washington was already filling up with sick and wounded. Women of the New York Central Association for Relief had already been pushing for the creation of a national relief effort, realizing that state relief agencies would not be enough. They had already sent lobbyists to Washington.

Dorothea Lynde Dix was not an experienced administrator. She made many mistakes and many enemies. She turned away many willing women because they were too young or too attractive. She was widely known as difficult. Women who were anxious to work as nurses often avoided her by joining the Sanitary or Christian Commissions, enrolled as regimental nurses, or with one of the state relief agencies. Sarah Sampson of Bath, Maine, called on her in June 1861 and later wrote, "...fortunately (I am confident) the lady was out, and I was waited upon by an elderly lady (Mrs. Healed) formerly of Maine." Sarah went on to work for Maine soldiers and the state of Maine.[52]

When Mary Livermore, head of the Northwestern Sanitary Commission, visited Dorothea Dix in November 1862, she noted:

> Unfortunately, many of the surgeons in the hospitals did not work harmoniously with Miss Dix. They were jealous of her power, impatient of her authority, condemned her nurses, and accused her of being arbitrary, opinionated, severe and capricious.... I knew, by observation, that many of the surgeons were unfit for their office; that too often they failed to carry skill, morality, or humanity, to their work; and I understood how this single-hearted friend of the sick and wounded soldier would come in collision with these laggards.[53]

Dorothea Dix did not view nursing as a career but as an extension of women's traditional role as mother and caregiver. Caring for sick children, husbands, and relatives was not much different from caring for sick soldiers. Her mission was to help the sick and wounded and she never gave up. Despite her lack of experience and opposition from all directions, Dorothea Dix managed to work with the system to ensure that large, well-designed hospitals were erected, with competent nurses assigned to each to keep them running smoothly. She investigated reports of ill- treatment of patients and pushed for the best care possible under some of the worst possible conditions.

By the end of the war she accepted the fact that her nurses should be paid

Mary Livermore, who became a nationally known relief worker during the war, visited Dorothea Dix in 1862.

(USAMHI)

for their services and she began to accept most women who applied for the work. Doctors, too, circumvented her and hired their own nurses.

After the war, she continued her humanitarian work until she was 80 years old. She retired to a home offered by the first hospital she set up in Trenton, New Jersey, where she died on July 17, 1887. She is most remembered for her work during the Civil War and honored for being instrumental in pioneering a whole new field of career opportunities for women.[54]

This circular sent out by Dorothea Dix listed requisites and qualifications needed to be a nurse in her service:

Washington, D.C.
September 17, 1864

No candidate for service in the Women's Department for nursing in the military hospitals of the United States, will be received below the age of thirty years, nor above fifty.

Only women of strong health, not subjects of chronic disease, nor liable to sudden illnesses, need apply. The duties of the station make large and continued demands on strength.

Matronly persons of experience, good conduct, or superior education and serious disposition, will always have preference; habits of neatness, order, sobriety, and industry, are prerequisites.

All applicants must present certificates of qualifications and character from at least two persons of trust, testifying to morality, integrity, seriousness, and capacity for the care of the sick.

Obedience to the rules of the service, and conformity to special regulations, will be required.

Compensation, as regulated by act of Congress, forty cents a day and subsistence. Transportation furnished to and from the place of service, not exceeding 300 miles.

Amount of luggage limited within small compass. Dress plain—colors brown, grey, or black, and while connected with the service, without ornaments.

No applicants accepted for less than three months service; those for longer periods always have preference.

D.L. Dix[55]

Mary E. Dupee

How can I collect my thoughts sufficiently to write you any kind of letter? The very idea is enough to drive me wild. Soon after I came (Saturday P.M.) a part of the 31st [Maine Regiment] reached City Pt. and being quite destitute came directly here for supplies. The Agency has been crowded ever since, and we came to the conclusion last eve that it must be an unusually full regiment. They are to leave today, and of course must be waited upon at once....

Thus begins a letter from Mary Dupee at City Point, Virginia to Mrs. Ellen Bacon in Portland, Maine. Mary had recently arrived at the Maine Camp Hospital Association's headquarters near Petersburg, Virginia, to work with Mrs. Ruth Mayhew and Miss Rebecca Usher, Mrs. Bacon's sister. The letter stopped and started several times and was written over a period of days. She wrote, "If friends at home could realize that every minute is occupied they wouldn't expect as many letters."[56]

This was not Mary Dupee's first experience with nursing and relief work during the war. In August 1863, Mary left Portland with Susan Newhall and others to begin work at the Naval School Hospital in Annapolis.

Susan Newhall had worked at the hospital in Chester, Pennsylvania, under the direction of Mrs. Tyler. When Mrs. Tyler was transferred to Annapolis, many nurses went with her. When Mrs. Tyler asked for more assistance, Susan Newhall convinced Mary Dupee to join them. In charge of thirteen wards, Mary remained for nearly a year, taking in some of the worst cases imaginable. Her patients were often former inmates of the Confederate prison camps including Libby, Andersonville, and Salisbury. Before breakfast each day, according to L.P. Brockett, she went into the wards to check the condition of her patients

Mary E. Dupee. (USAMHI)

and to see that their meal was properly served. Every afternoon she visited each patient to make him as comfortable as possible—not an easy task given the condition of her patients.[57]

In April 1865, she left Annapolis to join Rebecca Usher and Ruth Mayhew at City Point in Virginia as an agent for the Maine Camp Hospital Association for a three month period. They cared for, and distributed supplies to, the Maine soldiers who were laying siege to Petersburg, Virginia.[58]

After the war she married and moved to San Francisco, California.[59]

Harriet H. A. Eaton
(August 6, 1818–June 10, 1885)

Harriet Eaton of Portland and Isabella Fogg of Calais enjoyed a complex relationship while they worked together during the war. From vastly different backgrounds, the two were thrown together by the Maine Camp Hospital Association, one of Portland, Maine's relief agencies. Together they journeyed south as agents for that organization and together they convinced officials to allow them to do relief work in the field. They traveled throughout Virginia dispensing what comfort, care, and supplies they could, risking their lives and enduring great hardships from October 1862, until just after the Battle of Chancellorsville in May 1863.

Whereas Isabella grew up knowing hardship and loss and supported herself before the war, Harriet Eaton seems to have belonged to a more affluent group. She had been married to Jeremiah S. Eaton, minister of the Free Street Baptist Church in Portland until his death in 1857. She remained active with his church and worked with the Ladies Committee in collecting supplies to send south to needy Maine soldiers. When Mrs. Fogg returned from the front, suggesting a better way to distribute the supplies, the broader-based Maine Camp Hospital Association was formed. It appointed both Mrs. Fogg and Mrs. Eaton to serve as their agents in the South. On October 6, 1862, the pair left for Washington on what would be for both of them the adventure of their lives.

They arrived in the field in time to see the remains of the Battle of Antietam—wounded soldiers in every possible shelter left to die or recover as they would on their own. They worked day and night in the most unusual conditions, undoubtedly saving the lives of hundreds, if not thousands.

Harriet kept a journal which she must have intended to share with others. On October 28, 1862, upon visiting the camp hospital for the 1st Maine Cavalry Regiment near Frederick, she wrote:

> Oh these poor men, they have to dress their own wounds, wash themselves if they are washed at all and eat—I wish I could attach one of their rations to this book that it might be seen at home. The poor fellow, Edward B. Warren[60] of Standish Me, to whom I gave the shirt when we were here before, heard my voice and called to me. It is discouraging to go into this Hospital for the poor men are most starved I have not a doubt of it.[61]
>
> Nov. 2. Started early to visit Smoketown Hospital. Was quite disgusted with the place. Stench and filth dreadful. One ward, having a bad head ache, I could not enter. Men have not enough to eat. Dirty rags and other filth meet you at every turn. Men well enough to be up laying in bed for want of clothes...Smoketown is just the place for malarius diseases to prosper. Do not feel satisfied with travelling on the Sabbath but I believe we must go on; Hence to Bakersville to a school house where we found 23 men of the Maine 5th who had been left by some mistake with out any supplies. Promised to see that they had Sanitary supplies from Sharpsburg.[62]

On December 9 she wrote:

> ...have opened the Gorham box this morning and find it in good condition except the two bottles of tomato ketchup, which had both gone to smash. Are now waiting impatiently for ambulance to take us to the 17th [Maine Infantry Regiment]. Mrs. Fogg proposing to go to the 6th but I am afraid it will be too late to accomplish anything. Dined with Col. Roberts, Dr. Wescott and Col's son, the Adjutant [17th Maine] Mrs. Fogg and Mr. Hayes went to visit the 6th while I have remained to attend to the wants of the 17th. One of Capt Martin's camp, named Drew of Fryburg has died this afternoon.[63] I have made about 2 gallons of corn starch gruel and a large quantity of buttered milk toast, no conveniences but an out door fire.[64]

By December it was clear that Isabella Fogg and Harriet Eaton were having trouble working together. On Friday, December 12, 1862, Harriet wrote in her journal, "I am vexed with Mrs. Fogg. She started out for an ambulance and the next thing I know she has gone to the creek [Aquia Creek] for supplies and worn my rubbers thus preventing my going out all day. To be sure I can write letters but that is not very pleasant when there is so much else to be done."[65] All was forgotten the next day, however, with the commencement of the disastrous

Battle of Fredericksburg.
Harriet wrote:

C.C. Hayes, Maine State Agent.
(Maine State Archives)

> <u>An awful day</u>. The battle began early in the morning, and has continued all day. While Mrs. F. went to see about an ambulance I went over to the division Hos[pital] and there I found the sick men of the second maine about thirty of them. I staid there during the forenoon, made whisky punch and provided crackers, butter and marmalade for all the Maine men—Returned to camp of the 20th intending to work for them but found Mrs. F with an ambulance ready to go forward. Accordingly we drove over to the Lacey House, about 1/2 mile from the battle field, where they were bringing the dying and where lay the dead. It was my first experience and an awful one it was, but I find my nerves strong to endure where I can be of service. One poor fellow who had had both legs shattered called me to him and said "do let me see your face tomorrow. I am growing childish" and he burst into tears. Another from Worcester Mass. wanted me to write home a letter to his mother with my pencil, so that she might hear from him as soon as possible, as only his left arm was shattered and he was not killed. Two shells struck the house while we were in it and the noise of the musketry and cannons roar and flash was perfectly terrific. Mrs. Barton there with four ambulances and 7 men.[66]

The following day she wrote:

> I spent the day in washing wounds, oh! how many frightful scenes I have been witness to. The sight of the dead becomes a familiar one. Col. Varney of the <u>Second Maine</u> with his Adj.[67] and one of his captains is among the wounded. Mrs. F. has gone to Washington to get more supplies. How I wish I could hear from our Maine Reg'ts.[68]

By January of the following year, personalities were clashing once more. Harriet wrote, "I am told that an individual whose name may be passed by in silence, has talked of <u>me</u> in this regiment as being "the petted widow of a clergyman, who perhaps did well enough at home, but was unfit for the camp and yet was trying to get the reins in this business." Well I am willing to bide my time."[69]

Despite the unpleasant conflicts, work went on. On January 26, 1863, Harriet wrote:

> Today I have been (in company with Mr. Hayes, by the first train to which I was hurried by Mrs. F. without my breakfast) to the Windmill Point Hospital. First, we went to Aquia Creek, thence by "Fairy" to the landing, thence through 2,000 head of cattle to the Hos. Dr. Hawkins met us first and showed us attention. Soon the steward of the 2nd Maine came to our assistance. He first took us to Hodgkins but poor Grinell died this morning and already <u>dead</u>, yes, starved to death. Nothing to eat but hard tack and salt pork for 4,000 poor sick men! Just like all the army ... <u>No kettle</u> to cook with, not even <u>wash basins</u> for washing. Nothing nothing nothing but indifference.[70]

Harriet and Isabella continued their work throughout the winter, often working separately but keeping the same base camp. In April Harriet began thinking of home and seeing her two younger children, Hatty and Agnes, again. Although left in good hands, they were never far from her thoughts.

The Battle of Chancellorsville came between her and home. On May 3, 1863, she wrote, "It is a strange Sabbath. The battle has raged fiercely, as we rode up to our Hos. We saw on the field about 200 rebel grey backs who were prisoners. The lower part of the house was crowded with wounded. Capt. Goldman and Lieut Moore are laying on stretchers. All round the house the ground is covered, and there is indeed work enough to be done. The poor fellows are so glad to see women here. Capt Clark is here guarding telegraph."

> <u>Monday, May 4th</u>. Last night, I was cooking and feeding the hungry in the moonlight, till one oclock, they are constantly coming in. This morning quite an event occurred, it was about four o clock. I lay on the bare floor, in the little attic with a quilt around me, when <u>bang, whirrrrr</u> went the shells, a reb. Battery had got the range of the Hos. In the night and commenced shelling us. I felt very calm, perhaps did not realize the extent of the danger. However it seemed near enough to render it desirable to betake ourselves to a more remote place of shelter. The Rebs gave one of their hideous yells, the wounded men,

prisoners, ambulance drivers, horses and mules made one rapid skedaddle. One young fellow, cane in hand, limping along, offered to take my valise, and begged us to feel that there was no danger, while we could see the shells as they screeched over our heads and burst around us. Two men were killed, several wounded. The firing soon ceased and we returned to the house and went to work preparing breakfast, for the hungry.[71]

On May 10, 1863, Harriet Eaton began her journey home. She wrote, "I parted with Mrs. F. feeling a little bad to leave her alone though I imagine she feels competent to take the whole charge and now she will have no check to her schemes."

Despite the problems between them, Harriet Eaton would later admit that she missed the excitement of those times. She enlisted again to help the Maine Camp Hospital Association and went once more as their agent, this time to City Point, Virginia. Conditions were very different. Rather than traveling from camp to camp, there was one large camp. Instead of providing care and nourishment directly to the wounded soldiers, she provided "mess" (cooking) for doctors and other officers. Despite distributing much needed supplies to Maine boys, they came to her instead of her to them and it just was not the same. Shortly after her arrival she wrote, "They

The General Hospital at City Point, Virginia.   (Library of Congress)

have a 'mess' of Dr. O'Meagher, Div Surg of the 2nd Corps and Dr Der Horne...& this I do'nt fancy much. I had far rather live as I did before with the army, the fact is, I do'nt like the present work at all. We are not allowed to go to the Front, though there are continued calls."[72]

Harriet Eaton remained at City Point into December 1864. She continued to receive and distribute supplies and spent increasing amounts of time helping soldiers to find Jesus; but her thoughts turned more frequently to her children at home. When Mrs. Mayhew came on December 18, Harriet Eaton gladly relinquished her duties and started for home two days later. She confided to her diary, "My dear, dear boys, shall I never see them again, til we meet in heaven, I can never be thankful enough for the privilege I have enjoyed the last three months; only eternity can reveal the work."[73]

Harriet returned to Portland, and lived there until approximately 1867, when she moved to Hartford, Connecticut. She had been born in Hartford and still had family there. In 1871 Harriet found work as a pastoral assistant at the First Baptist Church on Main Street in Hartford where her husband had been pastor from 1839 until 1844.[74] She died in 1885 in Hartford and her body was transported back to Portland for burial in Portland's Evergreen Cemetery where her husband, Jeremiah S. Eaton and her children, Agnes and Hattie were burried.[75]

Harriet Eaton's grave in Evergreen Cemetery, Portland.

Isabella Fogg
(1823–December 23, 1873)

On November 18, 1865, General Joshua Lawrence Chamberlain wrote, "It gives me great pleasure to say that I regard the services of Mrs. Isabella Fogg, while in the vicinity of my command, in the Field, as of the greatest value. Her energy, untiring zeal and unstinted generosity, and indeed, the absolute devotion with which she gave herself to the high duty of caring for our suffering men, made her eminent among the Angels of Mercy who have shed a gleam of light upon the stern path of war."[76]

General Joseph Hooker wrote on June 5, 1865, to Isabella Fogg, "It affords me sincere pleasure to testify to the valuable services which you rendered in the Hospital Department during my connection with the Army of the Potomac. They were indeed precious, and, in my estimation, deserve the highest reward and consideration in the power of the Government to bestow."[77]

Dr. G.W. Baker, surgeon in charge of the 3rd Division of the 5th Army Corps wrote in 1864, "I have had the pleasure of her [Mrs. Fogg's] acquaintance and often of her assistance, in the care of the sick and wounded for the past two years. She is so generally known and appreciated it would seem unnecessary for me to say aught in her praise..."[78]

What seemed to be unnecessary to these and other highly respected officers in the field became very necessary for Mrs. Isabella Fogg to continue her work for the sick and wounded in Maine regiments. In November 1863, for some reason now unknown, the Maine Camp Hospital Association, for which she had been an agent since its formation, voted to disassociate themselves from her despite overwhelming testimony to her good work.[79]

Isabella was a daughter of Scotch immigrant parents who had settled in New Brunswick, Canada. She lived there until her marriage at the young age of fourteen to William Fogg. The couple lived in the Calais area of Maine. By the time the war started Isabella Fogg was a widow, supporting herself as a tailoress in Calais. When her 18-year old son Hugh enlisted in the 6th Maine Volunteer Infantry Regiment and left for the front in July 1861, Isabella felt that there was little to hold her in Calais. She, too, decided to lend her support to the Union.

She collected hospital supplies, and that fall she left for Annapolis, where she labored in hospitals for several months. When spotted fever appeared at one post hospital and one or two men were dying daily, she and Ruth Mayhew, another Maine woman, volunteered to nurse them—ignoring the danger of infection. They worked week after week throughout the winter and into the spring.

In May 1862, with McClellan's Peninsula Campaign raging, she left to work on the hospital ship *Elm City*, which the U. S. Sanitary Commission had equipped to transport the wounded from battlefields along the James and York Rivers to Northern hospitals. Those hospital trans-

Isabella Morrison Fogg
(Maine State Archives)

ports are credited with saving the lives of between 15,000 to 20,000 men and are heralded today as being revolutionary in concept. Never before had there been an organized effort to remove the wounded who previously would have, for the most part, been abandoned on the field.

At the end of May 1862, just as the Battle of Fair Oaks and the Peninsula Campaign was ending, Dr. John Swinburne asked for her aid at the front. Mr. Frederick Knapp of the Sanitary Commission relayed the request and her reply reportedly was, "Mr. Knapp, that is just where I would like to go."[80]

Throughout June 1862, she labored to feed the sick near the front at Savage Station, often protecting herself from the searing heat by wearing a wet towel wrapped inside her hat. When her son, Hugh, arrived for a visit, he described the suffering of his comrades in Hancock's Brigade at Chickahominy Swamp. She loaded an ambulance with supplies and headed west with him to where that brigade was encamped—within sight of the spires of Richmond. Here she delivered supplies, nursed soldiers with typhoid and diarrhea, and made plans to return permanently and better equipped.

The Battle of Gaines's Mill canceled all her plans. She had more than she could handle back at Savage Station as the Seven Days' Battle raged. There was fear that the sick and wounded would be abandoned to the Confederates as the Union troops fled. In fact 2,500 men were left in the field hospital and taken prisoner, including Dr. Swinburne. Isabella stayed as long as she could but was forced to retreat to Harrison's Landing on the James River with the rest of the army. There she began working with Dr. Letterman, preparing food for amputation cases, which she continued throughout July and part of August until the hospital was disbanded. She then made her way back to Maine.

In Maine, she spread the word about needed supplies and aid. As a result, a state agent, Colonel Hathaway, was appointed. His assistant, Mr. C.C. Hayes, Isabella Fogg, and Mrs. Harriet Eaton, of Portland, went south to Washington to ensure that supplies and aid reached Maine soldiers. They took along large quantities of supplies gathered by Portland ladies who would later organize themselves into the Maine Camp Hospital Association. Supplies collected from other local organizations went too.

Isabella worked with the wounded at Savage Station but was forced to flee with the rest of the army leaving the wounded to be captured. (Battles & Leaders)

Throughout October and November 1862, the pair traveled in the vicinity of Washington seeking out Maine regiments and distributing supplies. They were usually found with the 5th Corps of the Army of the Potomac since so many Maine regiments were attached to it. On November 10, 1862, Isabella wrote to Maine State Relief Agent Mr. Hathaway:

> ...We then went up to Smoketown Hospital, here we found 30 Maine men, this place is in a most miserable condition, the men complain very much although Mrs. Harris and several Penn. ladies, with a great quantity of supplies were there. The effluvia arising from the condition of these grounds is intolerable, quite enough to make a man in perfect health sick, and how men can recover in such a place is a mystery to me. We then went to Bakersville saw there 35 of the 5th Maine, left in a school house in care of the steward without supplies; found him making every effort to keep them comfortable. We inquired why he did not call on the Commission. He replied he had always found so many difficulties in obtaining them from this source he preferred purchasing himself. We told him we would go to the Commission and have what he required put up for him. Here we opened your box of jelly. We then came to Sharpsburg, the Maine troops had crossed the river, only five Maine men were left here, also Capt. Hill of the 20th in a private house. We did what we could for his comfort and then proceeded to Harper's Ferry. Here the sick are in a fearful condition, in every old house and church and hundreds on the ground. You no doubt think your ladies in Washington are doing a great work, but I can assure you, if they were here they would find the stern reality of want, privation and extreme suffering...[81]

They won the grudging respect of those who had, at first, argued against their plan to go to the front. On November 15, 1862, Chaplain George Knox of the 10th Maine Regiment wrote, "Seeing them so successful, I desire to inform you that the doubts which I expressed when in Portland a few weeks ago, are entirely dispelled; and I would earnestly encourage those now engaged in this labor of love and patriotism... Could you have been here during the last two or three weeks, you would have had most ample proofs of the need of just such persons as you have sent, and just such labor as they are performing."[82]

Frank Moore, in his book, *Women of the War*, reported that Isabella Fogg wrote in her diary:

Started with ambulance filled with necessary stores of all kinds, such as bread, soft crackers, canned chicken, oysters, dried fruit, preserves, condensed milk, dried fish, pickles, butter, eggs, white sugar, green tea, cocoa, broma, apples, oranges, lemons, cordials, wines, woollen underwear, towels, quilts, feather pillows, all invaluable among so many sufferers so far from home and its comforts. My first visit was directed to those regiments where the wants were most pressing; but my special mission was to those who languished under bare shelter tents, they being entirely dependent upon their rations, and seldom or never reached by sanitary hospital stores. In company with the surgeons, who always welcomed us, we made the tour of the camp, going from tent to tent, finding from one to three in each of those miserable quarters, suffering from camp diseases of every form, distributing our stores at the surgeons' suggestion. We left reading matter generally in each tent. Then we would hasten away to the General Hospital and pass the latter part of the day in reading the Bible to some dying soldier, or write out his words of final and touching farewell to the loved ones at home, then bathe fevered brows, moisten with water and refresh with cordials mouths parched with fever, and, adjusting pillows under aching heads, bid our patients farewell. Weary, but glad at heart for having it in our power to do so much for our boys, we sought our tents, which scarce protected us from snow and rain; but we were happy in a sense of duty discharged, and in enjoying the grateful love of our sacrificing heroes.[83]

On December 13, 1862, General Burnside made a disastrous attack on Fredericksburg, Virginia, which Isabella apparently witnessed from across the river. She and Mrs. Eaton labored incessantly for many days after that battle in camps all along the Rapahannock to the Potomac caring for the wounded.

Pneumonia struck her down in early March. Harriet Eaton tried to care for her, but Isabella was an extremely poor patient. She refused to take prescribed medication or follow the doctors' advice. Harriet Eaton wrote in her diary:

Wednesday, March 18th. [1863] Dr. Wixom came over today. He tells Mrs. F. that her disease is not dangerous, that it is bilious pneumonia, or congestion of the liver with an irritated state of the lungs. Dr. Hersom also called, medicines have been left, and mustard ordered on the chest. What shall I do? The Lord direct me. Dr. W. says I must not leave her for two or three days, while she says, if I do'nt go, to visit the Regts. she will start for Washington tomorrow. There lays the powder, she will not take it and there is the mustard draft, she will not have it on....[84]

Isabella gradually recovered and regained her strength by the beginning of the battle at Chancellorsville (May 3, 1863). For five days, she and Mrs. Eaton provided food to the wounded and weary soldiers at nearby United States Ford. At daybreak on May 4, she and Mrs. Eaton, exhausted, found an unoccupied corner in the attic of the building they used for a hospital. They had just lay down to sleep when shells and shot came smashing through the roof. All was chaos and confusion during the shelling as all who could walk or crawl tried to escape. Several died in the attack, including one soldier whose wounds Isabella had just bound. Soon, however, the Union forces made a more active defense of the site and the shelling ceased. Isabella Fogg and Harriet Eaton continued their efforts to keep men alive, but it was soon after this event, on May 10, that Harriet Eaton left for home.

Isabella Fogg stayed in the field. She was at Gettysburg on July 4, 1863, the day after the battle ended, distributing mail and what supplies she could scrounge to the Maine boys. She was joined by two other Maine women; Mrs. Ruth Mayhew, of Rockland, who had been sent by the Maine Camp Hospital Association to replace Harriet Eaton, and by Mrs. Sarah Sampson, of Bath. Isabella Fogg worked for nearly two weeks after the battle before leaving to follow the troops once more. Mrs. Mayhew and Mrs. Sampson remained to work at the Gettysburg hospitals. Isabella continued on to Warrenton, Culpeper, Bristow Station, Rapahannock Station, Kelly's Ford, and Mine Run, aiding the sick and wounded soldiers.

In early 1864, she went home to Maine once again. Armed with petitions and testimonials and despite being "dismissed" by the Maine Camp Hospital Association in November "in consequence of reports prejudicial to the character and usefulness of Mrs. Fogg as a nurse," she secured $200, a generous sum at the time, from the state legislature to continue her work.[85] Colonel Joshua Lawrence Chamberlain wrote:

Washington, D.C. February 1st, 1864

I consider Mrs. Fogg one of the most faithful, earnest and efficient workers in the humane cause in which she has been engaged for the last 3 years, that I have ever seen in the field. My opportunities for observing her efforts have been the most favorable, and I think it may safely be said that she is peculiarly qualified for such a service, and that her success is greater than that of many more assuming agencies.

I consider her services are too valuable to be dispensed with and trust that she may receive such countenance and support as may suitably recognize her past success and the high character she has sustained.

J. L. Chamberlain,
Col. 20th Maine Vols.[86]

Ulysses S. Grant was now commander-in-chief as Isabella returned to the front. His leadership style became evident during the Battle of the Wilderness in the second week of May 1864, where over 12,000 were wounded. Reportedly, she and Miss Dix, Superintendent of Army Nurses, took an ambulance to Fredericksburg, near the battle site. They found the city to be one huge hospital. According to Moore she wrote, "It was indescribable in its enormous woes, a sight demanding the tears and prayers of the universe—the awful price of a nation's existence."[87]

The army was concentrated around Petersburg, Virginia by late 1864. A pass issued to her by command of Lt. Gen. U. S. Grant on August 17, 1864 indicates that Isabella was there. However, Isabella was now associated with the Christian Commission, backed by the Bangor, Maine, branch. Many hospitals were established at nearby City Point and the Maine Camp Hospital Association set up a relief station there under Harriet Eaton, who arrived in October 1864. Isabella may well have left the area by the time Harriet arrived. In

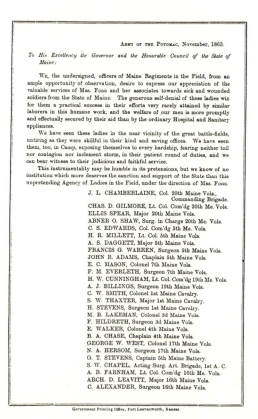

Petition supporting Isabella.
(National Archives)

October she was back in Maine collecting supplies when she heard that her son, Hugh, had been mortally wounded at the Battle of Cedar Creek. The Christian Commission helped her locate him. His leg had been amputated, but he was still alive in a Baltimore hospital where she cared for him. Hugh recovered but she herself fell ill and remained in bed for several weeks.

In November 1864, she applied to Mrs. Annie Wittenmeyer of the Christian Commission for a position. For the first time she was to help troops in the West. Mrs. Wittenmeyer assigned her to hospital boats around Louisville, Kentucky. It was there on the hospital transport *Jacob Strader* in January 1865, that she fell through an open hatch and was seriously injured.

In March 1866, she was still a patient at St. Luke's Hospital in Cincinnati. By then, Frank Moore was trying to collect material for his book, *Women of the War*.

Isabella wrote back to him, "in consequence of my being too ill to attend to the business required, and even now I am unable to do anything more than to send you a synopsis of my work.... I am aware that the synopsis I send you, might be made more interesting by giving more particulars, but I am now unable to make any changes, as I am entirely confined to my bed, and dependent on my friends to conduct my correspondence."[88] By May Isabella was well enough to write more specifically about her work during the war and those incidents were included in Frank Moore's book.

Unable to travel, in and out of hospitals for the rest of her life, she was de-

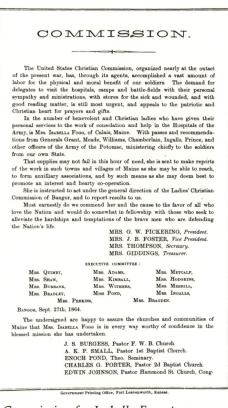

Commission for Isabella Fogg to serve as the agent of the Ladies' Christian Commission from Bangor.

(National Archives)

pendent on strangers for support. In 1866 she was granted a small pension ($8 per month) by a special act of Congress. She was one of the first women to receive a pension for injuries sustained during the war; but the pension was not enough to support her. In 1866 she wrote to Frank Moore, "During my sufferings I have written a few poems, one on the battle of Fredericksburg, another on Andersonville prison, and some other short pieces, which I am desirous to have criticized in order to ascertain whether they have sufficient poetical merit to warrant their publication...as the spinal injury I have received, will in all probability make me a cripple for life, it is important that I be able to do something for future support."[89] What became of those literary attempts is not known.

The pension was increased to $20 per month in August 1867. She asked for another increase in 1870. Major General George Meade, while writing on her behalf, mentioned that Isabella had failed to obtain any employment in the government bureaus of Washington. He went on to write, "I do assure you her case is most meritorious, and fully justifies her application being granted." The pension was increased to $30 in March 1871.[90]

Isabella Fogg died in Washington on December 23, 1873, at the age of 49. Her body was returned to Maine, and funeral services held at the Payson Memorial Church (The Second Parish Congregational) in Portland on January 8, 1874. She was buried in the Forest City Cemetery in South Portland, then forgotten for over 120 years.

In 1994, her grave was rediscovered. The stones had sunk into the earth, with the top stone falling backward, sinking until only its face and her name were visible. A group of concerned historians, with the help of cemetery officials, restored the stones to their original upright positions. A plaque commemorating her service during the war has been erected at the site and the American Legion has also honored her with a marker.

Isabella Fogg's grave, Forest City Cemetery, South Portland.

Ellen ("Nellie") Forbes
(September 1, 1837–December 4, 1908)

Ellen Forbes was born in Norridgewock, Maine, the daughter of Darius Forbes and Elizabeth Pottle Forbes. She was also the niece of Sidney Perham who happened to be serving in Washington as a Maine congressman at the time the war began. While visiting him in Washington, she realized how much help was needed to care for the wounded soldiers. She volunteered, and like many other nurses, paid her own expenses.

Ellen began nursing the wounded of the first Battle of Bull Run and continued until February 1863, when she contracted malarial typhus and was sent home. She endeared herself to her patients and received many letters from them afterward. One letter writer from Ohio wrote, "Since I left Washington one year ago I have often thought of the many kindnesses I rec'd from you while I lay there wounded & almost helpless. The many little deeds of kindness which, helped while away the long hours, that I rec'd from you shall never be forgot so long as my reason remains. Though I may never see you again I shall ever remember you. May God grant you a long and happy life."[91] Such letters she replied to, treasured, and saved.

Her letter-writing was of practical value, as well. Supplies were sent to her from various soldiers' aid societies in Maine. Most of these supplies came to her because she had written to the families of her patients. They, in turn, wanted to help the nurse who was caring for their loved ones. Ellen wrote to Abby Libby of Biddeford about her sick brother, John, in December 1862 and again when he died in January. Abby began to think of Ellen as a good and kind friend and

"Nellie" Forbes (USAMHI)

despite her brother's death, began working to save other soldiers. Wrote Abby Libby from Biddeford on January 28, 1863:

> I want to know where this clothing and other articles are going whether to the Hospital or otherwheres, whether it is for the sick and wounded, because the people of Biddeford have raised some money for this purpose and if we knew the particulars about it we get such things as you need most.... I have started out this afternoon to see what poor feeble I could do and the Lord has guided me this far and given good cause, and we are getting up a concert to raise money and then we will have the ladies to work making up the clothing you wish for. And I think it may be a sure thing. ...We will do all we are capable of doing....[92]

One of her patients was Eleazer Tolman of Milo, Maine, a member of Company D of the 2nd Maine Regiment. They married on April 8, 1864, and lived in Milo for a time after their marriage, later moving to Lawrence, Massachusetts. She continued to help soldiers by securing pensions for them, first as a volunteer, and later as an official pension agent.

A special act of Congress granted her a pension of $25 a month on May 18, 1886. In support of her petition were many prominent Maine men. Brigadier General George Beal wrote:

> While I was colonel of the Tenth Maine Regiment I know from personal experience that she gave her entire time in looking after the wants of and seeing that every care and attention was given to those in the hospitals. She became almost indispensable to the officers of my regiment in looking after their men; and any information as to their whereabouts or condition could always be obtained by sending to her. I take great pleasure in recommending her to the kind consideration of our Government, believing its bounties cannot be more worthily bestowed than in granting her a pension.[93]

Former Vice-President Hannibal Hamlin wrote:

> It was my pleasure to know and to be well acquainted with Mrs. E. B. Tolman. She did a most patriotic and Christian service in the hospitals in and around Washington during the late war. She was a long time in the hospitals; from my recollection more than two years. Her services were well discharged, and, I have understood, all voluntary.[94]

Colonel J.W. Hathaway and C.C. Hayes, Maine State agents; Sidney Perham, her politician uncle; and many others also wrote affidavits in her behalf. Her doctor, Dr. G. Howard, wrote:

> That she suffers from valvular disease of the heart, undoubtedly dependent upon or caused by stenosis of the pulmonary veins. There is also enlargement of liver and spleen, caused undoubtedly by malarial influences, contracted while in service in the various hospitals in and about Washington during the late war. She has been a great sufferer for many years from the above causes, and there is no probability that she will ever be any better. The condition of heart is such that exertion of almost any kind causes her much distress and suffering.[95]

Such testimony gained her the relatively generous pension of $25 at a time when most pensions granted were for $12 a month. With her pension secure, she continued to be active in the drive to grant pensions to all the nurses. She became a member of the Association of Army Nurses of the Civil War, an organization which lobbied for the passage of a bill granting nurses a pension. The former vice-president of the United States, Hannibal Hamlin, must have been supporting her work on behalf of the nurses when he wrote this introduction for her to President Benjamin Harrison:

> Bangor Me Jan 30 1891
>
> To the President
> This note will introduce to your acquaintance Mrs. Ellen M. Tolman a lady whom I have known for many years—She did excellent service as a nurse in the late war and was otherways a most useful woman in her aid to the country when it was much needed.
> I commend her to your kind attention as a most worthy lady in all respects.
> Very truly yours
> Hannibal Hamlin[96]

Ellen lived to see the passage of the act to grant nurses a pension in 1892. She saved all letters, poems and other articles given to her by the grateful soldiers. These were preserved by her family and are now part of the Maine Historical Society's collection.

Augusta M. Foster
(1838–November 19, 1901)

A Young Girl in the Battle. Miss Augusta Foster, daughter of the Second Maine Regiment, from Augusta, Maine, was upon the battlefield on Sunday, had her horse shot from under her and walked all the way from the scene of action to Alexandria, where she was ministering to the wounded at the hospitals.[97]

This interesting little newsclip appeared in Portland's *Eastern Argus* on Wednesday, July 31, 1861. It was copied from the *New York Tribune* and appeared in other Maine papers, including the *Maine Farmer*. Who was Augusta Foster and why was she on the battlefield?

The complete answer may never be known. The first Battle of Bull Run was the first major engagement of the war. Picnickers and spectators by the score had come out from Washington to watch the "entertainment." When the Union forces began to retreat, the audience became caught in panic and chaos.

But Augusta Foster is mentioned as the "daughter of a regiment" and not merely a spectator. The title "Daughter of the Regiment" was an honor bestowed by the men of a regiment upon a favorite woman associated in some way with that regiment. Some of them were wives or relatives of officers who acted as nurses or in other ways made life in an army camp a little easier. Some, like Kady Brownell of Connecticut, actually joined the men in battle, armed and ready to defend the flag. The 1st Maine Heavy Artillery adopted a Southern woman as their "Daughter of the Regiment"— a woman upon whose land they were camped and who graced them with visits and provisions. "Daughter of the Regiment" was an unofficial position and difficult to document. Augusta Foster is not mentioned in published accounts in connection with either the 2nd Maine Regiment or the 5th Maine, in which her husband served.

A month after the battle, N. P. Willis, a noted journalist who was originally from Maine, met Augusta Foster and, in writing about her, mentioned that she had followed her husband's regiment to war. If that is true, then it seems more likely that Augusta was the "daughter" of the 5th Maine Infantry Regiment. Willis had gone to Alexandria with Sanitary Commission officials Frederick Law Olmsted, Dr. Van Buren, and Dr. Agnew to visit the hospitals and report on conditions there. Willis wrote:

...her services had been found inestimable in the hospital since the battle. Miss Dix, finding her there, after a day or two, objected to her as too handsome for the position; but there had been such a universal protest among the patients, against her withdrawal, that the authorities had let her remain; and she is now quite the favorite nurse of the establishment. Dressed in a darkcolored calico loose gown, with her short-cut black hair fastened back by a round comb, and without any ornament whatever, she moved about among the sufferers, a "ministering spirit" indeed! It was quite evident that she was a woman of unusual tact and natural mental superiority, as well as of great goodness and benevolence. I wish she could have a "degree" conferred upon her, by and by![98]

The hospital was in the building of a former boys' academy on Washington Street, very close to an old church where George Washington was reported to have once worshiped. Augusta Foster remained there from July 1861 until the spring of 1862. In her application for a pension she wrote:

It was stated that I was at the hospital during January 1862. I could not recall the exact date; but remembered being there during the Holidays; which made the six months [needed to be eligible for a pension]. I now distinctly remember the departure of the 5th Regiment Maine Vols. I went to see it leave. My husband was there, & I hoped to see him, but they were in line for marching, & we did not meet, Dr Brickett tells me this was in March, 1862.[99]

Her husband, Charles, marched off with the 5th Maine Regiment and she never saw him again. His records show that he was promoted to sergeant and was honorably discharged in 1864 with the rest of the regiment. She never remarried, but went back to live in Augusta after the war. What happened between the two will probably never be known. Of her work she wrote:

I was appointed by the Sanatory Commissioner. My work consisted in keeping my Ward neat & tidy. When soldiers were brought in, many of them (with wounds which had been neglected) were alive with maggots. I washed & cleansed them of all impurities & vermin, as far as possible; then placed clean bed-gowns on them, gave them clean beds, & assisted the Surgeon in dressing their wounds. I did all in my power to alleviate the suffering caused by War. I gave each patient the food & medicine prescribed for him & fed those who were too feeble to assist themselves. And there were many who were fatally ill.[100]

Augusta included the following verse with her pension documents:

> I cheered them with Faith in that hour so trying,
>   When Hope in this life had fled,
> I received their last words, said prayers for the dying,
>   And closed the eyes of the dead.

Sarah Jane Foster
(October 12, 1839–June 25, 1868)

Sarah Jane Foster was one of many Northern women who volunteered to go to the South as a teacher/missionary to teach the former black slaves. Her diaries and letters cast a light on the trials and tribulations faced by such women. Sarah Jane's tribulations seem to have been greater than most because she defied her superiors in becoming friends with her black students—visiting their houses, allowing them to walk her home after school, etc.

Sarah Jane grew up in Gray, Maine. Her father, a shoemaker, was a church official in the Freewill Baptist Church which supported the abolitionists. Sarah Jane was no doubt influenced in that direction. An avid reader of both dime novels and literature, she wrote short stories and poetry as well, and was published in Portland's *Zion's Advocate*, *The Daily Press*, and Boston's *Home Monthly*.[101]

Before the war, Sarah worked as a domestic and as a teacher. During the war, while living in Portland, she became an avid critic of slavery, writing numerous letters to the editor of the *Daily Press* during the summer of 1863 condemning both slavery and those who refused to fight for principles. In one of her letters she wrote:

> Have we expended all our real patriotism? Are we going to give up while we have a man or a dollar left, because—*the rebels don't mean to be conquered?* Of course they don't, and the man among us who has any such intention is beneath contempt.... I know there is a large class of people, who will say I am thus earnest because I am of necessity a noncombatant; but Heaven knows that if there is one thing above another, which I regret, it is that I cannot be among the number who can offer their lives to so great and good a cause.[102]

In 1864 she applied to the Freewill Baptist Home Mission Society to teach the freedmen. In November 1865, she arrived in West Virginia with a small group of teachers and ministers, determined to aid the poor blacks any way she could. Her actions there, however, demonstrating her belief in the equality of the races, drew violent criticism from the local whites and church officials. She was forced to transfer from Martinsburg to Harpers Ferry, where she would be under closer supervision. In 1866, she returned home to Gray for a vacation, but while there, her teaching commission was revoked. She applied to teach again, this time with the American Missionary Association, and was hired to teach near Charleston, South Carolina, on an isolated, black-operated farm. In May 1868, in fear of the fever that was plaguing so many people of Charleston, she gave up her teaching to return to Maine. It was too late. Sarah Jane died on June 25 of yellow fever, and was buried in the Gray cemetery along the road near the fire house.[103]

Sarah Jane Foster   (Wayne Reilly)   *Sarah Foster's grave.*

Harriet L. Fox
(1824?–April 17, 1901)

As corresponding secretary, Harriet Lewis Fox was a key person in the day-to-day operations of the Maine Camp Hospital Association which sent hundreds, if not thousands, of boxes of supplies to its agents in the field. The *Portland Transcript* frequently requested donations to be sent to her at 49 Danforth Street in Portland, the home she shared with her mother, Elizabeth, and two brothers Augustus and William (Augustus enlisted with the 4th Maine Battery).

She wrote a well-written and complete summary of the association's activities in the year 1864 which was included in the Adjutant General's report for 1864/1865. "During the latter period," [November 1, 1863 through 1864] she wrote, "1,365 cases and barrels, containing every article of hospital stores for the use of our Maine soldiers, whether in the field or in hospital, have been forwarded directly to the Maine Agency at Washington, every city and town in the State having contributed to this great and noble object."[104] Included were 803 pairs of mittens, 288 flannel shirts, 397 pairs of flannel drawers, 75 cotton shirts, 2350 handkerchiefs and towels, 579 pillows and slips, 127 sheets, 84 quilts, 41 slings and swathes, 160 fans, 8 dressing gowns, 410 comfort bags and housewives,[105] 34 barrels of crackers, 487 cans of milk, 513 cans of meat, soup, and fruits, 75 pounds of corn starch, 11 bushels of corn and oatmeal, 202 pounds of tea and sugar, 49 pounds of butter, 1,000 bottles of wine, brandy, camphor, cologne, Jamaica ginger, pickles, jellies and preserves, 830 pounds of slat fish, 233 pounds of nutmegs, and numerous other items totaling in value $4,483. Many of these items must have passed through her house and Harriet probably counted them all and wrote and sent acknowledgements to all the donors.

Many soldiers' aid societies state-wide lasted only a few months, forming upon news of some fresh crisis and disbanding soon afterward, only to be re-formed with new leadership a few months later. The Maine Camp Hospital Association worked diligently from the time of its formation in November 1862 through the end of the war. Harriet remained at her appointed post, the most demanding in the organization, throughout.[106]

Harriet Fox never married. She is buried with her family in Portland's Eastern Cemetery.

Mary Germaine

Mary J. Barker of Hartford, Connecticut, married Dr. Charles N. Germaine of Boston in 1853. The couple moved to Rockland, Maine, to begin their married life. All three children born to the Germaines died very early in life. Their first, Julia, was born in 1855 and died January 9, 1857. Charles was born in 1856 and died January 20, 1857. Their last child, Oliver, was born in 1858 and died in August 1859.

When the war began, both Germaines threw themselves into the war effort. In 1862, Dr. Germaine was appointed examining surgeon of drafted men for Knox County. The following year he became examining surgeon for the state of Maine's applicants for pensions. His wife, Mary, meanwhile, began to organize the women and children of Rockland into work groups to prepare lint and bandages for the wounded soldiers. "Mrs. C. N. Germaine of this city [Rockland], associate manager of the Commission, herself alone, from the time the 4th regiment left Rockland till July, 1863, cut, rolled, and put up in packages for hospital use, 3824 yards of bandages."[107]

Cyrus Eaton in his *History* does not mention why she stopped preparing bandages in July 1863. When news of the Battle of Gettysburg reached her, she packed up her supplies and headed for Pennsylvania. She was there, tending the wounded, when Mrs. Goddard visited Gettysburg in September 1863.[108] Cyrus Eaton wrote that Mary Germaine was "known for her zeal in the cause of the suffering soldier."

After the war, the couple moved to Westfield, Massachusetts, where they spent the rest of their lives.

Abba A. Goddard
(July 20, 1819–November 26,1873)

On October 6, 1861, Abba Goddard left Portland with five other women to accompany the men of the 10th Maine Infantry Regiment. "Mrs. Goddard and Miss Merrill, will receive the blessings of our sick boys to the end of life," stated John M. Gould, author of *The History of the First, Tenth, and Twenty-ninth Regiments*.[109] He was a member and chronicler of those regiments. What exactly the nurses did was not recorded by Mr. Gould in his history. Instead, what is known of Mrs. Goddard is drawn mostly from her own reports which were published in the *Daily Press* of Portland. She gave lectures and solicited aid for the soldiers of the 10th Maine in November 1861, speaking in Saccarappa (Westbrook), Portland, Lewiston, and Gorham.

John Mead Gould's diaries, recently transcribed, edited, and published by William Jordan, offer a little more insight into the activities of Mrs. Goddard and Miss Merrill. According to him, many

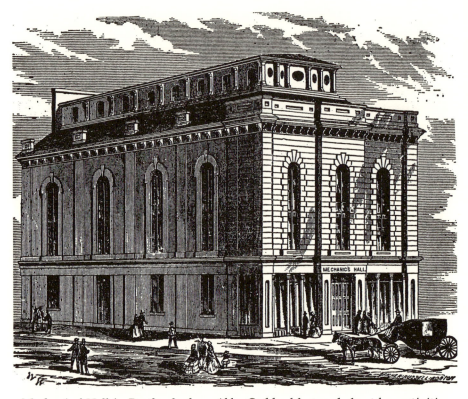

Mechanics' Hall in Portland where Abba Goddard lectured about her activities
as a nurse.   (Portland *Evening Express*)

men of the 10th Maine Regiment, and at least one nurse, did not get
along with the surgeon, Dr. Daniel O. Perry. On December 22, 1861,
Gould wrote, "The measles have now carried off two if not three of
our men and to me it seems owing to defectiveness in our Surgeon.
He is a mean, selfish man, and I don't believe from what I hear and
see that he is anything of a doctor. He spends most of his time and
energy in spiteing Mrs. Goddard."[110]

On February 5, 1862, Abba threatened to resign but Colonel
George Beal convinced her to remain. Gould wrote, "Miss Goddard
is the life of the Hospital and has the love of all the men."[111]

In March 1862, Dr. Perry finally had his way. He ordered her
and Miss Merrill discharged due to "irregularities in the hospital of the Tenth Me. Vols." The regimental hospital was closed
and the patients sent to hospitals in Baltimore. On March 7,
Gould wrote, "Band played a farewell to Mrs. Goddard and Miss
Merrill. I feel like shooting Perry every time I think of him."[112]

Dr. Perry, himself, finally resigned in July of that year. No doubt many in his unit rejoiced.

Meanwhile, Abba Goddard had not been idle. She was now the matron of the hospital in Harpers Ferry and had made a trip back to Maine, seeking more supplies and aid. In June General Banks made a disastrous retreat and abandoned Winchester, Virginia. The 10th was involved in the fighting. Abba reportedly visited every hospital in Winchester, Martinsburg, Frederick, and Baltimore, seeking out the sick and wounded men of the 10th Maine in order to determine what supplies were most needed and to make a complete report back to Maine.

The editor of the *Daily Press* wrote on June 28, 1862, "She has a variety of incidents of camp and hospital life-some peculiarly thrilling and tender, some heart-rending from their unpleasant features-which we hope she may find time to furnish for the columns of the PRESS."[113] Indeed, several of her letters were subsequently published. In July she wrote:

> It is useless to attempt to describe the feeling experienced when one of our 10th Maine boys comes in for a share of home charity. I am glad I can say, "your comrade, your mother, your sister, your wife helped supply these comforts; enjoy them and welcome!" Good Mrs. Jewett's pin cushions had a splendid run, and those checkerboards were hailed with delight. Indeed, slippers, socks, fans, pin cushions, towels and pocket handkerchiefs, in their rapid evolutions, quite excited my admiration.[114]
>
> In Baltimore I procured a barrel of soda crackers, and a hundred loaves of soft bread, and to-night, we shall have a jubilee. Hard bread and boiled fresh beef will lie upon the shelf this time, while tomorrow we intend to rejoice over a brimful kettle of hasty pudding. Our surgeon expresses great pleasure at the generous supply of clothing, etc, and wonders if Maine can stand such a draft frequently. I tell him that this is the only drafting Maine will allow, and that such drafts will be constantly honored.[115]

At that time she had 285 patients. Her letter on August 8 included an interesting description of her surroundings:

> I live on the warm side of a six-horse-power cook stove, kept at roasting point from 5 a.m. until 7 p.m. I try to sleep in a room just over that same cook stove nightly, and meanwhile the thermometer stands 96 in the shade. Hence, I conclude *there is a hot place*, and locate it in this especial region. Should you have any personal or political enemies toward whom you feel

disposed to use a popular expletive, and wish to send them to *the place*, get a pass direct to our kitchen. I think they will "fess" there is truth in "the doctrine."[116]

On August 11, 1862, she was preparing to leave. "Yesterday we received preemptory orders to remove the sick to Frederick, and close the Hospital forthwith." She did not plan to stay on at Frederick. "I shall go and deliver the packages belonging to those already there, and after that shall journey homewards, unless the spirit impels me to follow the fortunes of the Maine Tenth." In the same letter she wrote that, "some of the convalescents are wanting in what we call 'back bone;' that is, they dread returning to their various regiments. With the experience they have had, I do not much wonder; and yet I cannot help but wish for some of Dr. Bascom's hemlock plasters for them. If they would prove half as effectual in stiffening their backs as well as their courage, as his salve has in healing their sores, I should hope to see them with 'back bone' enough to do their duty to the last."[117] Her letter dated September 2, 1862, should have been her last from Harpers Ferry. "I am to-night the only white occupant of what was "Clayton General Hospital. Our sick were all sent off last week." She continued with a report of the supplies she had received from Maine and how she would distribute them. Once again, she expressed her extreme dissatisfaction with the cowardice of the troops. She called all the brigadiers "old grannies":

> One would think after fifteen months experience our men would get long past that;—yet surprises seem to be the order of the day....
> The other day we were surprised and lost 8,000 men! And this too, after some ten of fifteen other equally fatal surprises had been trumpeted through the country.... Two weeks ago, a body of Cavalry, 17 strong, were surprised and captured while in a field picking blackberries.

She listed several other equally surprising events and then concluded by stating, "I want to go home and electioneer for a commission... Then I want a thousand old—well my regiment wont be made up of 'old grannies,' I therefore want a thousand women not capable of being surprised at anything."[118]

She was still at Harpers Ferry on September 20. The day after she wrote her "farewell" letter of September 2, the hospital had been turned into barracks and occupied by some 300 "scared, weak-backed cowardly sneaks, who became suddenly afflicted with crick-in-theback, pain-in-the-stomach, weakness in the knees, etc,—contracted in anticipation of a visit from Stonewall Jackson."[119] The Confederate forces began firing on Harpers Ferry on Saturday, September 13:

> No less than 4 shells and a slug [fell] within ten feet of me. For about 2 hours they peppered us. As fast as a shell fell, I picked it up, and intend to carry home my own four or five proofs of narrow escape in time of peril. Some of our hospital tents were riddled by shell, but fortunately not one exploded, and consequently nobody was hurt. When we heard them whizzing, we dodged, and so escaped.[120]

Apparently the Union forces did not fire back, but instead abandoned the town. She bravely took a horse and wagon, loaded up supplies at the commissary and drove back as the Rebel cavalry arrived. When stopped, she told the officers that this was "private property" and to be respected. They let her through. With these supplies, she would be able to feed nineteen people for two weeks, and hoped rescue would come before then:

> I am almost tired of night-watching, and my revolver begins to grow heavy. It holds but five balls, but before secesh gets my seven ebonies [former slaves], my body will pay for the two balls wanting. Oh, this traffic in human flesh! Heaven send the day when the African shall cease to be born with a black skin. For this let Christians pray, instead of wasting breath in behalf of hard-hearted masters, for I am morally certain it would require a lesser miracle to change the skin of the negro, than the hearts of their owners.
>
> I had heard tell of the secesh army, but God forbid my ever looking upon such an ungodly crew again. Just suppose a meal bag dragged through the mud, dipped in bacon fat, and stuffed with rags, animated, and you have a decent representation of a live secesh; especially the live part—for the vermin frequently dropped from their clothes as they walked the street. Faugh! And then to think they drove our troops out of town like cattle! Well, it may be as secesh says; they say our men are so well dressed they don't dare fight, for fear of spoiling their clothes. I am sorry I cannot return the compliment.[121]

The Confederates, after seizing arms and supplies and blowing up the bridge, subsequently abandoned Harpers Ferry, and Union forces once again took control of the town.

In October 1862, Mrs. Goddard returned to Portland with "Aunt Jane," one of the freed negroes with whom she had been working. Both gave talks in the Portland area about their experiences. "Aunt Jane" had been the slave of several Virginia masters and forcibly separated from her children, as happened to many slave families.

By January 1863, she was back in the field. On January 15, she wrote from the 10th Maine Regiment's headquarters at Fairfax Station, Virginia, to say that she had visited many Union hospitals on her trip back:

> I wish some of our Portland Ladies' Committee could be here tonight, to hear what our men say when a woman from home enters camp. I brought dried apples, blackberries, raspberries, &c., some tinct.[tincture] ginger, two quarts of good brandy, some towels, socks, &c., for the sick in camp, and went into the hospital tent and gave each man a bouncing apple from the Pine Tree State. The old home smile was beautiful. One and all exclaimed, "You are welcome! You are the first woman we have seen since we moved from Berlin! God bless you!" Old faces came looming up and the warm hand grasp assured me words didn't express the half the heart felt. It is nonsense to talk of the camp being no place for a woman, that is, if the encampment is near comfortable dwellings.[122]

The 11,000 soldiers captured at Harpers Ferry the previous September were sent to Camp Douglas in Chicago until paroled or officially exchanged for Confederate prisoners. Included among them was her very special friend and abolitionist, Assistant Quartermaster John Parke Rutherford. She visited him there and on February 26, 1863, Abba and John were married by Reverend Tuttle, Chaplain of Camp Douglas. In attendance were two of John's children by his first marriage, and a nephew.[123]

In May John Parke was able to return home to his "mansion" house just outside of Harrisburg, Pennsylvania. Shortly after he was reassigned to South Carolina. Abba stayed behind in Pennsylvania.

June 1863 found her writing from Harrisburg just before the Battle of Gettysburg, now signing her letter "A.A.R." instead of "A.A.G." The marriage did not change the tenor of her letters back to Maine. The June letter from Harrisburg lambasted the patriotism of the Copperhead Pennsylvanian officials as they prepared to surrender to the invading Confederates.

She wrote from Webster, West Virginia, complaining of fleas, and from Harpers Ferry once more, saying she was glad to exchange fleas for bed bugs. From Harpers Ferry she journeyed to

Gettysburg, where thousands of wounded soldiers still remained even as the weather was turning colder. On September 24, 1863, she wrote from Gettysburg, apologizing for yet another tale from that now famous spot. She worked at what had been Spangler's Warehouse, at the corner of Carlisle and Railroad Streets (diagonally across from the railroad depot). While there, she found (or was given) a bible which came from a dead Confederate soldier's knapsack. About this bible she wrote:

> On the first cover of the bible (which fastens with a clasp) is the name of "Miss Almira Alice Wilson, Presque Isle, August 18, '52 (or '62)—I cannot clearly see which. On the first leaf is the name of "Moses C. Ames or Amors." Upon the opposite page is the name of "Wm. M. Nichols, Company F, 21st regiment, Georgia, V.A. May 27, 1863." Upon the last leaf and cover is written, "William Martin Nichols Book: picked up on the battlefield near Chancellorville, May 1st, 1863" To which I have added, "Taken from the knapsack of a dead rebel at Warehouse hospital, Gettysburg, July 1863." My theory is this: Miss Wilson gave the bible to William Ames: Ames like a loyal son of Maine, enlisted and fought at Chancellorsville. Either killed, wounded or a prisoner, his knapsack was rifled by a Georgian named Nichols. Nichols in turn was wounded and captured at Gettysburg, where he dies, and the bible falls into the hands of a nurse from Maine, who is anxious to restore it to the original owner. Will some one acquainted in Presque Isle tell Miss Wilson or some of her friends, what I have written, and say a letter addressed to Mrs. J.P.R., Box 130 Harrisburg, PA., will be promptly answered and the bible will at once be forwarded as a precious relic.[124]

Whether her theory is correct is questionable since there was no William Nichols listed as having been killed at Gettysburg. Mr. Moses C. Annas of Presque Isle, however, was wounded and sent to the Chester Street Hospital in Harrisburg, but by the time Mrs. Rutherford discovered that fact, he had been sent on to Fort Preble in Maine where his unit was then stationed. Mrs. Rutherford sent the Bible to the editor of the *Daily Press*, entrusting him to deliver it to Mr. Annas. It is hoped that it found its owner.

John Rutherford died in 1871 and was buried with his first wife, Eliza Rutherford. After his death, Abba moved to Charlestown, Massachusetts, where she suffered a stroke, paralysis, and died in 1873.

Lydia Gray
(February 22, 1813–April 9, 1901)

Lydia B. Gray of Durham, Maine, was one of the few women to receive a pension prior to the Act of 1892 which granted nurses pensions. She entered the hospital service under Miss Dix in August 1862 and continued until August 1864, when sickness and death in her family compelled her retirement.

Walnut Hill Farm in North Yarmouth where Lydia Bacon-Gray was born and grew up. The barn was added later.   (N. Yarmouth Hist. Soc.)

On November 26, 1862, Harriet Eaton, acting as agent for the Maine Camp Hospital Association, visited the "Navy Yard Hospital" which she called "a beautiful place, indeed. Found here a warm hearted company of nurses consisting of "Mother Grey" [Lydia B. Gray]" and others. There were some 50 Maine men in the hospital at that time. Harriet

Lydia Gray's grave in N. Yarmouth.

visited them all and was very impressed with the care they were receiving.[125] Lydia also held responsible positions in hospitals at Georgetown, Washington, and at Annapolis. According to testimonials in her pension file, her services were highly appreciated by Miss Dix and the several surgeons in charge.[126]

Lydia was born in North Yarmouth, Maine to Samuel and Ruth Bacon. Her childhood home was one of the featured farm buildings in *Big House, Little House, Back House, Barn* published by Thomas Hubka in 1984.[127] The farm is now known as Walnut Hill Farm. On November 6, 1835, she married Perez Drinkwater Gray, a sea captain, and they had two children, John and Julia. Perez died in 1850. She died in Durham in 1901, but was buried in the Walnut Hill Cemetery in North Yarmouth with her parents.[128]

Caroline Dana Howe
(August 21, 1824–October 30, 1907)

Caroline Dana Howe was not a nurse, or relief worker, not a crusader for the war effort, or the wife of a soldier who followed her partner into battle. In fact, Caroline Dana Howe was a poet, and an extremely unlikely candidate to have become enmeshed in those momentous events which enshrouded Washington. Yet for one brief week in 1864 she not only witnessed, but participated in, some most unusual occurrences connected with the final moments of the war.

Caroline Dana Howe, daughter of Apollo Howe, a laborer, and Elizabeth Dresser Howe, was born in Fryeburg in 1824. The family moved to Portland shortly thereafter and Portland became her permanent home. She attended school in the old stone schoolhouse on Spring Street, which later became an engine house and then a fire engine museum.

Even as a young student, she labored at her lifelong love of turning phrases into verses and verses into poetry. Her first poem was published when she was 20 years old by the *Portland Transcript*. She lived for awhile in Boston, where she taught school and began her poetry career in earnest. One volume entitled, *Willis Howard* was published for her by the Massachusetts Sabbath School Society. It sold out three editions.[129]

Her most enduring work was a slim book of poetry entitled, *Ashes for Flame and other Poems* [130] which was published in 1885. One Maine journalist noted, "She has such intuitive perception of the refinements of diction and delicacy in choice of melodious words that

Caroline Dana Howe
(Lewiston Sun Journal)

she may be compared to some sweet singer...."[131] This may well be why some 36 of her poems were set to music. This included her masterpiece, "Leaf by leaf the roses fall" for which she received a scant $3.00. Today, Caroline Dana Howe is remembered only as a minor poet, if at all.

In June 1864, she became involved, unwittingly, in several unusual events. She was staying with friends in Washington—influential friends—which included a congressman who was a member of the Committee on the Conduct of the War. According to her account, during her visit President Lincoln requested that the committee, which included Senator Benjamin Wade and Senator Zachariah Chandler, examine the Union fortifications around Petersburg and the preparations for the mine to be exploded. The committee members were allowed to take their wives, and Mrs. Howe was included in the party. They boarded the *Baltimore* and sailed down to Fort Monroe, where General Butler's wife and daughter joined them. A total of seven women were in the party, Mrs. Benjamin Wade, Mrs. Zachariah Chandler, Mrs. Kellogg, and newlywed Elizabeth (Libbie) Custer, among them. Mrs. Howe would later write a poem about Libbie's reunion with General George Armstrong Custer called, "Young Custer's Bride," a copy of which she sent to Libbie Custer after her husband's death.

From there, the party went to City Point to meet with General Grant. They remained there for two days. She wrote, "Generals Custer, Sheridan, Ingalls, and Weitzel were with us in a few hours after our arrival on the "Baltimore." We had a band and a quadrille that night on the steamer." It must have been that night, at dinner, when she struck up a conversation with General Grant who, according to her report, confided his dissatisfaction with a certain general (Hans Sigel?) in charge of a city to the north (Harpers Ferry?) but could do nothing since he was a Lincoln appointee. His comments were passed on to her friend on the Committee and thus to Lincoln. The man was soon replaced. According to the *Lewiston Sun Journal*, "This is the true explanation of the oft-repeated statement that during the war Mrs. Howe was given an important message by General Grant to carry to President Lincoln."[132]

From there the group sailed to General Butler's headquarters at Bermuda Hundred on the James River, where the committee was in the most danger. "Every fifteen minutes the death-dealing shells were seen and heard bursting over Petersburg from our line and the explosions were fearful to see as well as hear."

General Butler invited the ladies to watch him persuade the Rebels to come over to Union lines. His plan was to send messages to the Rebels attached to a huge kite which was going to be flown over the enemy earthworks.

Caroline Dana Howe wrote, "The tail of the kite was a huge mass of small strips of paper on which was printed the address to the rebel soldiers saying that if, because of their extreme destitution, they wished to come over to the Federals, they would be given plenty to eat, and not be obliged to fight against their own forces, but required simply to labor."

The slips were loosely attached, the wind cooperated, and the kite was launched. General Butler picked up one slip which fell as the kite rose and handed it to her. Reportedly, the general himself gave the string a hearty tug once over the Rebel lines and the slips fell "like a snow shower." That night, 28 Confederate soldiers deserted.

While watching this whole procedure, firing continued and a nearly spent bullet struck Mrs. Howe, grazing her ear. She wrote, "General Butler said it had force enough left to have destroyed my eye had it struck me there. He chased it and brought it to me hot. I still have it."[133]

She joined the nation in mourning President Lincoln's death, and wrote a heartfelt poem entitled simply "Abraham Lincoln," which appeared on the front page of the *Portland Transcript* on April 29, 1865. Capturing the mood and forebodings of the population, the final verses read:

Almighty Ruler of the earth and skies!
Bend thou in pity from thy throne of love;
Behold our lifted hands, our tearful eyes,
And guide our nation's clouded destinies,
While, chastened heavily, we look above!
Thou hast withdrawn our strong arm—
    and we drift.
Trembling and helpless, on the surging tide,
And we implore Thee, by that priceless gift,
Lent and recalled,—that great soul purified!
BE THOU OUR GUIDE!   *Portland, April 15, 1865.*[134]

After the war, life must have turned quieter for Caroline Dana Howe. She continued to write poetry, published *Ashes to Flame* and lived in her house on Cumberland Avenue in Portland. She died in 1907 and is buried in Portland's Western Cemetery, where her badly neglected gravestone has fallen and broken. Her parents' stones, which should be in the same plot, have disappeared.

Henrietta Crosby Ingersoll
(November 27, 1814–September 17, 1893)

Henrietta Crosby Ingersoll was renowned in the highest political circles of the capitals of both Maine and the nation. Her husband, George Ingersoll, well known in Bangor and Augusta, had been nominated for Maine attorney general when he died unexpectedly. She moved to Washington, D.C. with her children, and continued to move in political circles. James G. Blaine, Horace Greeley, Owen Lovejoy, Hannibal Hamlin, George William Curtis, and other political figures frequently stopped by her Washington home to get her opinion on various bills being considered.

Born in Dover, New Hampshire, the fifth child of a large family, she was, nevertheless, well educated. She married lawyer George Washington Ingersoll from Bangor and they had three children. Their daughter Alice married Daniel Chamberlain who became governor of South Carolina. Their son Edward Chase became a prominent lawyer in Washington. And their daughter Frances took a government job at the pension office and married Sumner Hutchinson, a farmer who was also involved in politics.

George was a graduate of Bowdoin College and a leading member of the House of Representatives in the mid 1850s. In 1860 he was elected by the Legislature to be Maine's attorney general. Before he could take office, however, he died of pneumonia.[135] She moved to Washington shortly thereafter and was there when the Civil War began.

Like many women of the time, as the horror of the war became known, she volunteered to do what she could to relieve the suffering of sick and wounded soldiers. Armory Square Hospital, just opposite the Smithsonian Institute in Washington, became her second home. Like many patients in the Armory Square Hospital, one doctor was also extremely glad to receive Mrs. Ingersoll's assistance. Dr. D. W. Bliss, surgeon in charge of the

Henrietta C. Ingersoll
(*Two Crosby Families*)

hospital, was under arrest by order of Secretary Stanton, when Mrs. Ingersoll intervened and pulled all the governmental strings she had at her disposal to free him.

The trouble started when Dr. Bliss dismissed a dishonest steward, who in revenge accused the doctor of misappropriating funds. Mrs. Ingersoll reportedly telegraphed Senator Hale and Senator Chandler and went to see Surgeon General Hammond, Charles Sumner, and Secretary Stanton. Dr. Bliss was released on parole, pending an investigation. Undoubtedly, the poor doctor was exonerated, since he never lost his position at the hospital.[136]

Henrietta was also active in the woman suffrage movement, serving as one of the vice presidents at the national convention held in New York by the Woman's National Loyal League on May 14, 1863. Organized by Elizabeth Cady Stanton and Susan B. Anthony, they pledged support for the Union in its struggle for universal freedom.[137]

In addition to nursing duties and political activism, in January 1864, Henrietta took up the duties of a newspaper editor, becoming responsible for the publication of the *Hospital Gazette*, the official paper of the Armory Square Hospital. It was a weekly publication printed by two of the patients and continued until August 1865.[138]

After the war, Henrietta Ingersoll continued to live in Washington, D.C. until her death in 1893[139] when her body was returned to Maine to be buried in the Mt. Hope Cemetery in Bangor with her husband.[140]

Addie Jackson
(June 3, 1830–July 10, 1927)

Addie Jackson was working in the mills of Lawrence, Massachusetts, when the Civil War began. She immediately enlisted as a nurse to serve with the 1st New Hampshire Infantry Regiment. Details of her service are sketchy. She served for some time with that regiment before accompanying another nurse (who had become ill) back to Massachusetts. She later returned to Baltimore and was employed making garments for the Union soldiers. According to her own testimony, she and her nephew, who were both in Washington at the time, planned to attend the play at Ford's Theater that fateful April night President Lincoln was shot, but changed their plans when the nephew became too ill to go out. She did see Lincoln's body lying in state a few days later.[141]

Little is known of Addie Jackson's early life, only that she was born in Kenduskeag, near Bangor, one of ten children of Michael and Sarah (Hutchins) Jackson. She attended schools in Bangor, and at the age of eighteen, went to work in the mills of Lowell and later Lawrence, Massachusetts. She was witness to the tragic fire of January 10, 1860, when 100 mill workers died. One of her cousins was General Joseph Clough of New London, New Hampshire, and he may have influenced her decision to aid the Union army. He began his military career as captain of the 4th New Hampshire Infantry in September 1861 and moved up the ranks to become Brevet Brigadier General U.S. Volunteers by July 1865.[142]

After the war, she met and married Edward Parmenter, a Boston businessman. She often assisted him in his express and trucking business, collecting bills and managing the business while he was ill. Mr. Parmenter was acquainted with such people as Henry Wadsworth Longfellow, John Greenleaf Whittier, and Charles Sumner, and Addie was delighted to make their acquaintance.[143]

When Mr. Parmenter died in 1891, Addie moved back to Maine to live in Old Orchard, where she had a cottage she called "Evergreen." In 1921, in failing health, she moved in with a friend until she died six years later at the age of 97. Addie Jackson Parmenter was buried with her husband in South Boston.[144]

Abba E. Jackson

(July 6, 1820–March 12, 1892)

The Honorable Congressman Thomas Brackett Reed, from Portland, introduced a bill to the U.S. Congress to grant a pension to Abba E. Jackson from Gorham, Maine.[145] His influence, and the influence of other powerful voices caused that bill to become law on June 21, 1888.[146]

Abba was born in Gorham, Maine, as Tabitha E. McLellan, one of thirteen children born to Tabitha and Samuel McLellan. She became the second wife of Chaplain E. W. Jackson in 1845. His first wife, Sarah McLellan, was Abba's older sister, who died in 1844.[147]

President Lincoln appointed Reverend Jackson as Chaplain in the United States Army on July 21, 1862. Assigned to the Armory Square Hospital in Washington, he served the dead and dying there from 1862 until July 1, 1865, during which time he conducted 1,500 funeral services. The couple built a house near the hospital and Abba used it as her base of operations to give extra care to the sick and wounded and to provide support for those who came to visit their hospitalized family members. Often family members came only to find their loved ones already buried.[148]

When Chaplain Jackson resigned in July 1865, Dr. Bliss, the head surgeon at Armory Square Hospital wrote him a letter which included the following:

> I can not close without paying a slight tribute to the benevolent and Christian labor of your devoted wife, who has been untiring in her devotion to the sick and wounded, unostentatious Christian devotion for the living, and with her own hands prepared and arranged the soldier's shroud, and placed the flowers of affection around his cold and lifeless form. In the absence of dear friends she has tenderly performed the part of the Christian mother and sister, which has won for her the love and esteem of all.[149]

She opened their home to all the needy, freely sharing food and money. Ex-governors of Maine Sidney Perham and Frederick Robie, and Lieutenant Colonel Henry Millett of the 5th Maine Infantry (who was in the hospital about four months) and several other soldiers who received her care, all wrote testimonials on her behalf concerning her service during the war.[150]

Both Rev. Jackson and his wife, Abba, occasionally wrote letters to be published in Portland's *Daily Press*, reporting on hospital conditions and the status of Maine soldiers staying at the Armory Square Hospital. In one such letter Reverend Jackson noted that Lt. Colonel Henry Millett was being allowed to return to his unit, "[He] is a gallant officer, with a good record, and has seen much hard fighting. His numerous friends will be glad to hear that he is again in the field."

Abba wrote to the Spiritualist Sewing Circle in Portland:

> In behalf of the wounded men I thank the ladies most heartily for their prompt response to our call for rags, lint, and bandages, &c. I think it must be pleasant to know that one's contributions are appreciated. I took some of the "soft crackers" to our Maine men and they were so delighted; one a Standish man said, "Well if that isn't a 'Blake cracker,'" as he saw that familiar stamp "E. Blake," "why," said he, "I have seen those every week since I can remember, till three years ago, and have not seen one since I enlisted." A little thing to be sure, but little things are often what make up the joys of a lifetime.[151]

Many years later, Mrs. Jackson wrote "[I] was assisted by [my] sister, Miss Mattie McLellan, who gave her life to her country's cause. After a service of two years and eight months in hospital life, in July 1865, borne on a stretcher by soldiers through the cities of Washington, New York, and Portland, she was laid in her bed at her childhood home in Gorham, Me., from which she went out no more."[152] Mattie McClellan (Martha) was born August 13, 1822, and died September 7, 1867. She is buried in the Eastern Cemetery of Gorham, Maine, with her parents and other relatives.[153]

Reverend Jackson died in June 1873. Abba struggled on, supporting herself as best she could until 1888 when she asked for, and received, a pension for her work during the war. She died in Springfield, Massachusetts, four years later.[154]

Mary Jane Johnson

> Yesterday a rather prepossessing lass was discovered on Belle Isle, disguised, among the prisoners of war held there. She gave her real name as Mary Jane Johnson, belonging to the Sixteenth Maine Regiment. She gave as an excuse for adopting her soldier's toggery, that she was following her lover to shield and protect him when in danger. He had been killed, and now she had no objection to return to the more peaceful sphere for which nature, by her sex, had better fitted her. Upon

the discovery of her sex, Miss Johnson was removed from Belle Isle to Castle Thunder. She will probably go north by the next flag of truce. She is about sixteen years of age.[155]

This supposedly was copied from the Richmond *Whig* and was included in the *History of the Sixteenth Maine*, where the author introduced it by stating, "The members of the Sixteenth were not all of the masculine persuasion. Company I boasted of the presence of one of the gentler sex in the ranks, who did good service at Fredericksburgh."[156] The story was picked up and repeated in various books and periodicals including Biddeford's *Union & Journal*, Louis Hatch's *Maine, A History* (1974), and Herbert Jones' *Old Portland Town* (1938). Although intriguing, it is difficult to substantiate such a story. Not surprisingly, there is no "Miss Johnson" listed on the muster roles or in the pension records.

But the story persists in different forms even beyond the state of Maine. Reportedly, a soldier named "Sprague," of the 13th Massachusetts, wrote on December 9, 1863, that there was a woman soldier in the 11th Kentucky Cavalry named Mary Jane Johnson at Belle Isle Island, who joined the army to be with a Captain who was killed in battle and she was taken prisoner.[157]

Libby Life was published in 1865 and written by a former prisoner, F. F. Cavada. He described the horrors of prison life and then wrote:

> But these horrors have not been endured by men alone. Lately, a woman disguised as a soldier, was discovered among the prisoners on Belle Isle. She had for more than a month endured the terrors of a situation which needs no comment, and had preserved her incognito unsuspected until compelled by sickness to repair to the hospital, where she confessed her true sex. She is a young girl of seventeen or eighteen years of age, of prepossessing appearance, and modest and reserved demeanor. She persistently refused to throw any light upon her previous history, or to reveal the motive which had induced her to adopt the garb and the calling of a soldier. She had served during more than a year in a cavalry regiment in the West, when made a prisoner. She had probably followed to the field some patriotic lover, or adventurous spouse. When these facts became known to us in the Libby, a sum was at once contributed by the officers, sufficient to purchase the female soldier garments suitable to her sex, wherewith she might present a more becoming appearance on her return to the Union lines.[158]

The true story of Mary Jane Johnson may never be known. It is quite likely that a woman calling herself by that name did, indeed, serve with the Union army until captured and taken to Belle Isle prison. Who she really was and where she really came from may never be discovered. The fact that Abner Small included this story in his history without denying its veracity lends some credence to the tale.

Hannah E. Judkins
(August, 1832–February 15, 1922)

A Skowhegan teacher, Hannah Judkins felt the need to contribute to the Union's war effort. She left Maine in August 1864 and traveled to Washington, D.C., where she reported to Dorothea Dix. Miss Dix sent her first to Carver Hospital for three weeks, then transferred her to St. John's Hospital in Annapolis, where she served for nine months. Dr. G. S. Palmer was the surgeon in charge, with about 1,200 patients and fourteen nurses. The patients were mostly paroled Union soldiers from Southern prisons. Hannah was there until the hospital was disbanded in July 1865:

> Pen cannot describe the first boat-load of half-starved, half-clothed, thin, emaciated forms whose feet, tied up in rags, left footprints of blood as they marched along to be washed and dressed for the wards. In many cases their minds were demented, and they could give no information as to friends or home, and died in that condition, their graves being marked "Unknown." The patience, bravery, and fortitude of our soldier comrades will ever be cherished in my memory.[159]

On April 4, 1866, Hannah married engineer Solomon B. Starbird of Fairfield, Maine in Portland.

Hannah Judkins-Starbird
(Our Army Nurses)

He was an 1858 graduate of Bowdoin College who served in the Union army for three years, first as a sergeant with the 127th New York Volunteer Infantry and later as 1st lieutenant with the 55th Massachusetts, one of the black regiments organized in Massachusetts. The couple moved to Denver, Colorado and had two sons, both of whom later graduated from the School of Mines of Colorado. Solomon Starbird died on September 29, 1889 in Denver. After his death, Hannah moved to Los Angeles, California and maintained an active role in the Army Nurses Association, serving as president of the California and Nevada departments.[160] She died February 15, 1922, having reached nearly 90 years of age.[161]

The Kilbourn Sisters
Hannah (1812–1880)
Mary Ann (1815–1890)

On July 20, 1864, the executive committee of the Portland Soldiers' Association met to procure a place in Portland for "sick, wounded and destitute soldiers passing through the city."[162] The group leased the first floor of the house that once stood at 14 Spring Street in Portland, at a rent of $150 per year. Hannah Kilbourn was hired at $3.50 per week as matron. Her sister, Mary Ann, was later hired to assist her. The soldiers' home, which could accommodate approximately 20 soldiers at a time, was open for thirteen months, closing in October 1865.[163]

Both women are buried together in Evergreen Cemetery in Portland, with their parents.

Amanda C. Kimball
(November 30, 1820–February 14, 1865)

Amanda Kimball, one of twelve children, was born in Rumford, Maine, to David and Lucy Wheeler Kimball. During the war, she served as a nurse at the General Hospital in Annapolis, where she caught one of the deadly diseases carried by the soldiers: typhus. An obituary clipped from the local paper read: "To her friends in this city, and to many a soldier languishing in hospitals— or at the front—or in winter quarters—this announcement will bring heartfelt sorrow. Devoted in her ministrations at the sick bed, her gentle influence has brought healing and comfort alike to the souls and bodies of her charge and her memory will ever be cherished in

Amanda Kimball   (Gay Gamage)

many a grateful heart, as that of a kind, sympathizing, devoted friend and sister."[164]

Mary A. Fitch, of Erie, Pennsylvania, was also a nurse there and in a letter dated April 3, 1889, she wrote (in listing nurses she remembered), "...Miss Amanda Kimball whose remains it was my sad duty to convey in a soldier's coffin to her waiting kindred in Worcester [Massachusetts] from whence they were taken to her home in Maine."[165] She is buried in the Rumford Center Cemetery with her friends and family.

Mary Kneeland
(January 1, 1829–January 11, 1920)

Mary (known as "Molly") Kneeland, Civil War nurse and spy, was said to be more dangerous than a regiment of soldiers. She had dealings with both the Union and Confederate armies and risked her life on numerous occasions carrying vital information to Union commanders and guiding Union officers through Confederate-held territory. Her house in Rogersville Tennessee, was used by the Confederates as headquarters for over a month. General Longstreet once personally guaranteed her and a neighbor safe passage to have their grain milled. Even while having such polite discourses with the Rebels, she was nursing Union soldiers and secretly housing runaway Union prisoners of war and helping them to escape.

Who was this brave and patriotic woman from East Tennessee? She was born in Byron, Maine, daughter of Hosea Austin and Vienna Holland Austin. The family ran a tannery and mill in Dixfield, Maine. In 1854, she married Dr. John Kneeland of New Hampshire. Because her husband was in poor health, he was advised to move to a warmer climate. Together, he and his new bride moved to East Tennessee and settled in the town of Rogersville in Hawkins County. He promptly set up his medical practice, but his health did not improve. He died the following year, in 1855, leaving Mary a widow in a territory far from home and far different from Maine.

Mary must have liked Tennessee, for she continued to live there, and was still residing in Rogersville when the war began. By remaining there, her life was touched by the war in ways that most Maine women could not imagine. Although Tennessee seceded from the North in June 1861, there were many Union sympathizers and pockets of resistance to Confederate rule, especially in the eastern section of the state. Mary was among them, and she said, "East Tennessee was intensely loyal, and sent no less than 20,000 men into the Union armies." Despite its loyalty, Rogersville was frequently overrun by forces from both sides. Mary described one of her most exciting adventures of the war during an interview which was printed in the *Lewiston Journal* in 1907:

> Things were looking badly for the union forces. Then it became necessary to send a message to Gen. Woods, who was in Rutledge, forty miles away. To reach him one must run the gauntlet of rebel forces nearly all the way, and it was thought best that a woman should undertake this job, as she would not be shot or caught. I had a reputation of being a fearless horseback rider, and also of intense loyalty, so the Union commander pitched on me to do the work.
>
> I was given a swift and strong horse and at daybreak commenced the ride of life or death. I had to cross the mountains in order to avoid the rebel pickets and this made my journey doubly hard. The journey was made, however, and at night I found myself in Rutledge. On attempting to deliver my dispatch to Gen. Woods I found that officer drunk and utterly unable to transact any business. I had hoped to ride back home under cover of darkness but now had to wait for the general to sober off.

The next morning I delivered my message and told him of the condition of affairs in Rogersville. Then I rode eight miles to the railroad and took the cars for Knoxville where I reported to Gen. Sam Carter who commanded the forces there. After receiving assurance that reinforcement would be sent at once I took to the saddle again and started back to Rogersville. So many rebel soldiers were on the road that I had to go the entire distance in hog paths over and through the mountains.[166]

Upon arrival home, she learned that a neighbor had betrayed her to Confederate General Vaughn, and she was about to be arrested.

The next morning Gen. Vaughan[167] and two aids came to my house. Of course I at once admitted them and then came a woman's wit in beating them. In my cellar I had a quantity of blackberry wine and I told my negro woman to bring up a bottle and set it before my guests. I knew the weakness of Vaughn and felt certain that I could get him drunk. As soon as the bottle was empty I had another one before them together with some cake. It was powerful liquor and Vaughn kept on drinking until he was nearly upset. All this time he had not said a word about my arrest, but finally he said in maudlin tones: "Madame, I came here to have you arrested but you have been so kind I shall not do it."[168]

By that time, she had already been hiding escaped Union prisoners in her house for almost two years. She wrote:

I cannot tell you more than a fraction of my war experiences. I remember of once secreting a Capt. Allen of an Ohio regiment who had been captured by the Rebels and escaped. He came to a negro cabin and sent for me. You understand I was noted far and near for aiding such cases. I furnished him with blankets and hid him in the woods. When I carried him food I took along some medicine bottles so if the Rebels stopped me I could say that I was going to visit a sick child. I kept a man watching the Rebel lines while I was taking food to Capt. Allen. Once I hung out a piece of red flannel which was a signal for him to come to my house for breakfast. There was another escaped prisoner with him, and I managed to keep them hid until I could get a guide to take them across the river to a railroad.[169]

Mary further recorded that, "Among our forces my place came to be known as a sort of underground railroad. The rebel and Union forces swayed backward and forth and with each turn of the tide I was in demand."

In early 1864 the Confederates made a surprise attack on Union forces outside of Rogersville. This began Mary's career as a nurse.

> The battle was a fearful one and the Rebels won. One Ohio regiment was completely cut to pieces. The Rebel commander then issued a proclamation giving permission to the Union women of the place to care for the Union wounded. many of these were packed into the hotel and a Mrs. Johnson, Mrs. Netherland and myself volunteered to nurse them. We cooked their food, dressed their wounds, and cared for them in the best possible manner. Strange to say, many of the Union forces that remained after the Confederates were gone, cut down our fences and used them for fuel, took our corn, oats and other property. The Rebels could do no worse. Years afterwards when Congress passed a bill to recompense us Grant vetoed it![170]

After the war, Mary met and married George W. Lynch. He died in 1879. In 1883 she moved to Kansas City, Missouri, and then moved again in 1907, back to Maine to live with her sister, Viola Chase, in Dixfield. Her sister died in 1914 and Mary died 6 years later, after a very long and adventurous life.[171]

Eliza Ann Leeman
(September 3, 1812–October 5, 1895)

Eliza Ann Dole married William S. (Cain) Leeman on January 8, 1833. He died November 14, 1883, at the age of 74. They had lost their only two children prior to the war. Ann Marie was fifteen when she died in 1854, and Charles was 22 when he died in 1856. Eliza became a matron at Cony General Hospital in Augusta, Maine, from August 1864 until April 1865, serving under assistant surgeon, J. W. Toward.[172]

In 1883, Eliza lost her husband. She applied for her pension nine years later when it first became possible for nurses to receive one. She was then 80 years old and had no means of support. The same Dr. Toward with whom she had worked so many years before, and who was now 76 years old, came forward on her behalf and testified so she could receive the $12 a month pension.[173]

Eliza and all of her family are buried in the Mount Hope Cemetery in Augusta, Maine.

Mary Lovejoy
(February 28, 1840–October 10, 1908)

Mary Lovejoy is possibly one of the most intriguing women from Maine actively involved with the Civil War. The story of her service is so fascinating that even her descendants question its veracity. No written record remains. Only the oral histories passed down through family members tell of Mary's unique role.

It is known that she was born in Auburn, Maine, to Azael Lovejoy and Esther Tracey Lovejoy in 1840. Family tradition says that she was the first woman from the Lewiston/Auburn area to volunteer to nurse soldiers, and that she continued that service throughout the four long years. Apparently, she was acquainted with Mary Todd Lincoln. Her daughter, Lottie Hartford, insisted that upon the death of President Lincoln, Mary Lovejoy "tore up her best black dress to make black bows for all the windows in her house and she went and stayed with Mrs. Lincoln until after the funeral. She even made Mrs. Lincoln's mourning dress." In gratitude for her friendship, report her descendants, Mrs. Lincoln gave Mary Lovejoy a small horse-hair trunk, a small book, and a few other items which once belonged to Abraham Lincoln.[174] A great-granddaughter of Mary Lovejoy Cotton remembers the trunk and believes that it once had a leather strap that was inscribed with "ABE." She remembered, also, that her aunt Leora cut the strap off many years ago to replace a broken skate strap.[175]

Unfortunately, there do not seem to be any records remaining of Mary's service as a nurse or as a companion to Mrs. Lincoln. Even the trunk has been lost. Yet stories such as these are often based on some kernel of truth. The lack of records about Mary Lovejoy is not unusual. And Mrs. Lincoln wore mourning clothes for the rest of her life. She must have had many outfits made by different women-one of whom could have been Mary Lovejoy. Also, there was a prominent politician in Washington at the beginning of the war—a representative from Illinois named Owen Lovejoy, a staunch supporter of Lincoln during his presidential campaign. Owen Lovejoy was born in Albion, Maine. Perhaps he was related to Mary Lovejoy or perhaps they met in Washington, and comparing names and backgrounds, became friends—enough that Owen may have introduced her to the Lincolns. We can only speculate on this aspect of the story.

After the war she married Dennet Cotton, a carpenter who had fought first with Company H of the 1st Maine Volunteer Infantry Regiment (a three-month unit) and then with the 14th Regiment Veteran Reserve Corps of Massachusetts. They had four children and "retired" to Mechanic Falls. Although Mary was active with the Women's Relief Corps, apparently she was also forced to support the family. When Dennet applied for a pension in 1891 it was stated that he was in feeble health, unable to work, that the family was destitute, and "the support

Mary Lovejoy-Cotton
(Rex Waite)

of the family to a great extent devolves upon the wife who does washing for the neighbors...." He was granted $8 per month.[176]

Iron marker on Mary Cotton's grave in Mechanic Falls.

Despite such hardships, her work during the war was remembered by more than just her family. A Daughters of Union Veterans chapter, or "tent," was formed in 1917 in Auburn, Maine, and named after her. It had over 60 members in the first year of its existence and continued to be active until 1960.[177] One of Mary's family now has a large photograph of her in her later years under glass in a beautifully ornate gilt frame. Over her image are the words "Our Army

Nurse" and under is "Mary W. Cotton." It must have once hung in the Auburn hall where the Mary Cotton Tent met, then given back to the family when the tent disbanded. It was the women of her tent who made sure that Mary's grave was properly marked with an iron marker inscribed: "Army Nurse."

Sarah Low
(February 2, 1830–December 14, 1913)

Sarah Low was a resident of Dover, New Hampshire when the war began. Born in South Berwick, Maine, in 1830 to Nathaniel Low and Mary Ann Hale, her family moved to Dover, New Hampshire in 1833. At an early age she began to write, publishing various articles in newspapers and producing a small book entitled, *May Duie* in 1858. In 1862, Sarah received this hurried letter dated September 8 with instructions from Miss Hannah E. Stevenson:

> Dear S
>
> Crowded with work; come at once to "Union Hotel Hospital, Georgetown" when you stop in Washington depot in the cars, tell a hackman to bring you to this place, between 2 & 5 miles, if you have a trunk, but if you send trunk by Adams Express, then let the coach take you to the horse cars near by as they pass this door. The night line, via Norwich is the easiest way to come connects with morning train from N.Y. at Jersey City; ticket through to Wash. Perhaps I can only give you a bed on the floor.
>
> Yrs trly
>
> H.E.S.[178]

Sarah Low   (USAMHI)

Sarah's Aunt Lydia was against her going to Washington, but nevertheless bought her a nice carpetbag for the journey, and stayed up very late sewing with other members of the family so that Sarah could leave the next day. Aunt Lydia was rewarded with many letters from her niece during the four years she was a nurse. Her frequent letters home often mentioned conditions in the hospitals. "The men are always asking what time it is. It is astonishing to see how grateful these men are for what the nurses do for them. They have a great horror of hospitals & are delighted & surprised to find anybody trying to make them comfortable." Sarah's presence in the hospital quickly incurred the wrath of Miss Dorothea Dix, and she wrote:

> Last Sunday some one came up to our ward saying that Miss Dix wished to see Miss Stevenson immediately. She went down. Miss Dix said to her, "Who are these two young girls I see about the house" (Can't think how she saw me as I never leave the ward except on some errand & I did not see her). "I presume one is my friend Miss Low," said Miss Stevenson. "Who is she?" Miss S. told her & she raved because her authority had been interfered with, as she said. Mrs. Ropes said that she did not see how Miss Stevenson could endure her talking to her in that way, but she is used to it. Miss Dix has always been very insolent to Miss S. She is arbitrary to them all. "My nurses," she calls them & does not look out for their comfort in the least. She wanted Miss Stevenson to send to Mass. for one hundred nurses, but she would not because she knew they would not be treated decently if they came.[179]

Miss Dix reluctantly agreed to allow Sarah to stay as "guest of the house" rather than as "nurse." Not too long after, Sarah wrote that the assistant attorney general paid a visit to their hospital and told them that Miss Dix only had authority over paid nurses, not volunteers. That seemed to settle the issue.

But Miss Dix was only one of many problems for the nurses at the Union Hotel Hospital. A mean-spirited, unscrupulous steward caused both Hannah Stevenson and Hannah Ropes to protest to authorities. The battle, plus poor food, drained Miss Stevenson to the point where she finally left for home (Massachusetts) on October 24, 1862.[180]

Shortly thereafter, on November 8, 1862, Sarah transferred to the Armory Square Hospital. Hannah Ropes wrote that Sarah "feared the steward too much to stay without [Miss Stevenson's] presence. The boys are all in tears; one on crutches has come to sit in my room, as the nearest approximation to his faithful nurses."[181]

Work at the Armory Square Hospital was easier for Sarah. It was known as a model hospital and was often visited by dignitaries. She praised Dr. Willard Bliss, with whom she worked. At one point, she gave reading lessons to a soldier named Charlie. Later she wrote, "I had been trying to think of something with which the patients could occupy themselves. The convalescents have hours in which they have nothing to do. In talking to some men I found they would like to study. We all have written home for books and are impatient for them to arrive."[182]

In April 1864 Sarah attended a reception at the White House. The place was mobbed and there was great difficulty in getting in and moving around. She described the event much as Rebecca Usher did of the "levee" she attended the following January. "The most astonishing people were there. Men with boots over their pants who looked as if they had been digging in the streets." The president said to her when she met him, "How do you do, marm."[183]

She wrote years later, "I joined Miss Stevenson as her assistant on the 10th of September, 1862. A few weeks afterwards Miss Stevenson's health compelled her to return to Boston, to the incalculable loss of the hospital. She was the most perfect nurse I have ever seen. When she left I went to the Armory Square Hospital, was the first unpaid nurse there. A month later Miss Anna Lowell came and we remained until after the close of the war."[184] During her service and after her return home she wrote about her wartime experiences under the pen name of Rachel Rollins. She brought back with her a black war orphan named John, whom she apparently raised herself. She did not marry.

In 1890, *The First Regiment New Hampshire Volunteers in the Great Rebellion,* by Stephen G. Abbott, was published. It contains the following tribute:

> Another who went forward as nurse, at the signal of duty, is Miss Sarah Low of Dover. Blessed with all that the world can give to make life a pleasure, this accomplished young lady left a cultured and distinguished family circle, and a home filled with treasures and associations of a historic past, in a noble old house that had known Washington among its guests, and took up the burdened routine of faithful hospital cares. It is said that when strangers in the national capital wished to go through a hospital, some one was sure to say "You must not fail to visit the Armory Square; it is kept with marvelous and exquisite neatness, under the supervision of Miss Low of New Hampshire." And only those who have waged war with arrogant,

Sarah Low, Rebecca Usher, and many other women were able to attend receptions at the White House and meet with President Lincoln. (*Library of Congress*)

careless, incompetent people such as appear as exceptions to the rules, in all public places, and with crowded conditions of illness and wounds, can form an idea of what it means to keep a military hospital in that fashion, during active hostilities between immense armies.[185]

Sarah Low is buried in the Pine Hill Cemetery in Dover, New Hampshire.

Ruth S. Mayhew
(*April 19, 1822–June 23, 1874*)

From City Point, Virginia (near Petersburg) on July 9, 1864, Ruth Mayhew wrote back to the corresponding secretary of the Maine Camp Hospital Association:

My dear Miss F[ox]: — Though nearly smothered by the dust and heat, and excessively annoyed by the flies which abound here, I will attempt writing you.

I left Washington on the 5th inst. in good health and arrived here on the 6th, after a passage of 20 hours, stopping two or three hours at Fortress Monroe on our way.

Mrs. Sampson returned to Washington on Monday, and Mr. Hayes left here for the same place this morning to be gone a few days.

There are about 1,200 soldiers in this hospital and 5 or 600 to the Cavalry Hospital. Nearly all these are slightly wounded or sick. Among them, of course, are many Maine men. A great many of them are able to come to our tent for themselves, and for those who are too sick to come, We try to ascertain their needs and supply them : for with the generous supply of nice things you send, we are able to do so, and for a multitude of brave soldiers from other states.

A number of other states are represented by similar agencies, but I think the Maine Camp Hospital Association better supplied as to quantity and quality. I have sent supplies to several of our regiments in the trenches during the week, and shall continue to do so as opportunity occurs. I am hoping to be able to go myself and take some in a few days. There must be pressing need of all we can get to them. I cannot imagine how the poor fellows live burrowed in the earth in this intolerable hot weather. I can give you no idea of the dust.[186]

Ruth Mayhew
(Maine Hist. Soc.)

Thus began what was probably teacher Ruth Mayhew's third venture south to care for soldiers. She had worked with Mrs. Isabella Fogg the first winter of the war, caring for spotted fever cases in Washington. She was back again just after the Battle of Gettysburg in July 1863, with Sarah Sampson, to care for the wounded as an agent for the Maine Camp Hospital Association. She made light of atrocious travel conditions, on that trip with crunched standing-room-only at the Hanover Station as they stopped to change trains. When some of the crowd left for Harrisburg, she described how those remaining washed and brushed their hair at the pump while waiting for the cattle cars to take them the rest of the way. When Ruth arrived in Gettysburg, she found that her supplies had not yet arrived, so she assisted Mrs. Sampson in distributing hers. "I wish those who send such nice things could see how much they are appreciated; it would repay them I think for all their labors and sacrifice."[187]

After the Battle of Gettysburg, Ruth Mayhew picked up where Harriet Eaton and Isabella Fogg left off—following the troops and distributing supplies for the Maine Camp Hospital Association. In early February 1864 she wrote to Maine Camp Hospital Association secretary Harriet Fox from somewhere near Brandy Station, Virginia:

> Heavy cannonading was heard distinctly out on the Rapidan all day yesterday. We have not heard the result. I hold myself in readiness at a moment's notice, to load my ambulance with such things as are most needed in an emergency, and go out to relieve the sufferings of the wounded.... On Monday and Tuesday last, the sick were sent from the army to Washington. They were brought from all the Corps except the 5th, to this station. On Monday morning we commenced at daylight, to prepare food for the poor sufferers. Four men volunteered to assist us. We had two fires, and filled four boilers, and two coffee-pots, and as soon as water could be heated, we made soup and tea. As fast as we prepared it, we carried it out to the cars and filled the kettles again, and so continued our work till the cars started at 12 o'clock. For those who were too sick to eat broth, we had farina and cornmeal gruel.— Mrs. P. and I went out alternately, one remaining at home to cook, while the other attended at the cars....[188]

During that day and the next, she and the unknown Mrs. P. fed over 500 soldiers.

Again in February 1864, she wrote to Harriet Fox, "I should have written you earlier, but we have been overburdened with work for the last week. Rising at half past six in the morning and working without intermission until eleven or twelve at night. But we enjoy the work. I only wish we were able to do ten times as much." One soldier, a lieutenant from the 7th Maine Battery, she reported, said he suffered most from want of good reading. "I mentioned every modern book I know, I found he had read everything except Parton's *Life of Butler*. He said they found copies of the Waverly novels in the Battery, given by the San. Com. to the troops that occupied the fort before them."[189]

[From the Portland Daily Press, February 6.]

State Agency at City Point.

FORT SEDGWICK, January, 29, 1865.

From articles which appear in the papers and from letters of enquiry I have sometimes received, I am led to infer that our friends at home are often at a loss to determine which of the two general Societies now operating in the field is most deserving of their patronage; I mean the Sanitary and Christian Commissions. Both these societies have done and are doing a vast amount of good in alleviating the condition of the sick and disabled soldiers, and nearly the only rivalry between them at front is, which shall accomplish the most. In a certain degree they are cooperative, laboring to the same end, but in the distribution of reading matter, the Christian Commission is purely sectarian, which feature is objectionable to some, and perhaps justly, for I believe that reading of a more general character is better adapted to the wants of the great mass of the soldiers. Each society commends itself to the warmest support of the benevolent public.

But it is not necessary for our friends in Maine, and particularly those who have relatives or friends whom they wish to aid, to operate through the medium of either of the above societies to accomplish their object. For all practical purposes the MAINE STATE AGENCY at City Point is the safest and best medium through which contributions from Maine to this army can be furnished, and from the able manner in which it is conducted it is deserving of the highest consideration, and our people should not suffer its operations to be impaired or retarded for lack of means. C. C. HAYES attends to the forwarding of and delivering of packages consigned to particular persons, and Mrs. Mayhew has charge of articles designed for general distribution. Mr. Hayes goes to Washington almost weekly —and sees that all goods are promptly forwarded; visits the army at intervals and looks up the Maine soldiers in the field hospitals and attends to their needs, and is indefatigable in his efforts to extend the benefit of the Agency to all entitled to them.

Mrs. Mayhew is equally efficient in her department. The agency is situated adjacent to the hospitals at City Point. She is engaged heart and soul in her benevolent and self-sacrificing labor and possesses rare qualities for the arduous position.

I spent an hour at the Agency a few days since and was surprised and delighted at the promptness and ability with which its affairs are managed. The ante-room was crowded with applicants all the time. One needed a shirt, another a pair of socks or drawers, another a quilt, another a little farina or corn-starch—another wishes for tea or sugar. Occasionally a surgeon from the front came in for a supply to take to the sick in the field hospitals. Numbers of pale convalescents came in from the hospitals and after receiving a bowl of hot coffee or some other luxury with a few words of motherly encouragement, retired looking, and doubtless feeling, many per cent better than when they came in. Mrs. Mayhew waited on all with promptness, had a kind word for each, and besides kept up a rambling conversation with those of us who did not come for aid, but only dropped in to see·

We hear but little said about this Agency; it is neither assuming nor pretentious; and yet in its own quiet way I believe it is of more real benefit to the *Maine* soldiers than all the other societies together. But its means of doing good are oftener limited for want of remittances from Maine, on which it solely relies.— Mrs. Mayhew informed me that from several entire counties in Maine she had never received anything, and yet soldiers from every portion of the State shared equally in its benefits.

Maine has done nobly in the war both in furnishing men and means, but this agency does not receive the support to which it is every way entitled. · Certain localities have done much; in others, nothing has been done. I believe that all who from condition or choice remain at home, should contribute something to alleviate the hardships of the soldiers, who are nobly sacrificing the comforts of the home circle for their sakes. If they would, though the offering of each may be small, the aggregate will be much. Hardly anything comes amiss. Shirts, drawers, mittens, socks, quilts, comfort-bags with their contents of needles, pins, thread and buttons—all are needful and sought for.

Those who have nothing else to give can contribute money. Money will purchase many things for the sick, such as canned meats and fruits, condensed milk, farina, corn-starch, etc.

Packages should be addressed, care of Geo. R. Davis, Portland.

If the generous and benevolent people of Maine will send their contributions through this channel, they can rest assured that they will be impartially and judiciously distributed, and that officers, which is too often the case, will not be permitted to appropriate the lion's share.   INDEX.

Mrs. Mayhew is Agent for the Maine Camp Hospital Association, and labors likewise for the Maine State Agency.

Broadside from Maine Camp Hospital Association about their work at City Point.   (Maine Hist. Soc.)

Ruth continued her good work at City Point, Virginia, while the troops encamped outside nearby Petersburg. There she remained until the war ended.

Ruth Mayhew was born in Orland, Maine, as Ruth Swett, daughter of David and Ruth (Coombs) Swett. She grew up on the Cranberry Isles and later lived in Surry with her sister Abbie and Abbie's husband Sabin Lord. In the early 1850s she married Reverend Andrew H. Mayhew of Rockland. After his death on January 25, 1856, she moved to Portland and was working as a teacher there when the war began. She immediately volunteered to nurse the sick and wounded soldiers of Maine.

When the war ended, she returned briefly to Rockland, then in September 1865 she traveled to Ottawa, Kansas, to teach at an Indian school. In 1868, when the Indians were removed to Oklahoma, she returned to Maine, bought a house in Rockland on Middle Street, and lived there with her sister and brother-in-law until her death in 1874.[190]

In 1891 a large monument was erected in her honor at her grave site in the Jameson Cemetery (also known as the Seaview Cemetery) in Rockland by the Women's Relief Corps. In 1923 the

Monument to Ruth Mayhew erected by the Women's Relief Corps in the Rockland Cemetery.

Daughters of Union Veterans of the Civil War established a "tent" in her honor in the City of Rockland. Called "Ruth Mayhew Tent #14," it was an active organization associated with the Grand Army of the Republic. Its purpose was to commemorate the contributions of veterans of the Civil War to our nation. It met regularly in the GAR Hall which is now the building known as the Shore Village Museum. The tent was still active in the 1990s.

Charlotte Elizabeth McKay
(August 2, 1818–April 10, 1894)

Charlotte McKay's army life began at Frederick, Maryland, on March 24, 1862. She arrived just in time to minister to the wounded of the battle of Winchester fought between General Banks and Stonewall Jackson. If she was looking for a way to forget the recent sad deaths of her husband and child, she had found it.[191]

Charlotte Elizabeth Johnson was born in Waterford, Maine, in 1818, one of seven children of Dr. Abner Johnson and Julia Sargent Johnson. Her family moved frequently while she was growing up: from Waterford, to Sullivan, to Cherryfield, Brewer, and Presque Isle, all within Maine. When she married William S. McKay of South Reading, Massachusetts on August 16, 1854, she moved there. William died on April 10, 1856. They had one child, Julia Sargent, who died on February 1, 1861 at age five.[192]

The war gave her an opportunity to bury her grief. She served some 40 months in various camps and hospitals from March 1862 through July 1865, and then volunteered to teach the freedmen after the war. Throughout the war, she kept a diary which she used to write the book, *Stories of Hospital and Camp*, which was published in 1876.[193] In her notes, she describes her service first at Frederick, which was taken over by the Confederates while she was there. She wrote:

> As the town could not be defended, the citizens prepared to give him [Lee] as silent a reception as possible. The home guard was sent off, also every hospital patient who could walk to the outskirts of the town, where teams were seized to convey them to a safe distance. Large quantities of Government clothing, blankets, and other hospital stores were collected and burnt on the grounds.[194]

The Confederates passing through reminded her of the old nursery rhyme, Hark! Hark! the dogs do bark, The beggars are coming to town. "So ragged were they, so filthy and squalid in appearance." The rebels left after a week's stay when the Union troops returned, led by the 1st Maine Cavalry. There was rejoicing, but not for long. The Battle of Antietam, which filled every hospital in and around Washington with wounded, began soon after.

By the beginning of 1863, Charlotte, armed with a pass from the War Department, joined the Third Corps to help set up a division hospital, remaining until after the battle of Chancellorsville. Her brother, Dudley H. Johnson, a lieutenant with the 17th Maine, was killed May 3, 1863, at Chancellorsville. She was there to hear the first report that he was wounded and the later report that he had been left on the field to die.

Charlotte began the day by loading an ambulance with supplies to take to the wounded near the front. She found a small house near United States Ford, being used as a hospital. She wrote, "Finding many wounded men lying in and around the house, I immediately commenced the distribution of stimulants and nourishment." After remaining there much of the day, she continued across the river to the Third Corps Hospital, which was then located in a large brick house. "As we approached we saw that wounded men were lying all along by the fences, all through the grounds, some under the little white tents, but more under the open heaven. They were on the piazza, under the piazza, in the cellar, through the halls, in all the rooms above and below, while cries and groans broke out where the agony was too great to be repressed." It was there that she learned of the fate of her brother. His body was never recovered.[195]

She retreated from Chancellorsville with the rest of the army. Charlotte continued to work with Isabella Fogg, Harriet Eaton, Mary Morris Husband, and others, tending the wounded and providing sustenance for demoralized Union troops.[196]

Falling close on the heels of the Battle of Chancellorsville was the Battle of Gettysburg. Like Isabella Fogg and many other women, Charlotte McKay traveled to Gettysburg as quickly as she could upon hearing of that horrible battle. She was there for six weeks. Of her time at Gettysburg, she wrote:

> My programme for a day at Gettysburg was to rise as early as possible in the morning, and send out everything that was available in the way of food to the wounded. An item for one morning was a barrel of eggs, and as it was impossible to cook them all, they were distributed raw, the men

who had the use of their hands making little fires in front of their tents, and boiling them in tin-cups, for themselves and their disabled comrades. Breakfast being over, I would ride to the town, and gather up everything in the way of sanitary supplies that I could get, from the Sanitary and Christian Commissions, the large and generously filled storehouse of Adams Express Co., or any quarter where they could be obtained. I would take butter, eggs, and crackers by the barrel, dried fish by the half-kettle, and fresh meat in any quantity, and having seen them loaded on an army wagon, would return in my ambulance, which was well filled with lighter articles, in time to give some attention to dinner. The remainder of the day would be devoted to the distribution of such stimulants as eggnog and milk punch,—which would be prepared in large buckets, and served to the patients in little tin-cups,—or supplying them with clothing, pocket handkerchiefs, cologne, bay rum, anything that could be had to alleviate their sufferings.[197]

In October 1863, Charlotte received a message from Colonel Joshua L. Chamberlain of the 20th Maine, requesting her services. She spent many days trying to track him down, going from place to place only to find he had just left. She finally found him at Auburn, Virginia, but the commanders decided not to establish a hospital after all, prompting her to return to Washington.[198]

With much of the Union army encamped outside of Petersburg, Mrs. McKay joined other relief workers at City Point, Virginia, working to provide the special diet needed by the sick and wounded of the Cavalry Corps.

After the war ended, Charlotte McKay continued to volunteer her services, teaching freed slaves around Poplar Springs, Virginia, about four miles from Petersburg.[199] She was one of the few women to be awarded the Kearney Cross for her work during the war. Given to her by officers of the 17th Maine Regiment, the award was created in memory of General Philip Kearny, killed on September 1, 1862, and was to be awarded to enlisted men who distinguished themselves in battle. Although she did not actually engage in "battle," Charlotte certainly distinguished herself on the battlefield. The medal was well-deserved.[200]

Charlotte McKay died in San Diego, California on April 10, 1894.

Emeline McLellan
(1842–Aug 10, 1922)

On October 27, 1862, a frantic Miss McLellan, then working at St. Elizabeth's Hospital near Washington, sent this note by special messenger to agent Watson, who was presumably then in Washington:

> A box left Brunswick Maine the 10th inst. If it has arrived will you please deliver it to the bearer. If it has not yet come will you notify me of its arrival at the earliest opportunity.
> Very Truly,
> E. E. McLellan[201]

The desperately needed supplies finally arrived at St. Elizabeth's on October 31, 1862.

Emeline Edmonds McLellan, daughter of Hugh and Abigail McLellan of Brunswick, Maine, first served as an army nurse under Dorothea Dix at the Union Hotel Hospital in Winchester, Virginia. She was there from April 1862 until mid-July of the same year. On May 25, she was taken prisoner during the Battle of Winchester and remained a prisoner until rescued by General Banks a week later. "We were kindly treated," she said of the experience. She spent a short time at the hospital at Point Lookout, Virginia, beginning in July 1862, before being transferred to St. Elizabeth's Hospital in Washington in September.[202] On May 16, 1864, the Superintendent of Army Nurses, Dorothea Dix, filled out a form for Emeline certifying that she was qualified and approved for the position of nurse. By then she had been working as a nurse for two years.

The Judiciary Square Hospital in Washington was her next and last assignment. She worked there until August 1864, when she was discharged. Her pension records state that she became too ill to continue her work.

Walter I. Himes was one of Emeline's patients at the Judiciary Square Hospital. A Michigan soldier who had been serving with the 1st Massachusetts Cavalry, he was wounded and sent to the hospital. He was discharged August 13, 1864. On March 28, 1865, Emeline married Walter Himes in Buchanan, Michigan. The minister who performed the service was Walter's father.[203]

Emeline and Walter moved to Nemaha, Kansas, to start their new life. It appears that after his death in the 1890s, she moved to Pittsburgh to live with her son and his family, and died there in 1922. Her body was sent to Buchanan, Michigan, to be buried with her husband.[204]

Eunice D. Merrill
(1824–April 2, 1880)

Eunice Day Quinby of Stroudwater, Maine, married Dr. John Merrill some time before the war.[205] What happened to their marriage is unknown, but when her sister Almira Quinby went to be a nurse during the war, Eunice went too. She worked at the Naval School Hospital in Annapolis under Mrs. Tyler with several other women from Maine, including her sister Almira, Rebecca Usher, Louise Titcomb, Susan Newhall, Emily Dana, Adeline Walker, Mary Dupee, and Mary Pearson.[206]

Eunice Merrill is buried in the Stroudwater Cemetery of Portland, Maine, along with her sister Almira Quinby and her friend, Louisa Titcomb.

Eunice Merrill, Louisa Titcomb, and Almira Quinby (all Civil War nurses) buried together in Stroudwater Cemetery, Portland.

Helen Merrill
(August 15, 1839–June 13, 1915)

Miss Dorothea Dix certainly would not have approved of Miss Helen Merrill serving as a nurse under her direction. Helen was far too young and attractive. Yet records show she did serve as a nurse at military hospitals. She may also have been the "Miss Merrill" who, with Mrs. A. A. Goddard and several other women in October 1861, accompanied the men of the 10th Maine Infantry Regiment when they left Portland.[207]

According to official reports, she served as nurse at the military hospital of Fort Schuyler in New York from March 1863 until January 1864. She then transferred to the Armory Square Hospital in Washington and remained in charge of Ward D until November 1864.[208] During her time at the Armory Square Hospital, the Maine Camp Hospital Association's records indicate that they shipped her at least one barrel of hospital supplies to help the wounded Maine soldiers hospitalized there.[209]

Helen Merrill (USAMHI)

Helen became the second wife of prominent Portland lawyer and former general George F. Shepley in 1872. They lived together for only a few short years in a beautiful house on State Street which is now known as "The Portland Club." George Shepley died July 20, 1878 of what was reported to be cholera.[210] Helen died of a cerebral hemorrhage in 1915 and is buried in Portland's Evergreen Cemetery with her husband.

In 1886, Helen wrote briefly of her experiences to a Colonel Arnold A. Rand who was collecting information about the nurses for a book. She wrote, "I think that all who have shared those eventful years, the interest in everything connected with them increases and deepens with every passing year—and our indebtedness is great indeed to those who have so ably carried forward the great work."[211]

The "great work" she referred to, the recognition of those who served during the war, was very important to her. She would remember the time she spent at the Armory Square Hospital for the rest of her life and she would be very pleased to learn there is still interest in those events to this day.

Formerly the home of the Shepley's on State Street in Portland.

Brig. Gen. George Shepley.
(USAMHI)

The Shepley's graves in the Evergreen Cemetery, Portland.

Sarah J. Milliken
(August 3, 1828–October 1917)

Although Sarah J. Milliken was born in Baldwin, Maine, she had been living with her brother for ten years in Lynn, Massachusetts by the time the war began in 1861. When hostilities erupted between the North and South, Sarah returned to her native Maine, where she worked to make army clothes for the soldiers.[212]

She soon grew tired of that form of service. Wanting to take a more active role in the war, she applied to Dorothea Dix for a position as a nurse. She and two other women, whose names she neglected to mention, left in September 1862 to become regular enlisted army nurses.[213]

The Battle of Antietam had just been fought and Washington was crowded with sick and wounded soldiers when she arrived. Every available building was in use as a temporary hospital. For nearly a month she worked in the court-room of City Hall before being transferred to the Judiciary Square Hospital to work with Dr. Hartsuff. The hospital had ten wards, each with 36 beds. Sarah was given charge of Ward Three and worked there until the spring of 1863 when, according to her own report, she was given charge of the whole hospital. The rest of the female nurses were dismissed or transferred. Without the aid of other women, Sarah was forced to rely on the assistance of convalescent soldiers and she directed them in the performance of those duties.[214] Mary Holland wrote, "She had under her charge the wounded from many a famous battlefield, and could relate many interesting and touching incidents which came under her immediate notice."[215]

Sarah Milliken-Sprague
(Our Army Nurses)

When she retired from nursing in January 1865 she received a recommendation from Dr. Hartsuff, who said, "Miss Milliken...has all the qualities of a good nurse and estimable woman." Considering the amount of antagonism that often existed between doctors and nurses, that is higher praise than it might first appear.[216]

In 1872, she married William N. Sprague of Lynn, Massachusetts, who had been a soldier in Company D of the 1st Massachusetts Cavalry. William died in May 1883 in Plainville, Connecticut. A pension was granted Sarah on June 27, 1890.[217] She died in October 1917 and is buried in the Pine Grove Cemetery in Lynn.[218]

Susan J. Newhall
(September, 1813–April 14, 1895)

Susan left her home in Portland, Maine, to work as a nurse at the General Hospital in Chester, Pennsylvania. Louisa Titcomb and Rebecca Usher worked side-by-side with her. They fed the patients, read to them, wrote letters for them, and provided company and comfort.

When the head nurse, or matron, Mrs Tyler, transferred to the Naval School Hospital in Annapolis, Maryland, Susan and Louisa followed. The work at the Naval School Hospital was far more grueling. Many of their patients were men who had been released from the prison camps in the South: from Andersonville, Georgia; Libby Prison in Richmond, Virginia; and the camp in Florence, South Carolina. Starvation, scurvy, and numerous other diseases made these men some of the worst cases of the war. One nurse wrote: "The hospital was often crowded with patients enduring the worst form of disease and suffering; and added to our former duties were new and untried ones incident to the terrible and helpless condition of these returned prisoners."[219] Records at the National Archives indicate that she served from about August 1863 until August 1864.[220]

Susan was the daughter of Albert and Susan Raymond Newhall. She lived in Portland, Maine, and Deering (now a part of Portland) after the war and was active in the Unitarian Preble Chapel where she taught Bible classes with Louisa Titcomb (who she worked with during the war) and Harriet Fox (secretary of the Maine Camp Hospital Association during the war).[221] She is buried in Portland's Evergreen Cemetery with close family members.

Sarah Elizabeth Palmer

(1832–January 19, 1894)

Sarah E. Palmer, who grew up in Dover, Maine, served as an army nurse under Dorothea Lynde Dix at the Carver General Hospital in Washington throughout most of the war. In response to a request for a photo and record of her work, she wrote in 1887:

> I have no record to give but did all I could for the brave boys. I left home in the fall of '62 and began duty at Carver Hospital Washington D.C. and remained there until the breaking up of the hospital. Was then transferred to Sleigh Hospital Alexandria Virginia and remained there until Aug '65.[222]

In 1889 Sarah applied for a pension. The report stated, "Her services seem to have been exceptionally meritorious and claimant is indorsed by C. S. Doughty Post, Grand Army of the Republic, of Foxcroft, Me. She is aged and infirm.... Her term of service was one of exceptional length and, according to a mass of testimony, of unusual value to the Government." She was granted $12 a month (less than half the amount originally applied for) on October 1, 1890.[223]

She died in 1894 in her home town of Dover, Maine, and is buried in the south section of the Old Dover Village Cemetery. Helen Beedy, in *Mothers of Maine*, wrote, "Upon the honor roll of the Maine women who were messengers of light and mercy to the sick and wounded soldiers, during the Civil War, should be written the name of Sarah E. Palmer."[224]

Sarah Palmer

(USAMHI)

Mary Phelps
(January 8, 1812–January 25, 1878)

THIRTY-NINTH CONGRESS. SESS. I. 1866.

July 28, 1866 [No. 103.] *Joint Resolution to reimburse Mrs. Mary Phelps, of Missouri.*

Be it resolved by the Senate and House of Representatives of the United States of America in Congress assembled, That there be paid to Mrs. Mary Phelps, of Missouri, out of any money in the treasury not otherwise appropriated, the sum of twenty thousand dollars to reimburse her for expenditures made by her, in raising and equipping troops for the United States in the late rebellion, and also for her expenditures made in behalf of the soldiers of the Union wounded in battle, and of the orphan children of soldiers of the Union.

APPROVED, July 28, 1866.[225]

In 1866, the United States government appropriated the unheard of amount of $20,000 to a woman for her work during the war! The appropriation of such an incredible amount of money to a woman at that time in our nation's history was absolutely astounding. But Maine-born Mary Phelps contributed much more to the war effort than the official reports indicate, plus she had connections with powerful government officials.

By some accounts, Mary was actually being rewarded for rescuing the body of Union General Nathaniel Lyon, who was killed at the Battle of Wilson Creek. Perhaps the resolution does not state this directly because of a possible cover-up by inept Union officers of what actually occurred. There are at least three widely differing accounts of what happened after that fateful battle—all involving Mary Phelps in some way.

Born in Portland, Maine, to a sea captain who died while she was still young, Mary grew up to marry an ambitious young lawyer, John S. Phelps, from Simsbury, Connecticut. John Phelps graduated from Trinity College in 1835. Upon their marriage in 1837, the couple promptly moved to Springfield, Missouri, where he began practicing law. His interest in law soon turned to an interest in politics. In 1844 he was elected to Congress from his newly adopted state and he served the people of Missouri continuously for 18 years through some of the most tumultuous times of Missouri's history. In the years before the war, the couple found themselves patriotic Yankees living among Confederate sympathizers.[226]

General Nathaniel Lyon was killed at Wilson Creek. Mary Phelps saved and preserved the body until it was claimed by the family.   (USAMHI)

Congress was deadlocked over the issue of whether Missouri should enter the Union as a slave state. Finally, in 1820, the Missouri Compromise allowed Maine to enter the Union as a free state if Missouri entered as a slave state. No other western territory above the 36°30' parallel would be allowed to enter as a slave state. However, the conflict over slavery was far from settled.

Pro-slavery sentiment could stir mobs to violence, and many in Missouri and surrounding territories were more than sympathetic to the Rebel cause. When Elijah Parish Lovejoy, originally from Albion, Maine, began his abolitionist newspaper in Missouri in 1833, his press was destroyed by a pro-slavery mob. He moved across the Mississippi River to Alton, Illinois, to continue his publication. Once more his press was destroyed. Again he replaced it. In 1837, the press was destroyed once again and in the battle to protect it, Elijah Lovejoy was killed.[227]

When President Lincoln called for four regiments to fight the rebellious forces in Missouri, Governor Claiborne Jackson's response was, "Your requisition is illegal, unconstitutional, revolutionary...inhuman, diabolical, and cannot be complied with." He then attempted to seize the Federal arsenal at St. Louis for the Confederacy.

Despite the danger, Mary and John remained loyal to the Union. When General Nathaniel Lyon came with his troops to Springfield, Missouri, to insure that southern Missouri stayed on the Union side, Mary offered her home as his headquarters. The Battle of Wilson's Creek, fought August 10, 1861, near Springfield, was one of the first major battles of the war. Leading his troops in a well-planned charge, the feisty Lyon was shot and killed. What happened next to Lyon's body depends on whose report is read.

According to reports by Union officers at the scene, Lyon's bodyservant, Lehman, and another aide, brought the body back to a place selected as a hospital and placed it in an ambulance with orders "that in no case was it to be removed from the vehicle."[228] But the orders were not followed. Lyon's body was removed from the ambulance and left on the field. This oversight was not discovered until after the battle, when the army had moved on to a new position. Under a flag of truce, Lt. Canfield of Company B, 1st U.S. Cavalry, was sent back with a company of men to recover the remains. This they accomplished without much difficulty and brought the body into Springfield where it was "decently laid out in the house which he had occupied as his headquarters." Although the army moved on the next day, Mary Phelps was asked to take care of the body, "which she did in the kindest and tenderest manner, and had it interred in her garden at the Phelps farm south of town."[229] In the book, *The Soldier in our Civil War*, the account goes as follows:

> He [Lyon] fell in the arms of his servant, saying: "Lehman, I am killed; take care of my body!" During the retreat which closed that eventful day, General Lyon's body was left on the field, whence the Confederate general Sterling Price sent it in his own conveyance to Springfield. When the Federal troops under Colonel Sigel retreated to Rolla, early the next morning, the body was again left behind, at Springfield. It was, however, carefully prepared for burial by members of the staff of the Confederate general J. B. Clark, and delivered to Mrs. J. S. Phelps, who had it properly interred.[230]

The most interesting version is told in the book, *Anecdotes, Poetry, and Incidents of the War: North & South* by Frank Moore:

> On the afternoon after the battle of Wilson's Creek, it was noised that the rebels had determined to cut out the heart of General Lyon, and preserve it as a trophy over the United States army. Mrs. Phelps, learning of this outrage on the slain General, armed herself, as she was accustomed to do for some time,

in order to preserve her life and the lives of her family from the murderous assaults of the secessionists. Thus armed, she drove to Price's camp by nightfall, and there, all alone, guarded the body of General Lyon. When ordered by the rebels to give up the body, she positively refused, and declared they must cut out her heart before they could get the heart of the General. There, all alone, she stood guard during the whole night, with her arms in readiness to defend her charge, regardless of her own life. —thus fearlessly passing the dreary night amidst the associations of the dead, the wounded, and the blood-thirsty men who were awaiting an opportunity to obtain the coveted heart of the noble Lyon.

After daylight, having made arrangements in reference to her precious charge, she repaired to her home, and sent a colored servant with a wagon and two horses to bring the remains of General Lyon to her residence, in order for burial in her garden on her farm, with all the respect in her power toward the commander of the loyal army. But as the wagon had not returned in due time, she drove again to Price's camp, found her wagon had been seized for the use of the rebel army, and her servant confined to it and gagged. As the horses had been unhitched from the wagon, with her own hands she again hitched them. When resistance was again offered to her course she fearlessly declared she would deal death with her revolver to any one who molested her. About the time she had released the servant, and got her precious treasure in the wagon, resistance was again threatened. She then pressed her way to the presence of General Price, who at her pressing instance, ordered her to have the body of the slain General, without further interruption.[231]

The true story is probably closest to the first account. The body, left on the battlefield on August 10, 1861, was retrieved and taken to the Phelps' house in Springfield which General Lyon had used as his headquarters. The Union Army, still in retreat and being pursued by the Confederates, hastily evacuated Springfield. Dr. Edward C. Franklin, the surgeon-in-chief of the army, was asked to care for the body as best he could. On August 11, Mary Phelps learned that the body had been left behind in Springfield and she came from her farm, south of town, to make arrangements for a coffin and proper disposition of the body. While these arrangements were being made, she and four other women kept watch over the slain general. When all was ready, the coffin was loaded into her wagon and she brought it back to the Phelps farm, where it was placed in the ice house and covered with hay. By this time the Confederates were in control of Springfield and some units were even encamped on the farm. Worried that the Confederates might mutilate the body of the fallen Union general, Mary had the body buried in her garden until family members could come from Connecticut to claim it. On August 22, over a week later, a delegation including Lyon's brother-in-law George Hasler and his cousin Danford Knowlton arrived. The body was then disinterred and taken back to Connecticut with a funeral procession which made stops in Cincinnati, Philadelphia, New York, and Hartford before finally reaching Lyon's home town of Eastford for a ceremony that was attended by some 20,000 people including two governors, three members of Congress, the mayors of Hartford and Providence, and numerous army officers.[232]

It would be interesting to hear what Mary Phelps, herself, had to say about the incident. Unfortunately, if she wrote an account, it did not survive.

The Battle of Wilson's Creek was fiercely fought. Outnumbered and poorly supplied, the Federal troops fought well. If Lyon had lived, the Union might have had a brilliant victory. As it was, General William Tecumseh Sherman (among others) blamed the next four years of strife and pillage in Missouri on Lyon's death.[233]

Meanwhile, John Phelps returned from Washington with the intention of raising his own regiment. Mary did not sit idly by; she helped raise money and helped to recruit men. When the regiment went to fight at the Battle of Pea Ridge in March 1862, Mary went with them and tended the wounded. When bandages ran short, she ripped up some of her own clothes to make more. After all the wounds were dressed, she made sure all the soldiers were fed.[234]

The battle over, Mary returned to Springfield and turned her home into a hospital for the rest of the war. She occasionally left Missouri to raise funds among her supporters back East. In March 1863 she returned to New England and Maine to solicit contributions for the relief of loyal Union citizens in Missouri and Arkansas who were suffering severely from the constant fighting there.[235] She made at least one other trip in January 1865.[236]

Her husband's six-month regiment was mustered out of service in 1862. President Lincoln then appointed him military governor of Arkansas, a position which he maintained from July 1862 until March 1863. John returned to his law practice in Springfield and ran in 1868 as the Democratic candidate for governor of Missouri. He lost. There were still far too many Southern sympathizers for him to be elected.[237]

In 1866, the 39th United States Congress voted to give Mary Whitney Phelps the extremely generous sum of $20,000 as a reward for her war efforts. She used the money to start an orphanage for children of soldiers, both Union and Confederate, who died during the war. The orphanage housed nearly 250 children at one time. Mary worked to find homes for these children and jobs for the older ones. She also became involved with helping several women of Springfield to establish a school for children of former slaves.

Even before the war, Mary's zest to participate fully in whatever came her way was evident. In 1859 a friend of her husband, John Butterfield, was racing mail across the country from California. When he reached Springfield, Missouri, he stopped at the Phelps' house. He invited Mary to ride with him in the stage to Tipton, about 100 miles to the north, where it connected with the railroad. Mary needed no urging. She grabbed a few things and her thirteen-year old daughter, and they were off. Her daughter (also named Mary) recounted many years later, "between Springfield and the first relay station my mother and I bounced around the driver's seat holding each other to keep on board." At the first stop Mary Phelps joined the mail sacks inside the coach.[238] It must have been a wild ride!

Later, she took an active role in the Missouri Womans Suffrage Movement. At one time vice president of the organization, she spoke before Congress on the issue. In 1869, she was one of the women who brought a petition to then Governor McClurg of Missouri asking for the right to vote.

The family's 1,000-acre farm in Greene County also took a lot of her time and energy. So did superintending the making of cheeses, which were reportedly delicious and very popular with people in the area.

In February 1876, Mary Phelps was a passenger on an ocean vessel, the *City of Panama*, returning home from the west coast, when she fell through three open hatchways—a distance of about 20 feet. Her fall was broken, at least partially, by soft cargo, but her right arm was shattered. That same year her husband was finally elected governor of Missouri. He took the oath of office in January 1877, but Mary was not there. Instead of becoming first lady of Missouri, Mary retired to the family farm and was seldom seen in public after her accident. Her balance had been affected by the fall and she fell again in 1877 on uneven pavement. Her daughter, Mary Phelps Montgomery, stood in her place as first lady and performed all the duties associated with that office for her mother.

On January 25, 1878, Mary Whitney Phelps succumbed rather suddenly to pneumonia. Her obituary contained flowery and glowing praise:

> Last Sunday morning word was silently passed from lip to lip, bespeaking the death of a cherished citizen, endeared to every one by a long life crowded full of the noblest charities. And, as each one heard of the death of Mrs. Mary Phelps, a warm word of encomium was spoken and a sigh of regret was breathed at a loss which the future might never replace.... Through all the days of want and poverty, through all the nights of ignorance and crime, she has ever been at her post of duty; now the heroine and nurse, then the alms-giver and helping friend, next the teacher and protector of the orphan and homeless.
>
> At the battle of Wilson's Creek she performed the duties of a veritable Sister of Charity, ministering to the wants of the wounded and dying, making her house a hospital for the reception of many a poor fellow far from home and in the land of the enemy.
>
> Her illness was of short duration, the disease, pneumonia, doing its work quickly. Her remains were interred on Sunday afternoon, the funeral taking place from the Episcopal Church. An immense concourse of people, estimated at five hundred, assembled to pay a last tribute to her memory.[239]

Harriet E. Pinkham
(January 2, 1824–December 7, 1914)

Harriet Pinkham was born in Boothbay, Maine, on January 2, 1824 to Thomas and Emma Abbott Pinkham.[240] She died there 90 years later, unmarried, living on her monthly pension check of $12.

Harriet served as a nurse, receiving what she called "soldier's pay" of $13 a month from the government from September 1863 until January 1864. She worked at McDougal General Hospital at Fort Schuyler in New York Harbor. By April, 1864, she had journeyed south to work at Division No. 2 (or St. John's College), General Hospital at Annapolis under Dorothea Dix, and was there until discharged from service in August 1865.[241]

According to Esther Hill Hawkes, her physician who had also served as a nurse during the war, Harriet suffered from kidney disease. She is buried in the Wylie Cemetery in Boothbay Center, Maine.

Harriet Pinkham, standing on the right.　(USAMHI)

Judith Plummer
(1828?–May 18, 1896)

On April 21, 1880, Judith Plummer applied for a pension. The claim stated, "while doing Hospital work and in the line of duty; and acting under orders [she] was compelled to sleep on the stone floor, contracted a severe cold which resulted in an enlargement of the right gland of the throat, and a chronic difficulty with which she continues to be afflicted." Belva A. Lockwood, the first woman lawyer allowed to present a case before the Supreme Court, and an ardent campaigner for women's rights, was her attorney handling the claim.

Judith Plummer was born in Levant, Maine, but at the time the war began may have been living in Aroostook County, where her family moved probably in the 1840s.[242] She and her sister Susan both left their home in the far northern reaches of Maine to volunteer their services. Judith began service at the Patent Office Hospital in Washington in March 1862 under Dorothea Dix. She was forced to sleep on a stone floor with only a thin blanket for a cover. Dr. J. W. Buckley wrote, "The result of this exposure was a severe cold and inflammatory or acute sore throat which nearly cost her her life. I performed a surgical operation at that time and one since. In the first operation in the Patent Office Hospital, I was obliged to lance her throat in order to reduce the swelling. In the second operation I removed tumors from both sides of her throat. The tumors being the result of the previous diseased condition of her throat."[243]

In August, she was working again at the Fairfax Seminary Hospital in Virginia. When she heard the news of the Battle of Gettysburg, she and her sister Susan made their way to Gettysburg and worked there until the general hospital closed. They then reported for duty at Slough General Hospital in Alexandria. William Frost, a hospital steward wrote, "I can testify to the fact how faithfully both sisters labored night and day in ministering to the sick and solacing the dying." Judith worked at the Slough Barracks Hospital near Alexandria until November 1864. After the war, she went back to Washington, working as a government clerk in the Treasury Department until 1882.[244] At that time she may have returned to her father's farm in Reed Plantation, Aroostook County, Maine, to live, but also spent some time in Lawrence, Massachusetts.

There are no records of Susan's service; we know only that she died sometime before 1889.

Judith Plummer clearly felt that the government was unfair in its treatment of women nurses. She wrote in her claim, "Because I am a woman I am obliged to petition Congress, instead of being pensioned in the regular manner."[245] Her original pension claim was denied in 1882, but she persisted and it was finally approved by special act in 1888. She died of cancer in Bangor in 1896.[246]

Arbella F. Pollister
(November 1, 1846–December 22, 1932)

One of the first female telegraphers in the United States is said to be Mrs. Arbella F. Pollister from Maine. She was born Arbella Pillsbury in Belfast, Maine, and grew up in Portland. Her home was at the corner of Atlantic Street and the Eastern Promenade. Although remembered for her contributions to help found the State School for the Feeble Minded at Pownal (later known as Pineland Center) and for her membership in the Women's Literary Guild, she is most remembered for her work as a telegrapher.[247]

Assigned to the provost marshal's office as an official telegrapher of the Union Army during the war, Arbella Pollister often tapped out in Morse code the casualty lists of the battles. She also had the distressing task of relaying the news of the assassination of President Lincoln.

She learned "to work the wire" as a young girl. Her skills were in demand during the war when so many male key operators left their jobs to enlist. Being from the same generation of "brass pounders" (as they were called) as Thomas Edison, she often worked on the same circuits with him. In fact, she visited with him at his home in Fort Myers, Florida, shortly before his death in 1931, and they swapped stories. Both vividly remembered receiving the tragic news of Abraham Lincoln's death to relay over the wires.[248]

She married George F. Pollister, a U. S. inspector of hulls and boilers from Portland. For a time after the war they lived in Hawaii. After his death in 1920, Arbella returned to Portland to stay at the Longfellow Inn on the Eastern Promenade until moving south to live with her daughter, Anna, in Fort Myers, Florida, where she died on December 22, 1932. The *Portland Press Herald* carried her obituary on its front page. Her ashes were returned to Portland and buried in the Evergreen Cemetery beside her husband's ashes.[249]

Sarah L. Porter
(November, 1826–March 3, 1907)

Sarah Porter was a resident of Bath, New Hampshire, when she left her home to become an army nurse at the Columbian College General Hospital for Dorothea L. Dix, where she served from December 1862 until July 6, 1865 with only brief temporary assignments to other hospitals. She was at Fredericksburg, Virginia, from May 12 until May 28, 1864 and at White House Landing, Virginia, for a few days in June 1864. She was at Winchester, Virginia, from September 26 until November 22, 1864, and at the Naval School Hospital in Annapolis in March 1865.[250]

After the war she moved to Bangor, where she lived with her sister at 39 West Broadway Street. She died at age 70 in Ashland, New Hampshire.

Sarah Jane Prentiss
(November 29, 1823–October 21, 1877)

Sarah Jane Prentiss of Paris, Maine, was an artist and writer as well as a nurse during the American Civil War. Sarah worked at various Union hospitals in Washington, including the Trinity Church Hospital, where Harriet Eaton visited her in October 1862 while preparing for her own career as an "angel of mercy."[251] Earlier, she had been in Frederick caring for the soldiers. Agent John Goddard had written to Maine's governor on June 6, 1862, saying that, "Miss Sarah Prentiss and another lady from Maine are here ministering to the wants of the sick and wounded to the utmost of their ability."[252]

During her tenure as a nurse in and around Washington, Sarah Prentiss was able to do some sightseeing. She described a trip into Virginia thus: "Soon afterwards I crossed the Potomac to the state once 'the birthplace of Presidents,' afterwards a hot-bed for rearing slaves for the rice and cotton fields, now the desolate battle-ground of destroying armies."[253]

In her spare time, Sarah delighted the convalescents with her watercolors. One was of a pansy and some violets which she had plucked in Virginia. Said a companion, "We had not known there were such: — Wild pansies! Magnificent violets! ...We have it yet,—almost more beautiful than at first; its green leaves, too, are fine in lace-like clefts."[254]

Atlantic Monthly occasionally printed Sarah's articles and she sometimes sent articles for publication to Maine papers as well. One appeared on the front page of the *Kennebec Journal* on October 28, 1864. In it, she described the noble work of Mrs. Almira Fales of Iowa, who often fed

Sarah Prentiss   (USAMHI)

Maine troops in the Army of the Cumberland and from her own front yard in Washington. Pleaded Sarah in the article, "Women of Maine! Will you not fill her ambulance for our brave boys in the valley of the Shenandoah?"[255] In a letter to a friend from the Finley Hospital in Washington, she wrote:

> My Ward is a barrack, long and low, the walls covered with plain strawcolored paper & the beams overhead hung with tissue paper cut in figures, forming lines of red, white and blue that has a very pretty effect as you stand and look across. There are thirty six beds on each side covered with blue counterpanes, occupied by "our conquering Haroes" as "Daddy" an old Irish Nurse calls them.... I have the Erysipelas and Gangrene Ward also; that is three tents on the other side of the hill in the middle of an orchard of blossoming fruit trees. This is not so nice as this. Yesterday I went and stayed a long time, combed their hair & talked with them, and was somewhat shocked by dirt and rough language. Made no comment on either, but when I went this morning I found the sick men's heads already combed & they talking of cleaning up things, & not a rough word spoken.[256]

An avid abolitionist, she applauded Lincoln's decision to free the slaves. "When one September morning, the Emancipation Proclamation came out at last, how I thanked God and took courage! My aching feet were never after burdened by a desponding heart."

She nursed sick and wounded soldiers for a good portion of the war, only leaving when her own health began to fail. She had apparently contracted malaria while working in the hospitals. Following the war, she went to Europe to regain her health and was there about three years. She returned to Maine to paint, and many of her landscapes were well received. She lived with her brother, Henry K. Prentiss, in Bangor, until her death in 1877. She was buried in the family plot in Paris, Maine.[257]

In *The History of Paris, Maine,* William Lapham wrote, "She is gratefully remembered by many wounded and sick Maine soldiers who were fortunate enough to come under her kind care during her hospital service.... She was kind-hearted, a friend to the poor, and the benefactor of many families in her native town who well ever remember her with gratitude."[258]

Almira F. Quinby
(1828?–October 11, 1909)

Almira Fitch Quinby was a member of one of the leading families of Stroudwater, Maine, and sister of Eunice D. Merrill, who also served as a nurse during the war. Almira first served as a nurse at the general hospital in Chester, Pennsylvania, and was responsible for enlisting Rebecca Usher for a position at that hospital. She wrote in October, 1862:

> Biddeford
> Oct. 17th/62
>
> Dear Miss Usher,
> Cousin Louise [Titcomb] tells me that you would like a situation as nurse in a Hospital. I therefore take the liberty to write to you, giving you an opportunity.
> Mr. Nichols has received an order from Miss [Dorothea Lynde] Dix for nurses—the number not to exceed four. One vacancy he wished me to fill. I've just written to Miss Newhall to see if she will take another place—and I thought you might like to go also.
> No particular qualifications or specifications are required— a common experience in nursing & plain, sensible clothing. Your travelling expenses are paid & we are allowed 40 cts per day. Mr. Nichols checks us through to Wash.—we go to Willard's where we meet Miss D. [Dix] & have our duties assigned us. I shall go, if Miss Newhall decides to go, but cannot get ready before the middle of next week. Miss D. would like to have us go as soon as possible.
> Please let me know your decision, if you wish for further information I will try to obtain it.
> Yrs. very truly
> A. F. Quinby[259]

Susan Newhall and Louise Titcomb went to work in the general hospital in Chester, Pennsylvania and Rebecca joined them a month later. After the Battle of Gettysburg, the war turned southward and the hospital was closed. Mrs. Adaline Tyler, the matron, was transferred to the Naval Academy Hospital in Annapolis, and many of the nurses went with her.[260]

Almira Quinby was already working at the Naval Academy Hospital when several other women from Maine arrived to work in August 1863. In May, she had sent to her brother, Thomas Quinby, of Biddeford, a copy of a letter she received from the parents of a boy who had already died:

O my dere son, John, how mother and me wold like to come and see you, but mother and me is to frail and weakly to stand the journey. I hope that God will spare my dere son. He is my only son and I hope that God will spare him to get home. My dere friend I hope and trust in God that you will try and du all you can for him and if he gets better, I want you if you pleis to send him to his mother for she will go crasy and I want him to come home and if he dies I want to come and fech him home and I will thank your for your kindness.

Almira Quinby (USAMHI)

It was, wrote Almira, only a sample of the many letters they received each day.[261]

The nurses worked under Surgeon Vanderkieft to receive and care for wounded men from battles such as Gettysburg. Later they nursed the returning prisoners from Confederate prisons like Andersonville, Libby, Salisbury, and Florence, where there had been little food, contaminated water, and no comforts of any kind. These were some of the most difficult cases any nurse ever dealt with:

> The sunken hollow cheeks, the parchment skin drawn so tightly over the bones, the great, cavernous, lack-luster eyes, the half idiotic stare, the dreamy condition, the loss of memory even of their own names, and the wonder with which they regarded the most ordinary events, so strange to them after their long and fearful experience, all made them seem more like beings from some other world, than inhabitants of this.[262]

Almira is buried in Stroudwater Cemetery with two other Civil War nurses: her cousin, Louisa Titcomb, and sister, Eunice Merrill.

Hannah Chandler Ropes
(June 13, 1809–January 20, 1863)

Hannah Chandler Ropes, an active abolitionist before the Civil War, had spent time in Kansas during its turbulent and troubled period. An acquaintance of General Nathaniel P. Banks, and a good friend of Senators Charles Sumner and Henry Wilson, she was known among some of the highest circles of the nation. An articulate and educated woman, she was not afraid to criticize when criticism was due. There is little doubt that if she had lived to publish her memoirs she would now be as well known as Clara Barton, Dorothea Dix, or any other woman who participated in the war. Unfortunately, her papers remained in private hands until the mid-twentieth century. Donated to a public institution, well removed from her New England home and not focused on study of the war, they remained unnoticed until the 1970s.[263]

Born in New Gloucester, Maine, the seventh of ten children of Peleg and Esther Parsons Chandler, Hannah grew up in a family that valued learning and thoughtful action. Her father was a prominent lawyer. Two brothers practiced law in Boston with John J. Andrew, a Freesoil advocate who may have influenced Hannah's abolitionist views. Conversation in the Chandler home, no doubt, included talk of social and intellectual issues.[264]

Hannah married William Henry Ropes in Bangor, Maine, in February 1834. An educator, William served as principal of the Foxcroft Academy in Maine from 1832 to 1835. He left to become principal of the Milton Academy, and then Waltham High School in Massachusetts between 1836 and 1840. The couple had four children; two survived to adulthood. Sometime around 1847, William left his family and moved to Florida where he died in 1864. Hannah was left to her own devices to raise her family.[265]

In 1855, her son Edward left their home in Massachusetts to claim a homestead in Kansas and support the Freesoil presence. Shortly thereafter, on September 11, 1855, Hannah and her daughter, Alice, left to join him, arriving in Lawrence, Kansas on September 23. Edward had already built a small cabin for them.[266]

There was much sickness in Lawrence, and Hannah cared for many of her new neighbors as well as her two children. Her letters home express understanding of the troublesome issue of slavery in the territories. Living in Kansas, the debates between pro-slavery forces and freesoil forces were no longer merely theoretical. The

Freesoil Party, formed in the 1840s, fought against the extension of slavery into the territories. The party sponsored groups of anti-slavery settlers to move into the territories and the Ropes family may have been members of one of those groups. Hannah wrote that she kept "loaded pistols and a bowie-knife upon my table at night, [and] three Sharp's rifles, loaded standing in the room" in case of attack by Missourians. The threat of violence became so great that six months later, Hannah returned home to await quieter times. She

Hannah Ropes (USAMHI)

arrived back in Massachusetts in April 1856. In May, the town of Lawrence was sacked by the Missourians she so feared and hated.[267]

Hannah Ropes responded by collecting the letters she had sent to her mother and others, and compiled them into an account of her sojourn in Kansas and an assessment of that turbulent situation. It was published in Boston under the title *Six Months in Kansas*. Clearly an abolitionist tract, it was a welcome contribution to the anti-slavery cause.

When war did come, her son Edward enlisted as a private in Company D of the 2nd Massachusetts Regiment. Hannah decided to volunteer her services as a nurse. She arrived in Washington with Julia Kendall of Plymouth, Massachusetts, on June 25, 1862, and soon joined Hannah E. Stevenson in service at the Union Hotel Hospital in Georgetown.[268] Her frequent letters home were carefully preserved just as she had instructed. She wrote, "Keep all my letters, gather them up everywhere you can. We live so much that I forget, and my discussions in letters are always the most graphic. Keep the ms. carefully...."[269]

The Union Hotel Hospital in Georgetown had been, as one might guess, an old hotel leased by the government to be used as a hospital. Capable of accommodating 225 patients, it was old, in need of repair, and broken up into many small rooms. Ventilation was poor, halls narrow, and little provision made for bathing. An attempt to close it was made in May 1862, but the pressing need for hospital beds caused it to be reopened again in July. On July 5, Hannah greeted her first batch of wounded soldiers. She wrote to her daughter, Alice:

> When we ran down the main hall stairs, such a sight met our eyes as I hope you will never witness. From the broad open entrance into the hall, to the base of the staircase, there bent, clung, and stood, in dumb silence, fifty soldiers, grim, dirty, muddy, and wounded.
>
> I thought of Neddie [her son], when he came down from the mountains, and it seemed as though these were he, in fifty duplicates.
>
> Miss Stevenson ran to the kitchen for the warm tea. I stood by the doctor as he took the name of each and handed each his bed with a ticket. Then they were led or lifted up over the great staircase, winding along, some to the ballroom, others to the banqueting room. When all were up, we each took our portion and commenced to wash them. We were four hours. Everything they had on was stripped off—and, weak, helpless as babes, they sank upon us to care for them. With broken arms and wounded feet, thighs, and fingers, it was no easy job to do gently. One quite old man, sick every way, and a bullet hole through his right hand, called me "good mother" when I laid his head on his pillow, and soon he slept as though he had come to the end of war, unto a haven of rest. That was the experience of one day—5th of July, 1862. You will live to tell your children of this.[270]

In October, she wrote to Alice again:

> I literally have no time to myself, and write at a running pace-for instance, in writing the above, I have got up to attend to a man who has just had his leg taken off—he is reduced in strength, and it is always a good deal of a job to bring a weak man safe out from the effect of the chloroform.
>
> Today we send off fifty men. Not half of them are able to go, but that is of no account to one head surgeon, who cares no more for a private than for a dog. Dr. Hays was a prince of a youth; but he would marry, and so had to go away. We upon the whole have had goodish men to rule over us. Still, between surgeons, stewards, nurses and waiters, the poor men in all the hospitals barely escape with life or clothes or money.

> The wars on James River [are] nothing compared with the fights I have with the stewards. We now have our fourth, as big a villain as ever walked unhung. I have entered a complaint to the Surgeon General but I don't suppose it will do any good at all....[271]

This steward was not the only man Hannah Ropes had heated "battles" with. It was her personal crusade to teach the doctors, stewards, and other officers that "God has made the private and officer of one equality, so far as the moral treatment of each other is concerned." The steward, Henry Perkins, to whom she referred, was eventually arrested under orders from the secretary of war.

On October 31, 1862, she found out that the steward had imprisoned a patient in a dark hole in the cellar of the hospital. This was too much. She had to free the patient and get the steward out of her hospital. She and Julia Kendall went immediately to seek the aid of General Nathaniel Banks, a personal friend of hers, but he was not available. Surgeon General Hammond would not see her (at least not immediately), but Secretary of War Edwin Stanton listened to her accusations and sent the Provost Marshal immediately to correct the situation. The steward and the surgeon were both taken off to the Capitol Prison.[272]

Before that eventful day, however, Miss Stevenson had already given up and gone home. Sarah Low left shortly thereafter. Dr. Clark was returned to the hospital after spending a week in prison. He blamed Hannah Ropes for his imprisonment, and let her know this in no uncertain terms. After he refused to release needed blankets and other supplies to the patients for more than two weeks, Hannah threatened to go back to Mr. Stanton. Clark, fearing arrest a second time, fled.

The hospital settled down for the rest of the fall. In December she wrote, "Don't worry about me. I shall send mighty quick if I am really sick, but...I shall go through the winter nicely."[273] Her last diary entry was dated December 27, 1862. On January 11, 1863, she again wrote to her daughter:

Dear Alice,
    Have not had time to write before, the house has been very sick and we nurses have fairly run down. Miss Kendall is in her room, to rest for a day or two. she would not give up till her knee fairly refused to bend at all! And so she is in bed, much to my relief. Miss Alcott, of Concord, began to cough as soon as she got here. the whole house of patients,

some in with lung irritations, [were similarly afflicted] and with her at first I thought it was purely sympathetic. Today she has "orders" from me not to leave her room and has a mustard plaster all over her chest. As for myself, the "head surgeon" placed me under arrest" the day before New Years and visits me twice a day. Mrs. Boyce wanted me to go home with her, but he would not yield. I have a promise that by next Sabbath I may go. My last patient, who was so crazy, whose hand I held so long till he fell asleep, upset me. It was, the Doctor said, "the drop too much." ...I will go home as soon as your *warm* time comes.

Your mother[274]

The U.S. General Hospital in Georgetown where Hannah Ropes died.
(The Soldier in Our Civil War)

At first Hannah's illness was not taken seriously. But as her condition worsened, Alice came to Georgetown to take care of her. Her care was not enough. On the evening of January 20, 1863, Hannah Chandler Ropes died of pneumonia. Senator Charles Sumner wrote, "Mrs. Ropes was a remarkable character, noble & beautiful, & I doubt if she has ever appeared more so than while she has been here in Washington, nursing soldiers. I regret much that incessant & most onerous duties here prevented me from seeing as much of her as I desired."[275]

Charles Sumner made the arrangements for the funeral, which was attended by hundreds of mourners.[276] She is buried in the cemetery on the Gloucester Hill Road in New Gloucester, Maine, with her parents and other members of her family.

Hannah's grave in New Gloucester.

Emeline B. Rose
(January 1, 1817–June 1,1880)

In July 1862, Emeline Rose set out for Iowa to visit her brother's family. It had been an arduous year back home in Maine, caring for victims of diphtheria. But the worst was now over and she felt she could now get away.

Emeline Proctor was born in Canton, Maine, one of eleven children. She worked as a teacher in Maine and a mill worker in Waltham, Massachusetts, before marrying Nelson Rose in 1851 and moving to Leeds, Maine, and later to Dixfield. Her journal prior to the war is filled with longings to feel the grace of God, listings of visits to friends and neighbors, callers, the travels of her husband, and remarks on the illnesses and deaths of many of her acquaintances. She joined a temperance band while living in Leeds and mentioned Harriet Beecher Stowe's visit to Livermore in 1854.[277]

Emeline's brother, Uriah, married a woman named Clara, and in 1855, the couple moved to Iowa with several other Canton area families. The land was supposed to be much easier to farm and much more productive. Uriah and Emeline wrote to each other frequently.[278]

Occasionally, Emeline de-
clared her satisfaction with
married life, writing in her journal more than once, "Mr. Rose
is the best of husbands." He
was frequently ill, however,
sometimes spending days in
bed. He apparently recovered,
however, for her next journal
entry would note his travel to
Portland, Farmington, or some
other town. But in 1861, Nelson
Rose did not recover. Diphtheria raged through the town and
claimed him as a victim.
Emeline noted, "The bell tolls
every day for another death in
our midst." She joined other
women in nursing the sick of
the community and was so
busy taking care of them that it

Emeline Rose

(Emma Bennett)

was not until April 23, 1861, that she wrote, "War has commenced at
the south—volunteers have gone from this place."[279]

She and other Dixfield women prepared clothing to send to the
soldiers. On October 28, 1861, she wrote, "The soldiers are marching around, there has been another battle in Virginia, I don't know
where Uriah is." Uriah, her brother who had moved to Iowa, had
enlisted.[280] Uriah wrote to her from Camp Herron, Missouri, in November, urging her to come west to visit his family in Osage, Iowa.

Camp Herron
Pacific City, Mo
Nov. 21st, 1861

Dear sisters,

I have neglected to write you since I left Dubuque. Clara
remailed your letters to me. I was in Benton Barracks Mo.
About 4 miles from St. Louis, one of the pleasantest places I
ever saw. We left there the 11th of Oct. And came to Camp
Somers 3 miles from here and were the only company that were
there. We had some high times. We could do pretty much as
we pleased. When we were at Camp Somers the Boys would
Draw Rations (steal) consisting of Chickens, Pigs and old Pigs,
Geese, Turkeys, Sheep, Beehives, Apples, Peaches, Sweet Pota-

toes and occasionally fat Cattle and other things too numerous
to Mention. You see we were not on very good terms with Secessionists. There are not many Rebels here. We came to Camp
Herron a week ago last Monday but we left with Regret for a
Soldiers life is obey Orders. We have a good Co and Regt. It
is said the best Regt. from Iowa. The 7th Iowa was badly used
at Belmont a short time ago. We have had no fight yet. Our
Regt are all Country Boys, most all farmers. We have a Smart
Man for a Chaplin, the best sermon I have heard for a long time
I heard last Sunday. The men are not allowed any Whiskey so
there is no fighting or quarrelling. We are well clothed and fed.
We do not get cakes or Pies but we have plenty of Fresh Beef,
Salt Pork, Bacon, Bread, Coffee, Sugar, Crackers, Beans,
Hominy, Rice, etc. We are in Tents—six men in a Tent. It is
warm here, we have had no snow nor no signs of any. I want
you to write. Tell all of my friends to Write Direct to me, Co. I,
9th Regt. Iowa Vol. Care of Capt. Powers. I have not heard from
maine since you wrote. I had a letter from Clara last Sunday.
They are all well. She wants you to come to Osage. If you do
come, the best way to Montreal, to Detroit, Chicago, Prairie
Duchien and then by Stage to Osage. I have no more time to
write as the drums Beat to fall in and there is no Excusing here.
Write soon.

Uriah A. Proctor[281]

Emeline resolved to go to Iowa when the diphtheria epi-
demic was over. She began her long journey in July 1863, taking the stage to Bryant Pond and the train through New
Hampshire, Vermont and into Canada. A ferry took her to Detroit, Michigan, and from there she again took a train to Chicago
and another from there to St. Louis, Missouri. A steamboat took
her up the Mississippi to McGregor, Iowa and from there she
took another stage to Osage, Iowa, the final leg of an arduous
journey. She was warmly welcomed by her brother's family.
Before long, she was working with women in Osage to prepare
relief supplies but she longed to do more. She wrote to Washington asking for a nursing position, but received word that there
was no vacancy.

On May 22, Uriah was wounded in the Battle of Grand Gulf,
the battle that convinced General Grant he would have to take
Vicksburg by siege. Uriah was taken to the Gayosa Hospital in
Memphis, Tennessee, shot in the leg four inches above the knee.[282]

Emeline immediately packed her bags and left for Memphis.
In Cairo, at the extreme southern tip of Illinois, she called on Gen-

eral Beaufort for a pass and then took the *Jacob Strader* to Memphis, arriving on June 20, 1863. Rushing directly to the hospital, Emeline later wrote, "They showed me up to Ward I. Uriah is as well as can be expected considering his wound. I staid with him till night & then went to the Soldiers Home, a very pleasant & beautiful place. The building is confiscated property—a large yard with trees, magnolias in bloom, roses and other kinds."[283]

Uriah had good days and bad. As Emeline cared for him she became aware of other soldiers' suffering. On June 28 she wrote, "2 died this morning in this ward both very young not hardly 18—one a drummer boy. It seems sad to come in here—suffer so much and die so far away from home, but for this WAR."[284] On July 3, Dr. Hartshorn sent for her, asking if she would act as nurse for the ward. She replied, "I am glad to do something for poor sick suffering creatures." She commenced work on July 6, receiving her commission from Dr. Erwin and Dr. Hartshorn. She wrote, "'T' is very had work I am so very tired, I hope I shall get along nicely without getting sick, but I like the business."[285]

Like many nurses, she spent long hours with some of the most fearfully wounded; reading, fanning, writing letters for the men, or just providing some company. Besides wounded soldiers, there were cases of lung fever, typhoid, diphtheria, small pox, and dysentery. The nurses hung up evergreens and, as she said, "Cleaned, cleaned, cleaned."

On September 9, 1863, her brother, Uriah, went home on furlough, but Emeline stayed even though she was very lonely without him.[286] She was still there for her birthday on January 1, 1864, when she wrote, "My birthday—47. Another year is past. The Ward had a nice dinner: oysters, chickens, mince pies, tarts & cakes. The men bought a barrel of apples & saved a whole lot for me which pleased me much."[287]

In May 1864, she began thinking of going home to Maine, but the surgeons convinced her to stay on. Uriah rejoined his regiment and was a member of Sherman's March through Georgia.[288] With renewed fighting large numbers of new patients poured into Emeline's hospital. By July, suffering from fatigue and the unaccustomed heat, she was granted her request to be relieved from duty. Emeline returned to Maine and, except for a few years in Boston, lived there the rest of her life. She died on the Rose Farm June 1, 1880, and is buried in the Greenwood Cemetery in Dixfield.[289]

When she left Gayosa Hospital, Dr. Horton gave Emeline a tribute which he had written for her:

To Mrs. Emeline B. Rose, Gayosa Hospital

Dear Madam. We tender to you our regards
For your sympathizing care in Ward I.
We pray you may have an abundant reward
And that happiness ever attend you
As an angel of Mercy, hast thou been here,
Ministering to each & to all,
Thy hands ever busy—a quick ready ear
And feet ever willing to run at our call.
Thy many acts of kindness shown to us here
Bring up fond memories, in holy review.
The kindest of sisters, the best Mother dear,
And a wife ever faithful, loving and true.
And now be assured, where ever we roam
Over land or sea, in peace or strife,
Wandering for abroad, or at home,
Thy memory, we'll cherish through life.
We claim for this, no praise to poets due
For its homely parts are plain to see.
But this humble verse, presents to view
Feelings we ever shall cherish for you.
Respectfully presented by your very obedient servant
Dr. Horton.[290]

Her journals, letters, and other personal items were found by her great niece in the attic of the Rose Farm in Dixfield in 1958, nearly 100 years after the war.

Sarah Smith Sampson
(1830?–December 22, 1907)

...there were a number of men that she wanted to send home—but the Surgeon had no power to send them farther than Alexandria. She went with them & when they arrived at Alex. she sent for the Surgeon & told him she wanted an order to take these men to Washington. He said he had no power to send them. But, said she, Dr. these men are dying, & if you let them go on, they may live to see their friends. He said he knew it was a hard case, but he could not help it; it was against his orders. Now, said she, Dr you just let me go on with these men—I know the Surgeon Gen. & as soon as I get to Wash. I will go to him & tell him that it is all my fault—that you could not help it; that I brought the men away in spite of you. She carried her point. As soon as she arrived, she went & called upon the Surgeon Gen. & told him what she had done. He was astounded at her audacity, & told her she must never do such a thing again.[291]

This was the second of three astounding stories about Sarah Sampson which Rebecca Usher recorded in her journal on Monday, January 23, 1865. "Mrs. Mayhew has been telling me about Mrs. Sampson of Bath. A very remarkable woman she must be as she always carries her point in spite of red tape," wrote Rebecca, who had just joined Ruth Mayhew at City Point, Virginia.

Another story involved Sarah going behind the back of a chief surgeon to have her friend, Dr. Garcelon, amputate the leg of a Maine soldier. One other incident occurred when she was short one stretcher, so she went into a general's tent, dumped everything off his bed and used that as a stretcher. Such audacity in the face of military protocol, although effective, often put women nurses and army surgeons and officers at odds, but clearly both Mrs. Mayhew and Miss Usher were impressed.

Sarah Sampson began her military career as one of the wives who followed her officer-husband south to the battlefields. Charles A. L. Sampson, a figurehead carver, was captain of Company D of the 3rd Maine Infantry Regiment. The Third Maine left Augusta for Washington on June 5, 1861, under the command of Colonel Oliver Otis Howard. Her first impressions of her new life were conveyed in a letter written on June 14 to Dr. Alonzo Garcelon, surgeon-general of Maine troops. Her journey, she wrote, "was to me truly delightful" traveling with the colonel and other officers. It took them three days to reach Washington, arriving at 8:00 on a Friday evening. She stayed at the luxurious Willard Hotel.[292]

The next morning, armed with a letter of introduction from Dr. Garcelon to Miss Dix, she wrote, "I made my way to the Capitol, but fortunately (I am confidant) the lady was out, and I was waited upon by an elderly lady (Mrs. Healed), formerly of Maine, but for eight years a resident of this city. From her I learned many items, that I trust you will assist me to appropriate to our advantage—State advantage I mean."[293]

It was then that she began pushing for a Maine general hospital and she wrote, "Female nurses are much more efficient than men. Our Surgeon thinks it exceedingly necessary that we should be provided with such. So does the Col. and our own people at home can readily see the advantage we should derive in keeping our Maine sick by ourselves. They would not then be exposed to diseases incident to the South, and it would save many a mother's and sister's tears to feel their dear one more tenderly cared for, by mothers and sisters from our own state."[294]

She cared for the sick of the 3rd Maine Regiment and other Maine units encamped nearby or within easy travel, and visited hospitals in the vicinity to check on conditions for Maine soldiers. On May 8, 1862, she went by herself through Baltimore to Fort Monroe in Virginia to visit the 7th Maine Regiment. She found steamers tied up at the dock loaded with wounded from the Battle of Williamsburg and the hospitals already full. She spent several weeks there, caring for Maine soldiers and distributing her supplies. On June 2, just after the Battle of Fair Oaks, she left for White House Landing, also in Virginia. "Among the first I saw was General Howard and his brother; the former with his right arm amputated, and the latter with a severe flesh wound of the thigh. At their request I returned with them to Fortress Monroe." After making sure they had medical attention she returned to White House Landing. She wrote, "Such suffering and confusion I never before witnessed. Many serious wounds had not been dressed for several days, and indeed, the loss of many limbs was the consequence of inattention to lighter wounds; but this was not from fault of surgeons, but from circumstances beyond their control."[295]

The Seven Days' Battle began on May 25, 1862. As White House Landing was being evacuated, Sarah found herself cut off from her supplies and without transportation. "My trunk containing my entire wardrobe, journal from the commencement of the war, and papers containing effects and items of priceless value to friends of deceased soldiers, were all at Mr. Dudley's house, which was demolished by the enemy that very day."[296]

The loss of her clothing and personal items was the reason she gave for returning to Maine that summer. But her husband, Charles, had been forced to resign from his post in July and that may have been the true reason for their return to Maine.

Having tasted adventure and not satisfied with returning home in disgrace, Sarah quickly arranged an appointment for herself and Mr. L. Watson, to run an agency sponsored by the State of Maine to care for Maine soldiers in the Washington area. It was called the Maine Soldiers Relief Association, located at 273 F Street, Washington, D.C. Sarah left home on October 1, 1862, to return to Washington. The agency's efforts paralleled and frequently intertwined with those of the Maine Camp Hospital Association. Perhaps they worked so well together because Sarah's brother, Lewis B. Smith, was an officer of the Maine Camp Hospital Association in Portland. Or perhaps it was because Ruth Mayhew and Mrs. Sampson worked well together. The two had traveled to Gettysburg together in mid-July, and stayed four weeks. By the end of the war the two organizations had, in effect, merged and the camp occupied by the Maine Camp Hospital Association agents at City Point was generally known as "The Maine Agency."[297] Sarah Sampson's lengthy report of her activities was, surprisingly, included in the *Report of the Adjutant General of the State of Maine, 1864/65.*

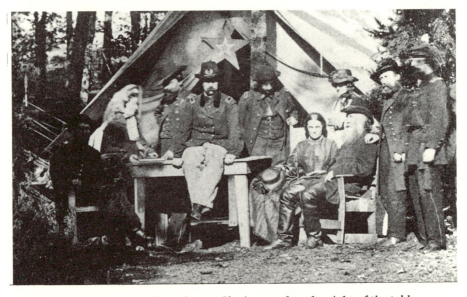

Sarah Sampson at Gettysburg. She is seated to the right of the table.

(USAMHI)

In 1866, Sarah Sampson established an orphanage in Bath originally for children of soldiers who were killed in the war.[298] Called the Bath Military and Naval Orphan Asylum, it was turned over to the state in 1919 and the name was changed to the Bath Children's Home. It existed until 1996 when it was forced to close. It was Maine's last state-owned residence for homeless teen-agers. Rising costs of upkeep on the building and the shift towards placing homeless children with families contributed to its closing.[299]

The Orphanage in Bath established by Sarah Sampson.

After her husband died in 1881, Sarah returned to Washington to work in the Pension Office. She also began receiving a pension of $25 per month in 1885. Although she never served as an official army nurse, the pension was granted based on her report published in the Maine Adjutant General's Report in 1865, testimonials from Hannibal Hamlin, Dr. G. S. Palmer, and others, plus the fact that her husband would have qualified for a pension.[300]

In 1906 Sarah returned to Maine for her last reunion with veterans of the 3rd Maine. A reporter from Bath managed to corner her for an interview about her life as an army nurse. "There is a good deal of the gypsy about me," she said laughingly, "and I always thought it would be fun to live in a tent. That was before I ever went into camp, but I never changed my mind about liking the life." When asked about her work, she said quite simply, "I was with many soldiers and did all I could to help them."[301]

When she died, she was buried at Arlington National Cemetery with several other Civil War nurses. The location of their graves was lost in official records until researcher Kathy Kleiman tracked them down. Her stone reads: "Sarah S. Sampson Volunteer Nurse Civil War Wife of Chas. A. L. Sampson Lt. Col. 3d Maine Vol. Inf." The veterans of the 3rd Maine Regiment placed a brass plaque on the stone which reads: "This tablet is dedicated in loving memory of Sarah S. Sampson by the Third Maine Regiment."

Sarah Sampson's grave in Arlington.
(Kathy Kleiman)

Harriet Scamman
(September 29, 1824–March 27, 1897)

Harriet Scamman, daughter of Nicholas Scamman, and a resident of Saco, Maine, served for seventeen months during the war at the Armory Square Hospital in Washington, from December 1863 until August 13, 1865, under the direction of Dr. D. W. Bliss, Surgeon. In March 1893, writing from her home at 19 North Street in Saco, claiming failing eyesight, age and ill health, Harriet applied for a pension.[302] She died of pneumonia in Saco, Maine, and is buried there in the Laurel Hill Cemetery where her stone reads, "She did what she could."

Susan Smiley
(1813?–?)

When Charles E. Smiley of North Vassalboro enlisted with the 11th Maine Regiment, Co. B, his mother, Susan Smiley, enlisted, too.[303] She said, "I enlisted in the United States service October 1, 1861, and was ordered to the front at Bell Plain, Virginia, to carry supplies and attend the sick and wounded." She served as the regiment's nurse for as long as she was allowed, then reported for duty at the Georgetown Hospital. She worked there until ordered by Miss Dix to Fort Monroe, where she stayed for about three months. She also worked at Stone Hospital (6 months), Columbia Hospital (1 year), and Harewood Hospital (8 months).

"In all," she later wrote, "I worked about 4 years; then was married in January, 1864." She and her husband, Daniel Babcock lived in Smithville, New York.[304]

Susan Smiley-Babcock
(Our Army Nurses)

Sarah P. Smith
(1836?–February 16, 1914)

Sarah Perry Smith was a descendent of Commodore Oliver Hazard Perry, the hero who fought the British in the War of 1812 and won a major naval battle on Lake Erie. Sarah continued the derring-do of her illustrious ancestor. Born in Norridgewock, Maine, daughter of Lyman Perry and Betsy Pishon, she was sixteen when she went to live with her sister Ann Elizabeth, who was married to Orrin Williamson, a hardware merchant in Augusta. There she met Lieutenant Hillman Smith of Company K, 8th Maine Infantry. On

August 28, 1862, they were married in a full dress military wedding. The ceremony was performed in Augusta by the chaplain of the regiment, Charles Nason of Kennebunk. According to her own reports, she was determined to be with her husband and share in whatever fortunes or misfortunes came to him.[305]

Shortly after joining her husband's regiment, stationed at Hilton Head in April 1863, they were sent to take part in the siege of Morris Island and she received her "baptism of fire." Bomb shells continually whirled through the air above her head and explosions were distinctly heard as the shells landed behind the Rebel lines. While the bombardment was going on, the Rebel artillery did not remain idle and "all compliments were returned." Although in constant danger, Mrs. Smith remained by her husband's side and became so accustomed to shot and shell that she scarcely noticed it.[306]

The regiment was later sent to Charleston, where Major Hillman Smith was put in command of the advanced picket line. This put Sarah even closer to danger. On one occasion, she took a short walk from camp and found herself unexpectedly in the midst of a Confederate picket camp. They made no effort to take her prisoner and later she noted that their tents were very shabby and they were lacking blankets and other important equipment.

She frequently went out riding on a nice shady road near Beaufort, South Carolina, where they were encamped for a time. On one excursion, she had ridden farther than usual; a Confederate picket jumped up from the side of the road and commanded her to halt. "Without a moment's hesitation she turned her horse and driving the spurs into his flanks, made a flying run back to the union camp."[307]

Sarah claimed to be a witness to an incident at Fort Greg [Battery Gregg] when, as she reported, the body of General Strong was thrown into a trench with black soldiers by the Confederates. She was most likely referring to the incident at Fort Wagner, when the body of Colonel Robert Gould Shaw was thrown into a trench with the bodies of the black soldiers of the 54th Massachusetts who had so bravely stormed that fort. General Strong was wounded at that battle and died twelve days later in Union hands. Battery Greg and Fort Wagner guard Charleston Harbor and she was in the vicinity. It seems unlikely, however, that she could have actually witnessed the event.[308]

Her sister, Ann, meanwhile, stayed busy helping the soldiers back home in Augusta. She collected supplies and sent them to the front throughout the war and was a leader in organizing the relief effort in her area. She went so far as to care for sick soldiers in her home when measles broke out. "She opened the doors of her home to the afflicted and tenderly cared for them, looking after their wants and writing many a letter for the young soldiers to their parents."[309]

Sarah's obituary indicates that she experienced many exciting adventures during the war. Apparently, she loved to talk about them and is still remembered by descendants of the 8th Maine Volunteer Infantry. On display in their regimental building on Peaks Island, off the coast of Portland, Maine, is a newspaper article about her adventures. Entitled, "An Auburn Woman at the Front," the article was clipped from what was probably the Lewiston *Journal* around 1905 and saved for future generations.

Sarah Smith was finally forced to leave the 8th Maine by the commanding general, Quincy Adams Gilmore, who felt conditions were too dangerous and too hard for a woman. She had just spent the last seven months proving him wrong, but there was no recourse.[310]

She and her husband settled in Auburn, Maine, after the war. They had five children, two of whom died in infancy. Hillman took an interest in local politics, serving as sheriff of Androscoggin County, warden of the Maine State Prison, and as mayor of Auburn for two years. He died August 1, 1905, but Sarah lived on in good health until just before her death in 1914.[311]

Emily Bliss Souder
(1814–December 22, 1886)

Like most Northern women, Emily was appalled by stories of the conditions faced by soldiers. She resolved to help. The women of Philadelphia set up the renowned "Cooper Shop Soldiers' Home" in Philadelphia, which provided shelter and served food and drinks to soldiers passing through their city. Emily helped out. It was a god-send to soldiers who were far from home in a strange city and often had little money.

Emily was the daughter of Stephen Thatcher. Her father, born in 1774, orphaned at age fourteen, became a well-educated preacher, serving in various communities until moving to Kennebunk, Maine. There he served as judge of probate from 1807 until 1818. It is likely that Emily was born in Kennebunk in 1814, one of fourteen children (three of whom died in infancy). Her brother, Peter, became one of

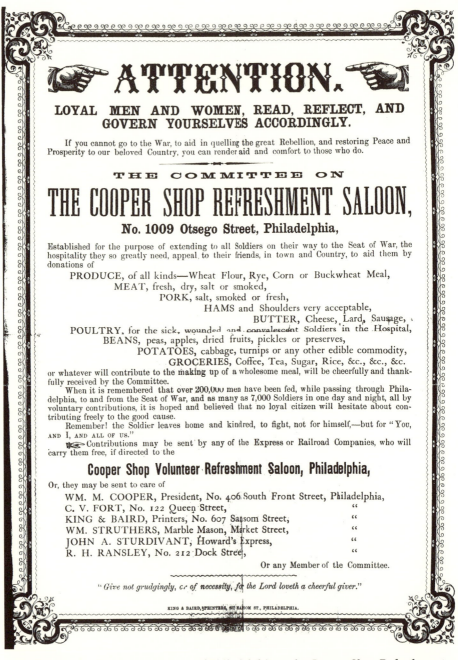

ATTENTION.

LOYAL MEN AND WOMEN, READ, REFLECT, AND GOVERN YOURSELVES ACCORDINGLY.

If you cannot go to the War, to aid in quelling the great Rebellion, and restoring Peace and Prosperity to our beloved Country, you can render aid and comfort to those who do.

THE COMMITTEE ON

THE COOPER SHOP REFRESHMENT SALOON,

No. 1009 Otsego Street, Philadelphia,

Established for the purpose of extending to all Soldiers on their way to the Seat of War, the hospitality they so greatly need, appeal to their friends, in town and Country, to aid them by donations of

PRODUCE, of all kinds—Wheat Flour, Rye, Corn or Buckwheat Meal,
MEAT, fresh, dry, salt or smoked,
PORK, salt, smoked or fresh,
HAMS and Shoulders very acceptable,
BUTTER, Cheese, Lard, Sausage,
POULTRY, for the sick, wounded and convalescent Soldiers in the Hospital,
BEANS, peas, apples, dried fruits, pickles or preserves,
POTATOES, cabbage, turnips or any other edible commodity,
GROCERIES, Coffee, Tea, Sugar, Rice, &c., &c., &c.,
or whatever will contribute to the making up of a wholesome meal, will be cheerfully and thankfully received by the Committee.

When it is remembered that over 200,000 men have been fed, while passing through Philadelphia, to and from the Seat of War, and as many as 7,000 Soldiers in one day and night, all by voluntary contributions, it is hoped and believed that no loyal citizen will hesitate about contributing freely to the good cause.

Remember! the Soldier leaves home and kindred, to fight, not for himself,—but for "You, AND I, AND ALL OF US."

Contributions may be sent by any of the Express or Railroad Companies, who will carry them free, if directed to the

Cooper Shop Volunteer Refreshment Saloon, Philadelphia,

Or, they may be sent to care of

WM. M. COOPER, President, No. 406 South Front Street, Philadelphia,
C. V. FORT, No. 122 Queen Street,   "
KING & BAIRD, Printers, No. 607 Sansom Street, "
WM. STRUTHERS, Marble Mason, Market Street,   "
JOHN A. STURDIVANT, Howard's Express,   "
R. H. RANSLEY, No. 212 Dock Street,   "

Or any Member of the Committee.

"Give not grudgingly, or of necessity, for the Lord loveth a cheerful giver."

KING & BAIRD, PRINTERS, 607 SANSOM ST., PHILADELPHIA.

Emily Bliss Souder helped citizens of Philadelphia at the Cooper Shop Refreshment Saloon—one of the best examples of women providing needed assistance to soldiers en route. (Maine Hist. Soc.)

Maine's earliest lawyers. Brother Ralph also became a counselor-at-law. Another became a state senator in Minnesota. Emily made her mark in other ways. She married Edmund A. Souder of Philadelphia. They were living in Philadelphia when the war began and when news of the Battle in Gettysburg reached her.[312]

She and three other women decided to travel to Gettysburg to assist, arriving about two weeks after the battle. Of her first day and her first trip to the hospital, she wrote on July 15:

> We saw the rifle-pits, the dead horses, the shattered windows and the stone walls, all scattered and many soldiers' graves. But who shall describe the horrible atmosphere which meets us almost continually? Chloride of lime has been freely used in the broad streets of the town and to-day the hospital was much improved by the same means; but it is needful to close the eyes against sounds of anguish and to extinguish, as far as possible, the sense of smelling.
>
> We dispensed buckets of milk punch and quantities of corn-starch, nicely prepared with condensed milk and bran, besides sundry cups of tea, an unwonted luxury, and broth made of beef jelly condensed, with many other services and a little chat occasionally with some poor fellow. I found a great many Maine boys; many from Wisconsin and Minnesota; scarcely one who had not lost an arm or a leg....[313]

She was glad that she brought a supply of paper and envelopes so that even when food supplies were not available, she could still be useful. She wrote:

> A surgeon from Ohio, who is waiting for the Harrisburg train, says he can take a man's leg off, if necessary and not mind it; but when a man says, "Can't you write to my wife and tell her how I died and tell her to kiss Mary," that I cannot do. This gentleman started from his home immediately after receiving tidings of the battle and walked twelve miles across the country to reach a railroad train, that he might arrive at Gettysburg as early as possible.[314]

> We rode in ambulance to the hospital of the Second Corps. The sights and the sounds beggar description. There is great need of bandages. Almost every man has lost either an arm or a leg. The groans, the cries, the shrieks of anguish are awful indeed to hear. We heard them all day in the field, and last night I buried my head in my pillow to shut out the sounds which reached us, from a church quite near, where the wounded are lying.[315]

We could only try to hear as though we heard not, for it requires effort to be able to attend to the various calls for aid. The condensed milk is invaluable. The corn-starch, farina, and milk punch are eagerly partaken of, and a cup of chocolate is greatly relished. A poor fellow with a broken jaw seemed to appeal, though mutely, for special attention. I beat up quickly two or three eggs, adding a spoonful of brandy and a cup of scalding hot milk, which he managed to draw through his scarcely opened lips, and at once seemed revived. The Union soldiers and the rebels, so long at variance, are here quite friendly. They have fought their last battle, and vast numbers are going daily to meet the King of Terrors.[316]

To her brother in Minnesota, on July 20, she wrote:

A great many Maine boys are here, especially of the 19th Maine, which was terrible cut up. We have several times visited the Adjutant of the 17th Maine,[317] a pleasant young man from Portland, who bears the suffering from an amputated limb with great cheerfulness. He is quartered in a private house in the town. On the opposite side of the street is a young captain of the same regiment, who has lost his arm, Captain Young.[318] He was wounded, I believe, in the first day's battle, and like many others laid several days in the woods without attention.[319]

Emily continued to write numerous letters during her stay in Gettysburg. Some went home to their society of supporters, some to her husband, and others to her family members back in Maine. These she collected in 1864 into a small volume entitled, *Leaves from the Battlefield of Gettysburg*, which she published, as she said, to give "a truthful picture of a portion of the field of labor, [and their sale] may also aid in providing needful supplies for our brave soldiers in the hospitals and on the field; for the Sanitary Commission, which, since the beginning of this dire rebellion, has been doing the work of the good Samaritan, 'pouring in the oil and the wine.'"

When Emily learned of the plans for a ceremony consecrating the cemetery and ground at Gettysburg in November 1863, she said, "I had felt as if I *must* be in Gettysburg whenever the ceremonies did take place."[320] She managed to be there, leaving home on Tuesday, November 17. The trip was extremely difficult since everyone seemed to have the same desire to be in

Gettysburg for the ceremony. It took her from 8:00 in the morning until 11:00 at night to make the 30-mile trip. She spent Wednesday revisiting sites of the battle, still finding numerous fragments of clothing, knapsacks, haversacks, and other items strewn over the ground. She was lucky to find a place to stay:

> The churches were lighted and warmed for the reception of those who could not find quarters elsewhere. The streets were filled with crowds of people. A band was playing the national airs in front of the house where Mr. Lincoln was staying, and eager calls were made for "the President," who finally stood a few minutes on the doorstep, and in response to the wishes of the people, made a few characteristic remarks, promising to speak at some length the next day.[321]

The next day, November 19, the day of the ceremony, began (as she remembered) dull and cloudy, but soon cleared. The crowd grew to enormous proportions:

> As the hour approached, heavy guns were fired at intervals, pealing like a solemn anthem on the air. The sadness of recent bereavement seemed to rest upon every heart. Soon we heard the sounds of funeral marches, and the long line of military passed through Baltimore Street toward the Cemetery. Then came the President, easily distinguished from all others. He seemed as chief mourner.[322]

In a time without public address systems, Emily probably never heard Lincoln's address. She noted:

> A beautiful flag floated over the platform, which was arranged with seats for the distinguished guests, but there was no place allotted for ladies.... It was long past noon when the procession returned. It was a magnificent sight. The long line of infantry with their bayonets gleaming in the sunlight, the artillery, the distinguished guests, the great multitude. As the President passed, every head was uncovered, and three hearty cheers were given for him.[323]

That evening, she paid her respects to the President and Governor Andrew Gregg Curtin of Pennsylvania before departing for home the next day. Emily returned to her wartime efforts at the Cooper Shop Soldier's Home.[324]

Lydia Spaulding
(April?, 1804–January 23, 1882)

In her book, *Stories from Hospital and Camp*, Charlotte McKay, referring to Lydia, wrote about a lady from Springfield, Maine who, hearing that her son, Liberty Spaulding of the 1st Maine Cavalry, had been wounded, traveled to City Point, Virginia, to find him. She arrived in mid-September, 1864:

> She had come without delay to look after him; but find-ing, to her great grief, that he had been lying in the little cem-etery five days, and seeing that there was much to do for the sons of other mothers who were far away, she forthwith sent her tears back to their fountains, and began to work for them, and soon became so much interested that she begged to be put on permanent duty in the hospital.[325]

She and her son are now both buried in the Springfield Cem-etery in Springfield, Maine, with other members of their family.

Harriet Elizabeth Beecher Stowe
(June 14, 1811–July 1, 1896)

Harriet Beecher Stowe is one of the few women who has never been forgot-ten for her association with the American Civil War. So much has been written about her and her famous family that little more can be added. Although usually not thought of as "a daugh-ter of Maine," Harriet Beecher Stowe was living in Brunswick, Maine at the time she wrote her greatest literary contribution, *Uncle Tom's Cabin.*

Harriet had married Calvin Stowe, a professor of biblical literature. In

Harriet Beecher Stowe
<small>(Life of Harriet Beecher Stowe)</small>

1850, he accepted a position at Bowdoin College in Brunswick, Maine. Harriet moved her family in April 1850, leaving Calvin in Cincinnati to finish his academic term.[326]

With the passage of the Fugitive Slave Act in 1850, which called for escaped slaves to be returned to their masters, Harriet was beseeched by friends and relatives to write about the issue. *Uncle Tom's Cabin*, a lengthy novel, included descriptions of the brutal and inhumane treatment of slaves in the South. First serialized in *The National Era* beginning June 5, 1851, it was published in book form in 1852. Her son Charles wrote, "It had been contemplated as a mere magazine tale of perhaps a dozen chapters, but once begun it could no more be controlled than the waters of the swollen Mississippi, bursting through a crevasse in its levees."[327] Harriet herself said, "I could not control the story; it wrote itself."[328] It was widely read throughout the United States and was so powerful that it helped to shape Northern attitudes on the issue of slavery. For its serial publication, she received a mere $300. For the book, she was to receive ten percent of the profits. She made nothing from the numerous plays and other

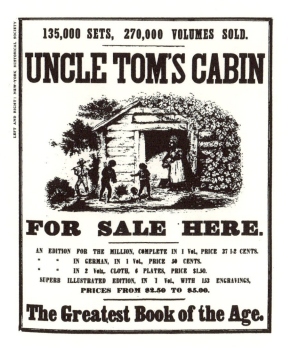

Advertisement for the book that began the war.

take-offs on the story. Still, after suffering years of poverty, the royalties paid her nearly $10,000 in the first four months of publication. It has not gone out of print since.

The money she received from the book allowed her and her family to move back to Massachusetts and near her family. Calvin accepted a professorship at the Theological Seminary in Andover, Massachusetts.[329]

Ten years after publication, in November 1862, when Abraham Lincoln met Mrs. Stowe he reportedly said, "So this is the little lady who started this great war!"[330] *Uncle Tom's Cabin* did not, of course, start the American Civil War, but it did, certainly, stir up Northern sentiment against slavery. It was widely read, especially in the North, and became a banner for the abolitionists.

Jane P. Thurston
(August 5, 1814–March 3, 1899)

In March 1863 Jane P. Thurston had a plan to end the war. It was not a plan President Lincoln or most loyal Republicans would have endorsed. Yet her plan shows striking similarities to the plan outlined by the Democratic Party platform unveiled at the end of August that same year. For those who were weary of the war and willing to compromise with the Confederates, the plan contained some interesting suggestions.

Jane was the daughter of Moses and Abigail Plummer and grew up in a large house with a large family at the corner of India and Fore Streets in Portland, just around the corner from Henry Wadsworth Longfellow's childhood home. Her father was a military officer and one of her brothers, a West Point graduate. Jane became an avid reader, scholar, and teacher before marrying Captain Henry Thurston in 1846.[331]

The Thurstons lived in an impressive house close to the Fore River on Tyng Street with a wonderful garden containing pear and cherry trees. There they had six children. Three lived beyond infancy; Henry Jr., Henrietta Maria, and Abbie Jane. When the captain sailed to foreign lands, his family often went with him. Tragedy struck in 1859. While on a voyage to Marseille, Henry Jr. died and his father became so ill that it was necessary for Jane to take command of the ship on its stormy return voyage. Although they made it back to Portland, Henry died early the following year.[332]

With the death of her sea captain husband, Jane Thurston suddenly found herself in reduced circumstances. It was immediately clear that the once-wealthy merchant had left his family with very little more than the house they lived in. Jane responded by setting in motion a bizarre legal campaign in 1861 to recover the property that she felt was rightfully hers. Some people admired Jane's original methods. Others thought she was completely mad.

While pursuing her claim that the Atlantic and St. Lawrence Railroad had illegally appropriated some of her land, Jane launched what may have been one of the most unique money-making schemes ever. She wrote a series of pamphlets which she offered for sale. One written in 1861 was entitled: *The Union of the States and the Union of Families of the United States and Great Britain: How They May be Preserved.* This was while her own family was dissolving. Her mother died in 1860. Her daughter, Abbie, died in 1862.

In March 1863 she wrote an even bolder treatise. It was a plan to end the war and she advertised its sale for $500. On March 26 the following letter was published:

> To the editor of the Press:
> I am ready to reveal my plan to the Editor of the Gardiner Journal, provided he will give me his note for $500, payable at any time when peace is declared, within six months. But I wish to annex the important condition, that the plan shall be adopted and tested at once; otherwise there is no prospect of the war terminating within a year. Of what use would it be to reveal the plan, if it is not adopted and acted upon? I am willing to make the note payable on the sole condition, that the plan shall stop the war, if acted upon in good faith, otherwise the note shall be void.
>
> Jane P. Thurston.[333]

Entitled: *The Plan to Close the Rebellion and Unite the States in Six Months*, it called for a series of steps to be taken. The first step was that all the loyal Northern states hold a convention to take action on her plan. Another part of her plan required President Lincoln "will be willing to leave his office." She felt Lincoln would do this for the good of the Union. Jane suggested George B. McClellan, Thurlow Weed, or Horatio Seymour be elected in his place. Her plan also called for all the Southern states to recognize the Constitution of the United States as the supreme law of the land. Lastly, she called for amnesty to all for their words and deeds during the conflict.[334]

Jane thought her plan would succeed because the Constitution was a covenant with God. Those who violated it would be declaring all contracts made under it null and void, marriage contracts included. When Southerners realized the gravity of what they had done, they would readily accept the Constitution and the union of the states once more.

Her plan did not address the fundamental issue of slavery. Neither did the platform put forth by the Democratic party six months later.

On August 29, 1863, the Democrats met in Chicago to ratify a platform and choose a candidate to replace Lincoln. New York governor Horatio Seymour gave the keynote address. By 1863 the number of Copperheads was growing rapidly and they were a strong force at the convention. They favored a quick, negotiated peace with the South. The platform called for an immediate cessation of hostilities and a convention of the states so that peace might be restored on the basis of the Federal Union of the States. Their candidate was George B. McClellan.[335] There is no record that they paid Jane P. Thurston her $500.

Jane fought other battles. She continued her legal claims and pamphlet writing. Since she had not been compensated for the taking of her land, she felt that both the State of Maine and the United States had breached the fundamental guaranties of their respective constitutions. She was therefore within her rights to seize their lands. Thus she claimed to be Proprietor of the State of Maine and Proprietor of the United States. She went so far as to appear before the Maine House of Representatives on January 5, 1870, just before the session was to begin, to auction off the state. Portland's *Eastern Argus* reported: "One Senator bid fifteen millions, and another seventeen. A Representative bid twenty millions, till at last she made one better and struck it off to herself and took her seat in the Speaker's chair." Amidst calls to "Put her out!" and threatened with being dragged out, she finally left the floor.[336] She later released the state back to Governor Joshua L. Chamberlain and tried to deed back the United States to President Grant.[337] She justified it all within the pages of her pamphlets.

In her latter years, Jane redirected her energies to researching genealogy. She published one genealogy on the Plummer family and another on the Norton family. Her earlier struggles, however, were never forgotten. When Jane P. Thurston died in 1899, the words "Empress of America" were carved on her gravestone. Unfortunately, the stone has since disappeared.

Mary Agnes Tincker
(July 18, 1831–November 27, 1907)

Novelist Mary Agnes Tincker, born to Richard and Mehitabel Jellison Tincker grew up in Ellsworth, Maine. She attended public schools and also went to the Blue Hill Academy. At age thirteen she began her career as a teacher in Ellsworth and at fifteen she began writing for local newspapers and magazines.[338]

In 1863 Mary Agnes procured a recommendation from Massachusetts governor John A. Andrew to be a volunteer nurse for the army. She secured a position at the Judiciary Square Hospital until she, herself became ill with some disease she caught from the soldiers and returned north.[339]

She settled in Boston and pursued writing full time. In 1873 she moved to Italy, where she spent the next fourteen years. She returned to Boston in 1887 and remained there for the rest of her life.

Mary Agnes Tincker was the author of eleven novels including *By the Tiber* (1881), *Aurora* (1886), and *Autumn Leaves* (1899). She also contributed to various magazines such as *Harper's*, *Putnam's*, and *Catholic World*.[340]

Louisa Titcomb
(December 20, 1823–July 15, 1905)

Louise was one of several Portland women who became nurses and relief workers during the war. The daughter of Sarah Titcomb and an unknown father, the Titcombs were a well-to-do family in Stroudwater, which is now a part of Portland, Maine. She and two of her cousins, Almira Quinby and Eunice Merrill, all served the army as nurses.

In 1848, Louise inherited the Partridge House in Stroudwater from her grandfather, Andrew Titcomb. She shared it with other members of her family including her cousin Almira. This arrangement gave her the freedom to volunteer her services during the war.[341]

Louise went to the General Hospital in Chester, Pennsylvania, in September 1862 and stayed until May 1863. When the matron of the hospital in Chester was transferred to Annapolis, Louise and several other nurses followed. The new hospital was officially called the General Hospital for Division No. 1. It was more commonly called the Naval School Hospital or the Naval Academy Hospital. Louise worked there from August 1863 until discharged in May 1865.[342]

She wrote often to her friend, Rebecca Usher, who she had known before the war, but they grew even closer as they worked together at the hospital in Chester. In October 1863, she wrote to let Rebecca know what items they needed for the soldiers. She also mentioned the great trouble she had caused by some remarks she had made in a letter about supplies for the soldiers. Her comments were misinterpreted by the Sanitary Commission when the letter appeared in the papers:

Louisa Titcomb

(USAMHI)

> They have brought down a torrent of bitter feeling against us all on the part of the San. Com. which has resulted in a serious matter to us here. That letter, and the one published in the Press from Miss Dana have been sent to Wash. as proofs that we have libeled the San Com.... I was never more astounded than when Dr. V[anderkieft] called my attention to it, nor was I ever more humiliated than when I was obliged to confess, that through the jealousy of our two prominent charities at home, my letter had been used as a peg on which to hang their personal animosity and spleen. I never dreamed that the San. Com. had not done their full shift here. Their work has been grand and glorious everywhere.... But does any person of even ordinary judgement suppose that this moving caravan of sick and wounded, who are passing by the thousands between City Point and this place would be clothed and fed by any Com. however mighty? Let such persons come here and see for themselves and then question if our calls for home supplies are disproportionate to the demand....[343]

In April 1864, she wrote to Rebecca on fancy hospital stationary with a letterhead showing a bird's eye view of the Naval School Hospital grounds:

Annapolis, Md. April 27, 1864

My dear Bep,

Have I ever sent you a view of our home. The buildings in the center of the grounds behind the tents are occupied by us. I have dotted the room I occupy, which commands river bay and country landscape far and wide. This day has been the most spring-like of the season, gay with showers and sunshine. The yards about our house are brilliant with peach bloom, hyacinths, lilies, and the richest beds of English violets, over which the South wind comes sweeter than ever. I have wished you here so many times today that I concluded, tired as I was, I must try and write a few lines this evening, acknowledging your last letter and the three dollars, so very acceptable at that time. I believe we now have all we need, except money, through the Sanitary and Christian Commissions. Of course I do not like to apply to friends at home for that, but you knew something of the need of this material in Hospital especially when the patients come as these have, from Southern prisons, without means to buy a letter stamp. To this purpose I appropriated the three dollars, and I assure you they have done such special good, in the relief they have given so many anxious wives and mothers. My own purse has run pretty low several times, and would have failed, but for reinforcements from home, for I am still a volunteer, and can not manage it with Sister Tyler to have pay. I suppose you know the Burnside Expedition has moved. The sick of their Regimental Hospitals were left with us, filling our wards completely. The work has been very hard, owing to the want of sufficient nurses and Police force. We have never been so nearly overtaxed before. The greater portion of the work is now done by colored soldiers, who are detailed from the colored Reg's stationed in this vicinity. We also have a section set apart for the col'd sick, who are treated with the same attention the other patients receive. It would have delighted your eyes to have seen the splendid colored Regm's from the North, march through Annap.to join Burnside. They had magnificent banners, full brass bands, and a more martial bearing than any belonging to the expedition. It was a severe "Spring medicine" to <u>Secesh</u>. but I think it will do 'em good! We have had Grant, Burnside, Gen. Smith, Graham and Quartermaster Meiggs here and Mr. Murdock gave a dramatic reading in our chapel to which Burnside and staff were attentive listeners. The latter looks precisely like his pictures, but I do not trace the same resemblance between Grant and his photographs. He is one of those men like Gough, who does not carry his character in his face. Last month Miss_Ellis and I went to Baltimore to do some shopping and stopped a few hours with Miss Kendall. She is dismally located, but likes her position, because she has as much control as any one, and as she expresses it, is free as air. Miss Southgate joined her last week, and Mrs. Dequindre must have done so by this time. Miss Ellis starts for home next week on a Summer furlough, and her place is already filled by a lady from Buffalo, who is to be reinforced soon by a blooming widow from Springfield. I doubt if we can all remain here through the summer. I would like very much to go North, in the hot months, but so long as I am well, shall stay, if I am very much needed. It is said we are to have the wounded from the next battle field. The paroled are being sent to the Baltimore Hosp. fast as practicable. Added to our daily duties we are rehearsing comedies for an entertainment for the benefit of a new Brass Band to be organized here as soon as the instruments can be purchased. We have a permanent stage now in the quartermasters building, ready for concerts tableaux etc. I have just heard our colored cook, a slave from Anap. declaim "Barbara Freitchie" in preparation for an exhibition to take place in their church tomorrow evening. This girl can not read a work and we are just beginning to teach her her letters; but among all the verses we produced she chose those and she does them better justice in recitation than most young ladies could, who graduate from our best schools.

I have noticed by the papers, that Jeanie is concert going.—glad her health will permit it, and wish I was there to hear. So you must lose Mr. Stebbins: I am so sorry for Portland, feeling as I do, that his loss can not be made up. I shall hope to have an article yet from you, for the Crutch. I have something to do with it every week and my time is so occupied day and evening, that a contribution for it is like drawing teeth. Do make Mat use her talent in this direction. Love to all, at home and at Salmon Falls, tell me all about friends when you next write....Write soon as possible and believe me Yours with <u>heaps</u> of love, Louise.[344]

In June 1864, she wrote to Rebecca, "Since I wrote you last, I have been appointed editor of the "Crutch" and supervisor of the officers' kitchen and wards."[345] The "Crutch" was the Naval School Hospital's newspaper which printed articles deemed of interest to the soldiers. She may still have been the editor at the time Adaline Walker, from Portland, died of typhoid pneumonia and the "Crutch" printed her very touching and flowery eulogy.

Rebecca and Louise remained friends throughout their lives. When Louise applied for a pension in 1892, both Rebecca and her

U. S. GENERAL HOSPITAL DIV. Nº1.

DR B.A.VANDERKIEFT.

(Surgeon in Charge.)

1. Tent of Medical Officer in Charge. 2. Tent of the Hospital Steward.

First page of a letter to Rebecca Usher from Louisa Titcomb. The letterhead shows the layout of the Naval School Hospital. (Maine Hist. Soc.)

sister Jane wrote a testimonial and her brother-in-law, Judge Nathan Webb certified the documentation.[346]

When she died in 1905, a glowing obituary appeared in the papers. It read, in part, "She was a patriot, a philanthropist and reformer. She has an enviable record as a volunteer army nurse. In the dark days of the Civil War she ministered with heart and

Louisa Titcomb's home in Stroudwater.

Louisa Titcomb edited "The Crutch."   (Lee Dionne)

hand, actuated by a broad and generous impulse, a love unbounded by section or race. She was an ardent advocate of human rights, and as such, deplored the conditions which deprived women of equal privileges with men in helping to direct governmental affairs...."[347]

Because she so loved the outdoors and flowers, her good friend and cousin, Almira Quinby, is said to have commented at the time of Louise's funeral, "I am glad it is summer time." She is buried in the Stroudwater Cemetery with her friends and cousins Almira Quinby and Eunice Day Quinby Merrill.

Sarah W. Tucker
(1822–?)

Sarah Tucker was a "contract nurse," working not as a volunteer, but for pay. At the time, many women frowned on taking pay for doing relief work, but often it was the only way some women could work for their country and support themselves as well. She was the daughter of Caroline and Gideon Tucker of Saco, Maine. Her sister, Caroline, married Reverend John Taylor Gilman Nichols, minister of the Second Parish Church in Saco, and well-known for aiding the wounded soldiers during the war.

She worked first at the Chester Hospital in Pennsylvania, along with Rebecca Usher (who had known her back in Portland), Susan Newhall, and Louisa Titcomb, beginning September 1862 and working through April 1863. By the fall of 1863 she was working at the Armory Square Hospital in Washington.[348]

On February 20, 1865, Rebecca Usher wrote home to her sister, Mat, to tell her about visiting Washington. She and some other ladies visited the Armory Square Hospital where Rebecca met Dr. D. Willard Bliss. "I asked Dr. Bliss if he remembered Miss Tucker. He said he did & considered her a very efficient interesting & fascinating woman & was very sorry to lose her."[349]

By July 1864, Sarah was working at the Cumberland General Hospital in Nashville, Tennessee. It is likely that she then took a position at the Union Refugee Hospital in St. Louis, Missouri, where records show a Mrs. Tucker, nurse and teacher, was working in March of 1865.[350]

The Usher Sisters

Rebecca Usher (August 31, 1821–June 2, 1912)

Ellen Usher Bacon (October 20, 1817–1902)

Martha Usher Osgood (May 1, 1823–1893)

Jane Usher Webb (October 12, 1836–July 11, 1920)

At a time when education for women was not considered of much importance, Ellis Usher, a prominent lumber dealer of Bar Mills, Maine, made sure his daughters were not only well-educated but could think for themselves. When the war broke out each of his four daughters did more than her part to help sick and wounded soldiers. Like many women of Maine the Ushers contributed supplies and money to the cause but their commitment went much further than most and their insightful commentary in letters and diaries that survive gives valuable insight into life during those years.

Ellis Usher came to Hollis at the age of twelve with a horse and a few dollars. By the time he died in 1855, he had amassed land holdings of tens of thousands of acres and owned one of the largest lumbering operations in the Northeast. He served in the state senate, was well known throughout New England, and often entertained prominent guests. Author Kate Douglas Wiggin and sculptors Benjamin Paul Akers and his brother Charles were frequent visitors. However, by 1855, his only son, Isaac, had moved West and his oldest daughter, Ellen, had already married a dentist, Eldridge Bacon, and moved to Portland. Apparently their mother, Hannah, was glad to allow Rebecca to manage the affairs of the estate.[351]

In October 1862, Rebecca received a letter from Miss Almira Quinby offering her a nursing position under Dorothea Dix. Rebecca at first declined. On October 19, her younger sister Mattie (Martha) wrote to a friend, "She had a very strong inclination to go, and I think the only reason she reluctantly declined is the short time for preparation—only a few days and our dressmaker is in Portland. It requires something of an outfit, as they do not wear hoops. She would require three or four plain dresses, and has not made a stitch on flannels etc. for Winter. If she should have another invitation a month later I am afraid she would go. I do not think she is strong enough for hospital service...."[352]

Meanwhile, Mattie [Martha] went on to recount that the sisters were all "working hard at our soldiers' meetings, much of my time goes that way." Mattie also expressed an interest herself in going to the front as a nurse, but sister Bep (Rebecca) "will not hear a word of my going...."[353]

A month later, Rebecca received another invitation. This time she accepted, joining Louise Titcomb of Stroudwater and Susan Newhall of Portland at the general hospital in Chester, Pennsylvania. Despite her sisters' misgivings, Rebecca thrived and wrote long descriptive letters home about the hospital and conditions there. On November 23, 1862, she wrote to sister Ellen:

Rebecca Usher around 1900.
(Maine Hist. Soc.)

> The main building of the Hospital was erected for a normal school. It is an immense building with large airy halls and high studded bed rooms— heated by furnace and lighted by gas. There are five wards, each ward containing three divisions, each division capable of holding 60 men. The wards are long one-story buildings plastered outside and inside—lighted by gas & heated by coal stoves. Miss Titcomb's ward the only one I have been through as yet, presents a very cheerful appearance. The beds are arranged on either side [of] the room heads to the wall, & the gas fixtures running through the center are ornamented with large wreaths of evergreen & artificial flowers & small United States flags.[354]

In another letter she wrote, "I am delighted with hospital life. I feel like a bird in the air or a fish in the sea, as if I had found my native element."[355]

She also took time to comment on national matters. On December 5, 1862, she wrote to Mattie, "I am delighted with the President's message; that part relating to emancipation. I think Abraham Lincoln has left his impress on the nineteenth century which will go down to the latest generation making him immortal with Washington."

Her remarks on more mundane matters indicated how hard Mattie and Ellen were working at home to support the soldiers in hospitals. She wrote to sister Ellen, also on December 5, 1862:

I have not time this morning to answer your letter but will only give you a few commissions for Mat's barrel. We need flannel shirts more than anything. Tobacco is very much needed. Louise thinks you might beg a box of Mr. Charles Rogers. I do not know but a box is too much to ask for from one person. We do not want to beg on too large a scale but it is pitiful to see men who left independent homes humiliated to the necessity of begging a pipe full of tobacco.[356]

At home the sisters were busy collecting supplies and money for the soldiers. Their Soldier's Aid Society in Buxton and Hollis was formally organized on October 1, 1861. Mattie, as secretary, reported later to the U. S. Sanitary Commission: "We were always received with civility though many families, and those among the most wealthy declined aiding in any way. But little opposition was expressed in words, though occasionally a person would tell us 'Those who made the war ought to take care of the soldiers'.... One woman gave us a nice new comforter, saying she knew they should need it that winter but she told her husband if they were cold in the night they could get up and build a fire, but the poor soldiers could not."[357]

The group started with some 50 members and raised money through a $1 annual membership fee and "by occasional contributions," a fair, concerts in which Jane (usually called "Jenny") frequently performed, making Christmas wreaths for sale, and ten dollars was sent from the Colonel of the 1st Maine Cavalry [possibly Colonel Goddard of Cape Elizabeth] in return for a sleeping cap which reached him through the Sanitary Commission.[358]

When Rebecca's hospital in Chester was broken up and the matron, Mrs. Adaline Tyler, sent to take charge of the Naval School Hospital at Annapolis, many of her nurses went with her, including Louise Titcomb and Susan Newhall. Rebecca, however, returned home to attend to matters there.

While Mattie was busy with the Buxton/Hollis Soldiers' Aid Society, sister Ellen became involved in Portland's Maine Camp Hospital Association, officially organized on November 17, 1862. Ellen was a member of the Board of Directors, along with several highly esteemed residents of the city including Lewis B. Smith, who had served as president of the Common Council, Railroad Commissioner, and Custom House official. Other members were George Bosworth, pastor of the Second Baptist Church, and Jedediah Jewett, mayor of Portland. At that time, the organization adopted two nurses to serve as their agents in the field: Mrs. Isabella Fogg, of Calais, and Mrs. Harriet Eaton, of Portland. The two were, in fact, already at work in Virginia distributing supplies they had taken with them in October. Harriet Eaton stayed until May 1863. Mrs. Ruth Mayhew, of Rockland, replaced her as agent just as the Battle of Gettysburg ended. Isabella Fogg was no longer an agent for the Maine Camp Hospital Association by 1864, when the nature of the relief effort changed and many organizations, such as the Maine

Ellen Usher Bacon   (USAMHI)

Camp Hospital Association, set up headquarters at City Point, Virginia—as close to Petersburg as they could get.[359]

Caring for the sick and wounded soldiers had been rewarding enough for Rebecca that when the Maine Camp Hospital Association began searching for new agents to send to City Point, Rebecca considered going south again. In fact, her sister Ellen, on behalf of the Maine Camp Hospital Association, urged her to go. In an undated letter (probably late 1864) Rebecca said, "I would go at once and gladly; but as we are situated now it is very difficult to be spared particularly just now as our man is drafted and our girl is to leave us the last of next week...say that nothing but a weighty sense of home duties prevents me from serving my country at the Front.... We have been very busy harvesting, selling timber lands, etc." She closed that letter by stating, "I feel strongly inclined to go for the Camp & Field [Maine Camp Hospital Association] but it is out of the question as you see."[360]

Conditions changed by the beginning of the following year. On January 12, 1865, she was in Washington, on her way to City Point. Rebecca did not miss an opportunity. While in Washington, she visited the still unfinished Capitol building and admired its east side, "the only one which is finished." She listened to speeches in the House and Senate, and visited Campbell Hospital, where she said,"They have a theatre, with a variety of scenes very tastefully arranged painted by the soldiers, all the carpenters' work and house painting done also by the soldiers. They have also a printing press, and a very good library, for all which they are indebted in great measure to the individual enterprise & energy of the Chaplain." She visited the Patent Office, Agriculture Building and most exciting of all—attended a "Levee" hosted by the Lincolns at the White House. In her diary, she wrote, "I have forgotten to say that Sat. P.M. [January 14, 1865] we attended Mrs. Lincoln's Levee & admired Old Abe for two hours & when he shook hands with me he said 'How do you do dear?'"[361]

She also wrote in a letter about the event:

> His pictures look just like him. He is not one whit handsomer than the homeliest of them. His coat looked as though he had fallen all away from it and had a tousled appearance, as if it might have come very recently from Iowa or Maine in a very crowded valise & was taken out & shaken & donned for the occasion.... I never saw anything so truly democratic. Everybody was there, who wanted to see the President—soldiers in their faded and war-torn blue coats, & ladies in silks and diamonds, officers in their regimentals, foreign dignitaries with their orders, and plain women in their bonnets.... It was far more imposing to me than any regal reception in any royal court.[362]

All was not so wonderful when Rebecca tried to obtain the proper passes to get to City Point. She finally appealed to Dorothea Lynde Dix, Superintendent of Army Nurses, to get the needed documents. Miss Dix complied in return for the favor of reporting back on the condition of the 9th Corps hospital where the nurses had been dismissed. Miss Dix continued to ask favors and reports of Rebecca throughout her stay at City Point. With the proper passes and stamps in hand, Rebecca boarded the government transport "Vanderbilt" and proceeded on her way. Her diary goes on to say:

> Mrs. Mayhew received me gladly and we harmonized at once. The Maine Agency is a stockaded tent with canvas roof & three rooms papered with newspapers. The first is the soldiers reading room with an open fire a table with newspapers & writing materials & long wooden benches—& three births one above another—the second is our sleeping room parlor & store closet combined, & is heated by an air tight stove of unique pattern & the third is our kitchen & pantry.[363]

She settled in once again to provide assistance—this time, especially for the Maine boys. Meanwhile sister Jane (Jenny) was continuing her own contribution to the war effort. The *Portland Daily Press*, on January 4, 1865, noted the following:

> The Buxton and Hollis Soldiers' Aid Society acknowledge the receipt of forty-seven dollars, the proceeds of a concert given in Buxton by Misses Usher and Bates, Messrs. Shaw, Colby and Marston, to whom they would tender their most grateful thanks.[364]

Rebecca wrote, "I had not heard a word from home for weeks, & knowing that the concert was pending, & fearing Jenny would get sick, & I not there to help, I had become very anxious." Rebecca's concern stems from the fact that Jennie was recovering from diphtheria and frequently suffered from colds. Mattie had written on January 27, 1863, "Jenny couldn't go [to a wedding] as she had a cold and was nursing herself up for a public appearance the next evening. She did as she usually does—went into Portland to arrange for the concert and took cold...." Rebecca wrote back, "I am thankful the concert is over for all concerned and that it was so successful!...The chick is growing brilliant!"[365]

Jane Usher Webb
(Maine Hist. Soc.)

Again in March, newspapers mention another concert in which Jennie performs:

> BLUE FLANNEL CONCERT. The seventh concert of this series for the benefit of the soldiers, will be given this evening at the house of Abner Lowell, Pearl Street. Performance to commence at 8 o'clock. Miss Jennie Usher and the Quintet Club will assist.[366]

Back at the front, Rebecca wrote, "It is very tantalizing to be in the midst of the army and so near the battlefield, yet know so little of what is being done. General Grant lives only a mile from here; yet rumors are so conflicting that we can tell nothing from them."[367]

In February, Rebecca wrote to Mattie: "Received your letter this morning & soon after came the glorious news that [General] Sherman was in Charleston [South Carolina]. I felt like throwing up my hat & giving three times three & a tiger" [the Union soldiers' cheer].[368]

On April 12, 1865, Ellen wrote:

> We have sent you splendid stores there must be all of 25 boxes on the way to you—I think at Washington—three cases of liquors—the very choicest too. We shall send tomorrow some peaches and you can spend your money as you choose— You know we go upon the principle that Our Agents can do no wrong.[369]

Ellen was at home in Portland on the night that news of Lee's surrender reached Maine. She wrote:

> What a world of events have been crowded into one week! I heard the first scream at midnight—looked at my watch, just 12. The watchmen whistled all round; the bells commenced ringing; pistols to go off—sky rockets went up— I thought of Lee the first scream, told Dr, B. [Dr. Elbridge Bacon, her husband] it was not a fire, could not move him, talked of a riot and hearing the fire-arms rapidly firing he got up and went out. In two minutes came back with the news. In a short time the whole city was illuminated, the streets were rapidly filling with people. We shut up the house and went out. Little Jenny said, "Oh, mother this is Happy New Year, Merry Christmas, Thanksgiving and everything else all-together." Went around the corner to hear Governor Washburn. The people would not hear speeches but they could cheer for Grant—for Lincoln—for the Flag— For the Union—for every thing that was good and patriotic. ...For once Portland was wild.[370]

Rebecca was at City Point when the war ended and, as there were still many wounded, stayed on for a time. On May 1, she wrote:

> While Mrs. Mayhew was at the Front, I was alone in my work with a house full of company, no help & very sick patients in the wards, but I bore up well under it until the news

came of the assassination of our beloved President. I could not believe it at first, but when the terrible truth was forced upon me I was almost paralysed. It seemed as if the sun would never shine again.[371]

After the war, Rebecca returned home to her family and friends. She continued to manage the family estate in Bar Mills and settled into a much more peaceful existence. In 1903, noted Maine author Kate Douglas Wiggin (and neighbor of the Ushers), wrote her enduring children's book, *Rebecca of Sunnybrook Farm*. She chose the Usher house in Bar Mills as the setting for the story. She borrowed Rebecca's name for its heroine and she based the characters of the two aunts, Miranda and Jane, loosely on Rebecca Usher. In the story, Aunt Jane supposedly served as a Civil War nurse.[372] Although the book has been a perennial children's favorite, the real life of Rebecca Usher was far more interesting. She died June 2, 1912, and is buried with the rest of her family at the Tory Hill Cemetery in Buxton, Maine.

Martha (Mattie) also settled back into a more peaceful existence in Bar Mills, living with Rebecca at the family estate. She died in 1893 and is also buried at the Tory Hill Cemetery in Buxton.

The Usher home in Bar Mills. Today it looks almost unchanged.
(McArthur Library, Biddeford)

Jane continued her interest and participation in local musical events after she married Judge Nathan Webb. She was the leading vocalist in the choir at the First Parish Church in Portland for a number of years, and studied with Professor Hermann Kotzschmar. She was active in the Portland Rossini Club, founded in 1871, whose object was "the mutual improvement in the art of music." Jane, the youngest and last remaining sister, died July 11, 1920, at the age of 84 after attending services that morning at the First Parish Church. She is buried with her husband in Evergreen Cemetery in Portland.

During the course of the war, the Soldiers' Aid Society in Buxton and Hollis contributed over $3,000 worth of goods to the various relief organizations, including the U. S. Sanitary Commission, the Christian Commission, the Maine Camp Hospital Association, and directly to various hospitals, thanks, in large part, to the efforts of the Usher sisters.

The family's collection of diaries and letters now at the Maine Historical Society in Portland gives a glimpse of a warm, loving, and vibrant family during one of the most trying times in American history.

The Usher family graves in Buxton.

Adeline Walker

(1830–April 28, 1865)

Adeline Walker gave her life to aid the wounded and support the Union cause. One of several women who left Portland in 1863 to nurse soldiers, she was working at the Naval School Hospital in Annapolis, Maryland when she caught one of the most dreaded diseases that raged through the army: typhus. The superintendent of her hospital, Maria M. C. Hall, wrote for the hospital newspaper, *The Crutch*:

> She slept at sunset, sinking into the stillness of death as peacefully as a melted day in to the darkness of the night. For two years and a half—longer than almost any other here—she had pursued her labors in this hospital, and with her ready sympathy with the suffering or wronged, had ministered to many needy ones the balm of comfort and healing. Her quick wit and keen repartee has served to brighten up many an hour otherwise dull and unhomelike in our little circle of workers, gathered in our quarters off duty.
>
> So long an inmate of this hospital its every part was familiar to her; its trees and flowers she loved; in all its beauties she rejoiced. We could almost fancy a hush in nature's music, as we walked behind her coffin, under the beautiful trees in the bright May sunshine.
>
> It was a touching thing to see the soldier-boys carrying the coffin of her who had been to them in hours of pain a minister of good and comfort. Her loss is keenly felt among them, and tears are on the face of more than one strong man as he speaks of her. One more veteran soldier has fallen in the ranks, one more faithful patriot-heart stilled. No less to her than to the soldier in the field shall be awarded the heroic honor.[373]

Adeline Walker's grave in Evergreen Cemetery, Portland.

Adeline once said, "It is noble to die at one's post, with the armor on; to fall where the work has been done."[374] And that is exactly how she died. She is buried in Portland's Evergreen Cemetery, close to the monument for Civil War soldiers.

Harriet N. Warren
(September 21, 1830–January 24, 1898)

Harriet N. Warren was the wife of Surgeon Francis G. Warren of the 5th Maine Volunteer Infantry. Born in Brunswick, Maine, daughter of Thomas and Marilla Welch Roberts, when she married Francis Warren on November 16, 1848, she probably was not expecting the adventurous life they led during the war. She accompanied him to the South, as did a number of officer's wives. While encamped with the troops in the fall of 1861, she took an active interest in the soldiers' welfare and wrote at least one letter back to Maine addressed to the editor of Biddeford's *Union and Journal*. It read:

> Mount Eagle, Fairfax County, Virginia.
> Sept 30, 1861
>
> Mr. Cowan: Sir: I take the liberty to address a few lines to you in behalf of the sick in our regiment [the Fifth Maine], now lying in hospital. They are very destitute of bedding, not having enough to make them comfortable.
>
> Saturday I visited the 3rd Maine Regiment and the contrast between the 2 hospitals, I assure you, is very great. They have nice bed cots, pillows and comforts, while our sick have as you may say nothing—lying on coarse sacks filled with straw, nothing under their heads, and nothing over them excepting a blanket; the nights are now very cold, and one blanket is rather thin covering for chills and fever.
>
> Knowing you to be a kind-hearted as well as patriotic man, I wish you to call together the benevolent ladies of our city, who will no doubt, with willing hearts and hands, do all in their power for the welfare of our sick soldiers far from home, in a strange land, no wife or mother to bathe the aching head or moisten the fevered lip.
>
> We need most some pillows and comforts. We have now in hospital about forty. This I believe is about the average number. You will please tell the ladies this, and they will know how many we shall need.

I would not call upon them were it in my power to do differently, but these things are so very much needed I thought it time some one interested themselves, and that speedily.

Dr. [Warren] sends his regards to yourself and family, and wishing you success in this generous undertaking, I am

Yours with respect,
Mrs. Harriet N. Warren[375]

By mid-October, nurse Amy Bradley was with the 5th Maine at Camp Franklin and in charge of their hospital. With her connections to the Sanitary Commission and the supplies solicited by Mrs. Warren, the 5th Maine's hospital was soon in excellent condition and deemed the best in the brigade.[376]

Both Harriet Warren and her husband survived the war. Dr. Francis G. Warren practiced medicine and later opened a pharmacy in the City Building in Biddeford, Maine. Active in city affairs, he served as mayor for three years and chairman of the committee in charge of constructing the new City Building. She continued to help other, less fortunate people; volunteering for various charitable causes and donating both time and money. They had one child, Frank, who also became a physician. Her obituary stated, "She was a careful reader and a good conversationalist and possessed a grasp upon current affairs of the day that few men or women possess."[377] Her husband died two years after she did, and they are buried together in Saco's Laurel Hill Cemetery.

Amanda Watson
(1828–October, 1894)

State Historian Henry Burrage mentioned several Maine women who contributed much to the war effort. Amanda Watson-Bowler was one of those women.[378] She was also one of the few women to get a pension before the year 1892. On September 26, 1890, an act granting her pension was approved by the Senate and House of Representatives. The Secretary of the Interior was directed to "place on the pension-roll the name of Mrs. Amanda Watson Bowler (formerly Amanda Watson), an army nurse to Union soldiers who were held as prisoners at Memphis, Tennessee, at the rate of twelve dollars a month."[379]

Amanda was born in Fayette, Maine, to Permelia and Richard Watson, a clergyman. She worked as a nurse at the Crittendon General Hospital in Louisville, Kentucky from January 1865 until August 1865. She married Reverend James R. Bowler on November 10, 1883. He died at the Maine General Hospital in Portland on January 19, 1891. Amanda, who taught music to support herself, suffered from muscular rheumatism, and died from it four years later.[380]

Harriet J. Wright
(April 10, 1825–March 21, 1915)

Harriet (Hattie) Chamberlain Wright resigned from her position as nurse at the Slough Hospital in Alexandria on July 14, 1865 after, Surgeon Edwin Bentley noted, "long continued and faithful services in these [Alexandria, Virginia] hospitals."[381]

She began nursing in March 1862, serving briefly at the Union Hotel Hospital in Georgetown, the hospital where Hannah Ropes served and died, before being attached to the Armory Square Hospital in Washington. Dr. W. C. Robinson, of Portland, Maine, who was a surgeon at the Armory Square Hospital, testified to her efficiency and faithfulness. On October 8, 1862, he wrote: It gives me pleasure to state that Mrs. Harriet J. Wright has acted as a nurse in the ward under my charge for the last four weeks and that she has been faithful and efficient...." She also worked the Mansion House Hospital of Alexandria under Dr. Koechling, who wrote, "I can bear testimony of her efficiency and cheerfully recommend her as worthy of reliance in the care of sick and wounded."[382] She well deserved her honorable discharge.

Walt Whitman, who refused to fight in the war but served his country by nursing soldiers, also wrote about her, "There are many women in one position or another, among the Hospitals, mostly nurses here in Washington, and among the military stations; quite a number of them young ladies acting as volunteers.... The presence of a good middle-aged or elderly woman, the magnetic touch of hands, the expressive features of the mother, the silent soothing of her presence, her words, her knowledge and privileges arrived at only through having had children, are precious and final qualifications. (Mrs. H. J. Wright, of Mansion House Hospital, Alexandria, is one of those good nurses. I have known her for over two years in her labors of love)."[383]

Hattie cared deeply for her patients and, though not well educated, she tried to keep the families of hospitalized soldiers informed on how their sons or husbands were doing. When she believed a soldier named Charles Coleman was dying, she wrote to his family in New York. He recovered, however, and they continued to correspond. She wrote to him from Saco, Maine, in December 1865:

> I was glad to heer that your health was so good. Your Pet Leg is better than I ever expected it would be. i was supprised to have you say that you could walk without a cane but feel vary thankfull that you are so well as that. I trewly hope you will get a situation as boat keeper. I think such (—?—) as any of you cripoled boys have should entitle you to all such positions in every case where you are qualified for them, and I doubt not but what you could do well I do not think any well man should have any of those situations where a cripol can do just as well. With me those that have sacraficed for the love of contry should in <u>all cases</u> have the preferences to those that have remained at their homes in safety and had their homes protected.[384]

Charly Coleman saved her letters and they were passed down through generations to another Charles Coleman, who is now researching the career of his namesake.

Harriet moved to Abingdon, Massachusetts after the war, where she applied for and was awarded a pension of $12 per month in 1892. She later moved back to Saco where she had lived for so long, but, in 1904 moved once again, this time to Washington, D.C., where she died in 1915 at age 89 years and 9 months.[385] She spent the last years of her life as a member of the household of a former patient, one Dr. Foster. He invited her to live with his family in gratitude for her kindness during the war. According to her obituary, she was buried in Arlington National Cemetery with other honored Civil War nurses.[386]

Mehitable Jane Young
(June 30, 1836–October 12, 1925)

Mehitable Jane was born in Greenville, Maine, daughter of Elijah and Mary H. Young. The family moved from Hollis, Maine, to be among the first settlers of Greenville. According to family members, she served in hospitals in Washington, D. C. for most of the war. Her brother Leonard, and father, Elijah, also served, both in Company I of the 2nd Maine Infantry. Leonard died on October 29, 1862. The father, listed as Eli Young in the Adjutant General's report, was discharged January 18, 1862.[387] In 1867, she married James Sumner Hamilton of Old Town, and they moved to Wisconsin in 1888.[388]

Other Maine Women who Served in the War

While reading accounts of women who served during the war, many names were mentioned, but all too frequently no further information was available. Either the government did not keep the records or the records have been lost or buried in some understaffed historical society. Or, perhaps, they still exist with their descendants. Whatever the case, the following women were mentioned in various accounts as having been from Maine. It is hoped that more about their service and their lives will come to light in the future:

Aberl, Mrs. S. W.
Served as a nurse at the Fort Preble hospital in Cape Elizabeth (now South Portland, Maine).

Barnum, Mrs. Wheeler.
Mentioned in the 1864/65 Maine Adjutant General's Report as helping to feed the soldiers.

Chapman, Miss G. D.
Reportedly from Exeter, Maine. Took charge of a school for children of Black refugees. She resigned due to ill health after several months and was replaced by Sarah E. M. Lovejoy (daughter of Owen Lovejoy, Senator, who was born in Maine).

Davis, Jenny.
Reportedly from Wellington, Maine, and nursed the wounded at Gettysburg in 1863.

Davis, Lydia.
Worked as a cook at the Cony General Hospital in Augusta from February through April, 1865.

Grafton, Jennie.
Nurse with the 4th Maine Infantry Regiment.

Graves, Miss
Nurse with the 3rd Maine Infantry Regiment.

Hall, Mrs. George W.
Formerly from Vassalborough. Sometimes accompanied Sarah Sampson when she visited the troops and distributed supplies. Mentioned in Sampson's report to the Adjutant General of Maine in 1864/65.

Holt, Jane (? – Feb 23, 1913)
> Her husband died in 1859. She lived in Boston after the war, then moved to Nova Scotia, where she died. Worked as a nurse at the General Hospital of Fort Schuyler in New York Harbor from December, 1862-October, 1863, and at the Crozier Hospital in Chester, Pennsylvania and Columbian College Hospital in 1864. There is an unconfirmed report that, at least at one time, she lived in Maine.

Lawrence, Sarah Warren (? – January 15, 1922)
> Sarah Warren was from Bangor, Maine. She married Enoch Lawrence shortly after he enlisted July 28, 1861 with the 1st Maine Heavy Artillery. She went with the regiment as a field nurse. According to her obituary, she worked both as a field nurse and in the hospitals of Washington. She died in Brewer, Maine at the home of her daughter.

McDonald, Mrs. (Mary or Florence?)
> Nancy Atwood-Gross worked with another nurse from Maine whom she said was Mrs. Mary McDonald, from a neighboring town, possibly Corinth, Maine. There was a Florence McDonald who was a matron at the Armory Square Hospital and also served at the Seminary Hospital.

Packard, Orissa A. (December 2, 1837 – ?)
> From Rockland. Compositor for the *Rockland Gazette*. Served as a nurse with the 4th Maine Infantry Regiment.

Pearson, Mary G. (1836 – ?)
> Mary Pearson was one of the women from Maine who worked at the Naval School Hospital in Annapolis beginning in August 1863 and served until about October 1864.

Rea, Dorcas.
> Widow of Albus Rea, and secretary of the Ladies Committee in Portland which collected supplies. Her reports and letters can be found in Portland papers and at the Maine State Archives.

Sherburn, Jane A.
> Matron at Cony General Hospital in Augusta, Maine, March-June, 1865.

Smyth, Adaline A.
> Adaline Smyth of Lewiston was granted a pension of $12 per month by the U.S. Congress on August 17, 1888. The reasons

cited were for her services "tendered immediately after the battle of Gettysburgh" and for her work at the Judiciary Square Hospital which lasted a period of seven months.

Snow, Hediah.
From Portland. Worked at the Columbian College Hospital from December 26, 1862 – April 1863.

Southgate, Miss (Helen or Harriet?)
Reportedly lived in the Portland area. Served at the Seminary Hospital in Georgetown.

Titcomb, Emma.
Matron at Cony General Hospital in Augusta, Maine.

Towle, Susan (March 4, 1830 – ?)
Lived at 91 State Street in Bangor, Maine. Worked as a contract nurse at Armory Square Hospital in Washington from approximately February 1865 until after the war in September 1865.

VanHorne, S. L.
The Maine State Archives has an interesting letter from her postmarked Portland, Maine, October 5, 1862, addressed to Governor Washburn, in which she pleads to be appointed to a regiment as a field nurse. She states she has already been asked to go to the Armory Square Hospital but she would rather work in a camp hospital. There seems to be no record that she did either.

Varnum, Elizabeth Widgery (May 24, 1836 – December 11, 1917)
Daughter of a very prominent Portland family, she taught black children in the South during the last days of the war and after. She never married and is buried in Portland's Eastern Cemetery.

Watson, Mrs. L.
Mrs. L. Watson of Farmington, Maine, was mentioned in the *Kennebec Journal* (Sept. 9, 1864) as working for the Maine State Agency with Mrs. Sampson around Washington. She may have been the wife of Maine relief agent Mr. Leonard Watson.

Whitman, Angelina.
Mentioned by the *Portland Daily Press* (November 8, 1862) as going to work as a nurse in the war.

Undoubtedly many more women served in some capacity during the war. Perhaps someday their names, too, will come to light and they will finally be given the honor they deserve.

Susan Towle is just one of many Maine women who served as a nurse during the war but little more than that is known. (USAMHI)

Chapter 6

The Unfinished Battle

> We often hear the remark that these are days that try men's souls. I believe they try women's souls, too. I shall remember you and all the noble women of the North when we are at peace.

These prophetic-sounding words were spoken by President Abraham Lincoln to the nurses of the Judiciary Square Hospital shortly before he was assassinated.[1] Exactly how he would "remember" the women is certainly subject to debate, but one interpretation could be that he would recognize their wartime service with support for greater rights, possibly voting rights and pensions similar to those of the soldiers.

Even before the war Abraham Lincoln had been quoted as stating, "I go for all sharing the privileges of the government who assist in bearing its burdens. Consequently, I go for admitting all whites to the right of suffrage who pay taxes or bear arms - by no means excluding females."[2]

How did these noble women wish to be "remembered?" Did they feel that women deserved greater rights and a greater role in society? How did they feel about pensions and voting? These questions may be somewhat easier to answer than determining President Lincoln's intentions.

The women's suffrage movement (the struggle to obtain voting rights for women) had its start in 1848, when Elizabeth Cady Stanton and Susan B. Anthony organized the first convention in Seneca Falls, New York. During the war most of the members agreed to cease their lobbying efforts. Some believed the war itself was a struggle for "liberty to all; national protection for every citizen under our flag; universal suffrage and universal amnesty."[3]

Before 1860, the suffrage movement had little support and was subject to ridicule from a great portion of the population. The war changed everything. The American Civil War, wrote Samuel Clemens, "uprooted institutions, changed the politics of a people, transformed the social life of half the country, and wrought so profoundly upon the national character that the influence cannot be measured short of two or three generations."[4]

The institution of slavery was, of course, the most profoundly uprooted by the war. Close behind was the social institution which prohibited women from becoming equal partners in determining the course of government.

Women from every state in the Union reacted to the crisis of war with an unprecedented outpouring of support, volunteering time and resources in a massive effort to aid their husbands, brothers, sons, friends, neighbors, and the Union cause. The experience gained from the effort changed the way women viewed themselves and their role in society forever.

With husbands and breadwinners off fighting the war, women grew more self reliant as they were forced to make major decisions for their families without the advice of their partners. Some also became quite self-sufficient—forced to support their families themselves when their soldier-husbands failed to send the promised pay. In addition, there were many businesses that needed women to fill now vacant positions. Societal needs forced changes in the 19th century perception which viewed women as either incapable of participating in business, politics, and public matters or above such squalid affairs. Social upheaval was the inevitable result:

> It is safe to say that during the four years of the war more than half a million men were withdrawn from occupations which could be followed by women and the very necessities of production to provide for the war itself increased the demand for service in all these occupations.... It was thus that war...brought to women an opportunity to compete with men in occupations which they could follow.[5]

Isabella Fogg, Abba Goddard, Louise Titcomb and other women who left their homes and participated more directly in the war, experienced even more profound changes in their lives than those who worked at the homefront. After the war, many continued to work as nurses, clerks, teachers, pension office agents, and in other occupations. The choices were still extremely limited, but the war effort had made it far more acceptable for women to earn a wage outside the home. The nursing profession itself was created and legitimized by the war. Some Civil War nurses such as Nancy M. Hill of Massachusetts who served at the Armory Square Hospital, found they had a knack for treating the sick and wounded and went on to become physicians. Esther Hill Hawks and Susan Barry, who were already trained physicians, worked as nurses and resumed their medical practices after the war ended.

With the end of the war, most of the Maine women returned to their former lives as teachers, mothers, and housewives; some married, others moved away and disappeared from record. Ruth Mayhew went on to teach Native Americans in the West for a time. Amy Bradley founded a school system in Wilmington, North Carolina, for poor white children. Sarah Sampson founded an orphanage in her home town of Bath, Maine, for children who had lost a parent in the war. She later returned to Washington to work in the pension office since she could not find work to support herself in Maine. Mrs. Caroline Cowan became the official postmaster of Biddeford, appointed by President Grant, after serving in her husband's stead for several years. Harriet Eaton left Portland to become a pastoral assistant for the First Baptist Church in Hartford, Connecticut.

At the end of the war, many women volunteered to go south to teach the freed slaves for the Freedman's Bureau or for various missionary groups. Sarah Jane Foster of Gray, Maine, was one of these. So was Elizabeth Widgery Varnum, the niece of Portland's "Grand Dame" of society, Charlotte Julia Thomas, who was an active abolitionist before the war and a supporter of women's rights. The Portland Freedman's Aid Association was run by several of Portland's most prominent citizens. It included individuals who, during the war, were involved in Portland's Maine Camp Hospital

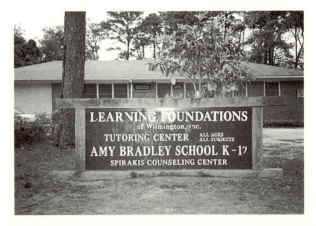

Educational facility in Wilmington named after Amy Bradley.

(Kimberly MacIsaac)

Association. Harriet Eaton, until she moved away from Portland, was one of the officers. According to one contemporary newspaper article, dozens of Maine women volunteered to go south to teach either the freedmen or the poor whites. "They perceived that all reconstruction must be based on the education of the poor whites and especially of the freedmen and they gladly offered themselves for the work."[6]

The Freedmen's Bureau was established near the end of the war. This agency was set up to assist the freed slaves to find food, shelter, jobs, and to provide education. By 1869, there were 9,000 teachers for the former slaves in the South. More than half were women.[7]

Whatever they turned their hands to after the war, these women had been exposed to appalling and enlightening events which they never would have experienced otherwise. Many were active in the fight to abolish slavery, both for blacks and for themselves. Elizabeth Cady Stanton was quoted as saying at an American Antislavery Society meeting in 1860, [A woman is] "more fully identified with the slave than man can possibly be...while the man is born to do whatever he can, for the woman and the negro there is no such privilege." The struggle to free slaves was, for many, the first step in the struggle to free themselves.

Many local soldiers' aid societies discussed the principles of civil liberty as they gathered to stitch comfort bags and knit socks for the soldiers. And equal rights must certainly have been discussed in the home of Portland's Charlotte Julia Thomas who knew, and often entertained, such notables as former slave and black leader Frederick Douglass, abolitionist William Lloyd Garrison, Senator Charles Sumner, author Harriet Beecher Stowe, relief organizer Mary Livermore, suffragists Lucy Stone and Susan B. Anthony, and General Benjamin Butler.[8]

On May 14, 1863, representatives from numerous women's groups gathered in New York City for a meeting called by the "Women's National Loyal League" to debate whether women should support women's rights as well as the emancipation of slaves. One of their resolutions called for woman's suffrage. Another more immediate and visible outcome was: they collected one million signatures on 400,000 petitions calling for a Constitutional amendment to end slavery. At the time, petitioning the government was the only political action available to women and they were now beginning to resent that limitation.[9]

Charlotte Julia Thomas' house in Portland.

(Maine Hist. Soc.)

During the war men and women worked together on many projects for a common cause. Their experiences gave them new insight into their place in society. Many women came into direct conflict with male doctors, stewards, and others in positions of authority. Hannah Ropes of Gray, Maine, was one who stood her ground to have a chief surgeon dismissed. So did Amy Bradley of East Vassalboro. They were "answering to a higher authority" as Mary Ann Bickerdyke had attested when she too caused a surgeon to be dismissed for incompetence and neglect of his patients.

One particular incident opened the eyes of Mary Livermore, while she was organizing the Northwestern Sanitary Fair in Chicago. A new hall was needed to house machinery contributed to the fair. She and Mrs. Hoge obtained the necessary permits for a temporary wooden structure, but were amazed to learn that under the law, even though they were handling thousands of dollars for the Sanitary Commission, they could not enter into a contract with a builder. He said, "You are married women and by the laws of Illinois your names are good for nothing, unless your husbands write their names after yours on the contract." When Mrs. Livermore suggested that they pay in advance out of their own earnings, and receive in return a promissory note for the construction, the builder's reply was, "The money of your earning belongs to your husbands, by the law. The wife's earnings are the property of the husband in this state. Until your husbands give their written consent to your spending your earnings, I cannot give you the promise you ask." Mrs. Livermore wrote:

Here was a revelation. We two women were able to enlist the whole Northwest in a great philanthropic, money-making enterprise in the teeth of great opposition, and had the executive ability to carry it forward to a successful termination. We had money of our own in the bank, twice as much as was necessary to pay the builder. But by the laws of the state in which we lived, our individual names were not worth the paper on which they were written. Our earnings were not ours, but belonged to our husbands.... We learned much of the laws made by men for women, in that conversation with an illiterate builder. It opened a new world to us. I registered a vow that when the war was over I would take up a new work—the work of making law and justice synonymous for women.[10]

Mary Livermore was not alone in that vow. Elizabeth Akers Allen of Maine discovered a similar lack of rights when trying to support herself through her writing. When she inquired why she had not been paid the $50 for articles accepted for publication by the *San Francisco Chronicle*, she was outraged to discover that her earnings had been handed over to the husband who had long since abandoned her, and wrote, "By the shameful law at that time, he could have thus taken every cent I earned...."[11]

After the war, she and Mary Livermore corresponded about this and other issues. Apparently, Mrs. Allen had exchanged "words" over woman's suffrage with one Mrs. Johnson. The Livermores received a letter from a friend concerning the controversy. Mary Livermore wrote to Elizabeth Allen and described the letter which "recounted your bouts with Mrs. Johnson, whose chief stock-in-trade is the worn-out saw that 'since women cannot fight, they should not be allowed to vote.'"[12] They were, she said, sending Elizabeth a copy of Mr. Livermore's pamphlet containing a chapter called "Female Warriors." The "pamphlet" was actually a 224-page book entitled *Woman Suffrage Defended by Irrefutable Arguments and All Objections to Women's Enfranchisement Carefully Examined and Completely Answered*. It was published in Boston in 1885.

Elizabeth became a member of New York City's Sorosis Club, which was founded in 1868 in protest to the New York Press Association's refusal to admit women. It was the president of the Sorosis Club, May Riley Smith, who officiated at Elizabeth Akers Allen's funeral.

Portland-born Mary Whitney Phelps became active in fighting for women's rights in Missouri after the war. In February 1869, leaders of Missouri's suffrage movement petitioned the legislature for the right to vote. History records that the delegation, which included Mary Whitney Phelps, was received by Governor Frances McClurg. Not until 1919, however, did Missouri enfranchise women.[13]

By the end of the war, women had become accepted as nurses, relief workers, organizers, and political activists. The number of women wage-earners rose by 60 percent in the 1860s. New vistas were opening for them (or so they believed). They had cause to hope that after the war, injustices would be corrected. Slavery would be abolished, and both blacks and women would be able to vote. Clara Barton, who was now head of the American Red Cross, stated at the 1888 Memorial Day ceremony in Boston, "Woman was at least 50 years in advance of the normal position which continued peace...would have assigned her."[14] Women felt entitled to compensation for their war-time efforts; they pushed for pensions and suffrage. Neither were immediately forthcoming.

In 1866, Ulysses S. Grant, who became president in 1868, was the first to sign a petition on behalf of the former nurses. It stated in part:

> Large numbers of these women are absolutely destitute and suffering from common comforts—They ask for no special renumeration. They simply ask and pray for compensation for actual, absolute and indispensable labors performed under the advice &, in many instances, by the pressing request of Surgeon General Hammond of the United States.[15]

This was, perhaps, one of the first attempts to secure pension rights for women who served as nurses in the war. Unfortunately, a bill granting pensions to nurses was not passed until 1892. By then, many of the nurses had already died. Those remaining were often frail and elderly with severe disabilities, and were reduced to pleading for a few dollars to sustain themselves.

Instead of gaining rights, women seemed to be losing them. In 1862 women in New York lost their right to equal custody of their children and their right to use their deceased husbands' estates for the benefit of their children.

The Fourteenth Amendment to the Constitution was passed in 1868. It contained the first reference in the Federal Constitution to male citizens in determining the right to vote. The women who had ceased their suffragist efforts during the war began to regret that decision. If the passage of the Fourteenth Amendment and the loss

LECTURE !

MISS CLARA BARTON,
OF WASHINGTON,

THE HEROINE OF ANDERSONVILLE,

The Soldier's Friend, who gave her time and fortune during the war to the Union cause, and who is now engaged in searching for the missing soldiers of the Union army, will address the people of

LAMBERTVILLE, in

HOLCOMBE HALL,
THIS EVENING,

APRIL 7TH, AT 7½ O'CLOCK.
SUBJECT:

SCENES ON THE BATTLE-FIELD.
ADMISSION, 25 CENTS.

Many nurses continued their work after the war. Clara Barton made sure her work was not forgotten.
(USAMHI)

of rights in New York set off warning bells for women, the wording of the Fifteenth Amendment thoroughly alarmed them. It clearly spelled out that the right to vote "shall not be denied or abridged by the United States or any State on account of race, color, or previous condition of servitude." For nearly a decade, abolitionists and women's suffrage supporters had worked hand-inhand pushing for both blacks' and women's rights. Now that partnership was being abandoned.

The wording of the Fourteenth and Fifteenth Amendments caused male blacks to reassess the alliance. Realizing that their chances of gaining the vote would be better without including women's suffrage, they disassociated themselves from that issue. Frederick Douglass, the foremost black leader, said on May 14, 1868, "I have always championed woman's right to vote; but it will be seen that the present claim of the negro is one of urgent necessity. The assertion of the right of women to vote meets nothing but ridicule."[16]

Acknowledgement of the important service women made to the war came very soon after the war ended. Books such as Frank Moore's *Women of the War* (1866) and L.P Brockett's *Woman's Work in the Civil War* (1867) were published. Maine's Governor Cony, in his state of the state address in January 1866, said:

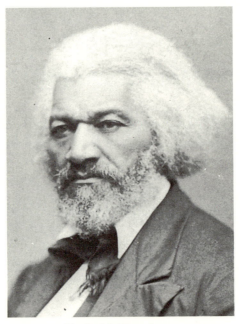

Frederick Douglass
(Library of Congress)

The agencies for the care of our soldiers have been discontinued and the various organizations maintained, especially by the ladies of the State, for their relief, have closed their labors. To these, as well as to the noble women who have gone to the front, and with that patience and tenderness belonging only to their sex, have watched and waited by the couch of the sick, wounded and dying soldier in his agony, I tender the thanks and acknow-ledgement of the State.[17]

Such recognition was not enough. Miriam H. Fish of Illinois wrote to Susan B. Anthony, "...notwithstanding the mean position that we are compelled to occupy, I feel like upholding the Government as the best that is, feeling quite sure that the kindness and good sense of our rulers will give us something a little more like justice after awhile."[18]

Clara Barton spoke at a woman's suffrage convention on January 19, 1870. To the men in the audience she addressed the following plea: "Brothers, when you were weak, and I was strong, I toiled for you. Now you are strong and I am weak—because of my work for you, I ask your aid. I ask the ballot for myself and my sex and as I stood by you, I pray you stand by me and mine."[19]

The Fifteenth Amendment, granting former slaves the right to vote, was passed in 1870, the same year as Clara Barton's impassioned plea. Three years later 3,000 women participated in a "Centennial Tea Party" in Boston to reaffirm that "taxation without representation is tyranny."[20] The protest had no effect. Despite their heroic service, despite the fact that thousands of women proved their patriotism, courage, and effectiveness to aid the Union cause, women continued to be denied the right to vote for more than a half-century after the war. In August 1919, Maine ratified the Nineteenth Amendment granting women the right to vote. The amendment was finally adopted by the Federal government on August 26, 1920.

Badge presented to Civil War nurses by the city of Portland during a national G.A.R. encampment held there probably in 1929.   (Bedford Hayes)

Chronology of Events

1820

Maine becomes a state as a result of the Missouri Compromise which allowed Missouri to enter the Union as a slave state and prohibited slavery above latitude 36 30'.

1849

Elizabeth Blackwell graduates from Geneva Medical School in New York.

1850

January 29   Henry Clay introduces the Compromise of 1850 to settle increasing disputes over slavery in the territories.

1852

Publication of *Uncle Tom's Cabin* in book form by Harriet Beecher Stowe.

1854

May 30   Kansas-Nebraska Act passes, allowing the spread of slavery into the territories.

1859

May 12   New York Infirmary for Women and Children established by Elizabeth and Emily Blackwell. It trained nurses for the Civil War.

1860

Florence Nightingale's *Notes on Nursing* is reprinted in Boston.

November 6   Abraham Lincoln is elected president of the United States with Hannibal Hamlin of Maine as his vice-president.

December 20   South Carolina is the first state to secede from the Union.

1861

February 4   The Confederate States of America formed in Montgomery, Ala.

February 9   Jefferson Davis elected president of the Confederacy.

April 12   Fort Sumter fired upon by the Confederates; begins the war.

April 15   President Lincoln calls for 75,000 volunteers to defend the Union.

April 15   Soldiers' Aid Societies begin forming throughout the North.

April 19   President Lincoln proclaims a blockade of the South.

April 20   Dorothea Lynde Dix begins work as Superintendent of Army Nurses.

April 29   Formation of the "Women's Central Association for Relief" in New York.

May 8   Richmond, Virginia, is made capital of the Confederacy.

May 14   2nd Maine Inf. leaves for the war, the first regiment from Maine.

June 13   The Sanitary Commission's plan of organization is approved by Lincoln.

July 21   Union troops are defeated at the Battle of Bull Run (Manassas).

Alonzo Stinson of the 5th Maine Inf. is first Maine soldier killed.

August 3   Female nursing is made legal in Army hospitals by Act of Congress. Pay is set at 40 cents and one ration per day.

1862

January 1   Maine Agency for the relief of Maine soldiers formed. George R. Davis, agent.

January 28   Christian Commission organized.

February 23   Nashville, Tennessee falls to Union troops.

March 9   Confederate iron clad ship *Merrimac* engages the Union *Monitor*.

March 17   General McClellan begins Peninsula Campaign to take Richmond.

April 6-7   Battle of Shiloh in western Tennessee. Union victory.

April 25   New Orleans captured by the Union.

April 25   Hospital Transport Service of the Sanitary Commission begins with the commissioning of the first ship, the *Daniel Webster*.

May 31-June 1   Battle of Fair Oaks on the Virginia peninsula.

June 1   Robert E. Lee made commander of the Army of Northern Virginia.

June 23   Dr. Jonathan Letterman made medical director of the Army of the Potomac.

June 26-July 2   Seven Days' Battle. Union forces retreat to Harrison's Landing and Savage Station is overrun.

July   Surgeon General Hammond issues order that at least one-third army nurses be women.

August 2   Dr. Jonathan Letterman creates an ambulance corps for the Army of the Potomac.

August 3   Army withdraws from the Peninsula.

August 27-30   Confederates victorious in the second Battle of Bull Run.

September 1   Maine State Agency established in Washington.

September 16   Sanitary Commission establishes a hospital directory to help locate wounded men.

September 17	Battle of Antietam at which the Union forces prevail with great loss of life.
October 6	Harriet Eaton and Isabella Fogg leave Maine for the front.
November 17	Maine Camp Hospital Association established.
December 13	Union forces defeated at Fredericksburg.
	Mary Walker becomes a volunteer surgeon.

1863

January 1	Emancipation Proclamation frees slaves in Confederate states.
May 2-4	Union forces are defeated at Chancellorsville.
May 14	The "loyal women of the nation" meet in New York City to form the Women's National Loyal League and demand the abolition of slavery.
June 20	West Virginia admitted as 35th state.
July 1-3	Confederate forces are defeated at Gettysburg.
July 4	Vicksburg surrenders to General Grant.
October 27	Northwestern Sanitary Commission Fair in Chicago opens.
November 19	Gettysburg Address given by President Lincoln.
November 26	First national observance of Thanksgiving.
December 14-21	Boston Sanitary Fair is held.

1864

February 1	Lincoln calls for 500,000 more men.
March 12	U. S. Grant made commander of all Union troops.
May 4	General Sherman begins his march through Georgia.
May 5-7	Battle of the Wilderness. Both sides lose 30,000 men.
May 8-17	General Grant victorious at the Battle of Spotsylvania.
June 3	Union suffers heavy losses at the Battle of Cold Harbor.
June 16	Siege of Petersburg, Virginia, begins.
August 5	Union victory in Mobile Bay.
September 2	Fall of Atlanta, Georgia, to General Sherman.
October 5	Mary Walker commissioned as assistant surgeon.
October 12	Harriet Eaton sets up station at City Point for the Maine Camp Hospital Association.
November 8	Lincoln reelected.
December 21	Fall of Savannah, Georgia.

1865

January 31	Passage of the Thirteenth Amendment to the Constitution abolishing slavery.
March 3	Freedmen's Bureau established by Congress to aid former slaves.

March 4	Lincoln's second inauguration.
April 2	Petersburg falls.
April 3	Richmond surrenders.
April 9	General Lee surrenders to General Grant at Appomattox C.H.
April 15	Lincoln is assassinated by John Wilkes Booth.
May 23-24	Grand Review of the armies in Washington.
May 26	Last Confederate forces surrender.

1870

Women win right to vote in Utah and Wyoming territories.

March 30	Fifteenth Amendment to the Constitution ratified which makes it illegal to deny anyone the right to vote because of race.

1873

December 15	Centennial Tea Party in Boston. Three thousand women protest taxation without representation.

1892

March 1	52nd Congress passes law granting pensions to army nurses.

1919

March 19	Maine women are enfranchised for presidential elections.
November 4	Maine ratifies the Nineteenth Amendment.

1920

August 26	Nineteenth Amendment giving women the right to vote is passed.

Appendix B

Hospitals

Maine women served as nurses at many hospitals in and around Washington, D. C. and in the vicinity of major operations. This is a list of some of the major hospitals which were established by the Army's medical department referred to in text. Also included is a short description and the names of the Maine women who are known to have served at these locations.

Armory Square Hospital: August 15, 1862-September 1865.
Located in the "Mall," bordered by 7th Street and Smithsonian, Washington, D. C. 1,000 beds. Eleven long pavilions placed parallel with each other. Each ward 149' x 25' x 13' high. Surgeon-in-chief, Dr. D. W. Bliss. One of the newer, better organized temporary hospitals located close to transportation. Often visited by President Lincoln.

Henrietta Ingersoll	Abba Jackson	Sarah Low
Martha McLellan	Helen Merrill	Harriet Scamman
Susan Towle	Sarah Tucker	Harriet Wright

Auger Hospital: January 14, 1864 until closed.
Located on the grounds of "Rendezvous of Distribution," Alexandria, Virginia. 668 beds. Surgeon-in-chief: Dr. G. L. Sutton. Camp Convalescent existed in approximately the same location from August 1862-January 14, 1864. Originally tents replaced by wooden barracks.

Amy Bradley

Carver Hospital:
Located on Meridian Hill, two miles north of Pennsylvania Avenue, 14th Street and Georgetown Road, Washington, D. C. 1,300 beds. Surgeon-in-chief: Dr. O. A. Judson.

Mary Chamberlain	Hannah Judkins	Sarah Palmer

Chester General Hospital:
Chester, Pennsylvania. Centered around a college building that housed the staff quarters, administration, etc. 878 beds. 5 long units of 3 wards each with poor ventilation and poor placement of privies. Surgeon-in-chief: Dr. T. H. Bache.

Mary Dupee	Susan Newhall	Almira Quinby
Louisa Titcomb	Sarah Tucker	Rebecca Usher

Clayton General Hospital:
Harpers Ferry, West Virginia. Surgeon-inchief: Dr. E. W. Dawson.
Abba A. Goddard

Columbian College Hospital: July 14, 1861-July 10, 1865.
Located on Meridian Hill, Washington, D. C. Just south of Carver
Hospital. 43 wards. 844 beds. Each ward building 80' x 16', made of
white-washed planks. Surgeon-in-chief: Dr. T. R. Crosby.

Jane Holt	Sarah Porter	Susan Smiley
Hediah Snow		

Harewood General Hospital: September 4, 1862-May 20, 1866.
Located on 7th Street. Corcoran Farm, Washington, D. C.
Last general military hospital to close after the war. Located on a
farm and consisted of a brick farmhouse and wooden barracks in pa-
vilion style. Each ward was 187' x 24' x 20' high. 15 wards, 2,000 beds.
Covered walkways between buildings. Surgeon-in-chief: Dr. R. B.
Bontecou.

Hannah Babb	Mary Brown	Susan Smiley

Hygeia Hospital (also known as Hampton Hospital): May 20, 1861-
August 25, 1862.
Fort Monroe, Virginia. Located in a former seaside resort hotel ad-
joining the fort. 3,487 beds. Surgeon-in-chief: Dr. E. McClellan.

Elizabeth Bent	Mary Chamberlain

Judiciary Square Hospital: March 28, 1862-July 6, 1865.
Located in public square, between City Hall and Pension Building,
Washington, D. C. First pavilion style hospital. Built on cedar posts,
3' above the ground. 5 wards, 84' x 28'. 510 beds. Surgeon-in-chief:
Dr. E. Griswold/Dr. Hartsuff.

Sarah Milliken	Emeline McLellan	Adaline Smyth
Mary Agnes Tucker		

McDougall Hospital: Ft. Schuyler, New York.
1,184 beds. Surgeon-in-chief: Dr. S. H. Orton.

Jane Holt	Helen Merrill	Harriet Pinkham

Naval School or **Naval Academy Hospital**: Annapolis, Maryland.
Division No. 1 hospital: 1,562 beds. Surgeon-in-chief: Dr. Vanderkieft.
Division No. 2 hospital: 600 beds. Surgeon-in-chief: Dr. G. S. Palmer.

Emily Dana	Mary Dupee	Lydia Gray
Hannah Judkins	Amanda Kimball	Eunice Merrill

Susan Newhall	Mary Pearson	Harriet Pinkham
Sarah Porter	Almira Quinby	Louisa Titcomb
Sarah Tucker	Adeline Walker	

Seminary Hospital: June 30, 1861-June 14, 1865.

Behind Union Hotel at the Female Seminary, Georgetown. Corner of Washington and Gay Streets. Formerly a female seminary. Brick building with narrow hallways, no provisions for bathing or toilet facilities. In 1861, it had 30 beds and 135 patients. 121 beds. Surgeon-in-chief: Dr. H. W. Duchachet.

    Nancy Atwood   H. Southgate

Slough Hospital: May 23, 1864-May 1, 1865.

3rd Division Hospital, Alexandria, Virginia.

1,350 beds. Surgeon-in-chief: Dr. E. Bentley

    Judith Plummer   Susan Plummer   Harriet Wright

St. Elizabeth's General Hospital: November 11, 1861-May 31, 1864.

Uniontown, Washington, D. C. Used for the insane of the various military branches.

    Emeline McLellan

Union Hotel Hospital: May 25, 1861-May 15, 1862 and July 1, 1862-March 1863.

Corner of Bridge and Washington Streets, Georgetown, Virginia.

An old building with many problems (small rooms, narrow hallways, lack of ventilation and provision for bathing & toilets) capable of housing 225 patients.

    Sarah Low   Hannah Ropes   Harriet Wright

In Maine:

Cony General Hospital: June 1, 1864-November 30, 1865.

Camp Keyes, Augusta, Maine. 816 beds.

Surgeon-in-chief: Dr. George E. Brickett.

    Lydia Davis   Eliza Leeman   Jane Sherburn

    Emma Titcomb

Fort Preble Hospital:

Cape Elizabeth, (now South Portland) Maine.

    Mrs. S. W. Aberl

Gymnasium Hospital: June, 1864-?

Bangor, Maine.

    Nancy Atwood

Appendix C

Maine Contributions to the U.S. Sanitary Commission

The following Maine towns had Soldiers' Aid Societies, which were affiliated with the United States Sanitary Commission and filed reports with the Commission at the end of the war. The reports varied in detail from a simple statement that no records were kept to listings of items sent, to long narratives describing the activities the ladies undertook to raise money for the cause. The records are included with the United States Sanitary Commission Collection in the Special Collections of the New York Public Library.

Andover
Anson
Ashland
Athens
Auburn
Augusta
Bangor
Beddington
Belfast
Bingham
Brunswick
Burke & East Burke
Buxton & Hollis
Calais
Castine
Center Lovell
Cherryfield
Dixfield
Dover
Dresden Mills
East Machias
East Northport

East Pittston
Eddington
Ellsworth
Fort Fairfield
Freedom
Frankfort
Gardiner
Garland
Gouldsboro
Hallowell
Harrington
Hiram
Hodgdon
Howland
Kennebunk
Lagrange
Levant
Lewiston
Liberty
Montville
Monroe
Limington

Lincoln
Lincolnville
Lisbon
Livermore Falls
Livingston
Lovell
Machias
Mercer
Newfield
Norridgwock
North Anson
North New Portland
Northport
Palermo
Prospect Ferry
North Waterboro
North Yarmouth
Orrington & Orland
Parkman
Passadumkeag
Portland R. F. Society
Portland Ladies Sanitary Commission

Presque Isle
Readfield
Rockland
Rockport
Sabattusville
Saco
Sandstone
Sanford
Searsmont
Searsport
Skowhegan

Solon
Somerville
Mt. Desert
South Fayette
South Paris
South Thomaston
Springfield
Stockton
Stockholm
Steuben
Upper Stillwater

Unity
Wales
Waterford
Wells
Wesley
West Brooksville
West Buxton
Whitefield
Winterport

Note: this list was copied from a hand-written index to the Maine reports. It is unknown why Burke and Sandstone were included since there are no such towns in Maine.

Endnotes

The Union is Dissolved!

1. "From Augusta," Bangor *Whig and Courier*, 19 April 1861.
2. Cyrus Eaton, *History of Thomaston, Rockland, and South Thomaston*, Vol. II (Hallowell: Masters, Smith & Co., 1865), 40.
3. "Immense Union Meeting!" *Lewiston Evening Journal*, 22 April 1861.
4. "Flag to be Raised by Ladies," *Portland Eastern Argus*, 22 April 1861.
5. "Patriotic Feeling in Portland," *Portland Eastern Argus*, 23 April 1861.
6. "Secession—The News," *Brunswick Telegraph*, 28 Dec. 1860.
7. Samuel Langhorne Clemens and Charles Dudley Warner, *The Gilded Age* (New York: Harper & Bros., 1901), 200.
8. "Hurrah for the Old Patriots," *Lewiston Daily Evening Journal*, 29 April 1861.
9. "Supplies for the Soldiers," *Lewiston Daily Evening Journal*, 29 April 1861.
10. Relief Agencies Collection, Maine State Archives.
11. Gail Hamilton, "A Call to My Countrymen," *Atlantic Monthly*, March 1863, 346.
12. "A Noble Response," *Lewiston Daily Evening Journal*, 3 May 1861. The soldier was Elijah M. Shaw, formerly of Lewiston, who served with the 1st and 10th Maine Infantry, rising to the rank of captain.
13. Relief Agencies Collection, Maine State Archives.
14. Abner Small, *The 16th Maine in the War of the Rebellion* (Portland: B. Thurston Co., 1886), 90.
15. "A Lady was Drafted in Lewiston," *Portland Transcript*, 25 July 1863.
16. Mrs. VanHorne to Israel Washburn, 5 Oct. 1862, Relief Agencies Collection, Maine State Archives.
17. Ira Gardner, *The Recollections of a Boy Soldier in the 14th Maine Volunteers* (Lewiston: Lewiston Journal Co., 1902), 24.
18. Lauren Cook Burgess, *An Uncommon Soldier: The Civil War Letters of Sarah Rosetta Wakeman, Alias Private Lyons Wakeman, 153rd Regiment, New York State Volunteers* (Pasedena, MD: Minerva Center, 1994), 3.
19. "Maine's Only Woman to Shoulder a Musket in the Civil War Now Afflicted With Strange Malady," *Portland Sunday Telegram*, 14 Sept. 1930.

On the Homefront

1. R. H. Stanley and G. O. Hall, *Eastern Maine in the Rebellion* (Bangor, 1887), 31.
2. *Ibid.*, 31.
3. "The Feast of the Doughnuts," *Baltimore American*, 29 June 1861.
4. Elizabeth W. Hatch, *Report of the Kennebunk Soldier's Aid Society (1866)*, Special Collections, Kennebunk Free Library, Kennebunk, Maine.
5. *Union and Journal* (Biddeford, Maine), 15 Nov. 1861.
6. *Union and Journal*, 27 March 1863.
7. Hatch, 25.
8. *Portland Transcript*, 25 July 1863.
9. Eaton, 55.
10. William Howell Reed, *The Heroic Story of the United States Sanitary Commission: 1861-1865* (Boston: Geo. H. Ellis Co., 1910), 10.
11. Eaton, 55.
12. Rebecca Usher to Ellen Bacon, 23 Nov. 1862, Rebecca Usher Collection, Maine Historical Society.
13. Harriet Eaton to Harriet Fox, *Portland Transcript*, 14 Feb. 1863.
14. *Report of the Adjutant General of Maine, 1863* (Augusta: Stevens & Sayward, 1864), 47-48.
15. Tolman/Pottle Family Papers, Maine Historical Society.
16. U. S. Sanitary Commission Collection, New York Public Library.
17. *Union and Journal*, 28 Feb. 1862.
18. Rebecca Usher Collection. A comfort bag was usually a small sewing kit consisting of needles, thread, buttons, etc., to help soldiers keep their clothing repaired.
19. Frank Moore, *Women of the War: Their Heroism and Self-Sacrifice* (Hartford: S. S. Scranton & Co., 1866), 489.

20.   Maine Camp Hospital Association flyer, Broadsides Collection, Maine Historical Society.
21.   Adelaide Smith, *Reminiscenses of an Army Nurse During the Civil War* (New York: Greaves Pub. Co., 1911), 113.
22.   *Report of the Adjutant General of Maine, Vol. I: 1864-65* (Augusta: Stevens & Sayward, 1866), 85-91.
23.   U. S. Sanitary Commission Collection.
24.   *Report of the Adjutant General of Maine, Vol I: 1864-65*, 73.
25.   Asa Dore to Elizabeth Dore, 17 Feb., 1864, private collection.
26.   *Ibid.*, 19 March 1864.
27.   Eaton, 41.
28.   Duck is a cotton cloth somewhat like canvas but slightly lighter in weight. Drill is a coarse cotton cloth with a diagonal weave.
29.   Dane Yorke, *Men and Times of Pepperell* (Boston: Pepperell Manufacturing Co., 1945), 50.
30.   Catherine Clinton, *The Other Civil War: American Women in the Nineteenth Century* (New York: Hall and Wang, 1984), 92.
31.   *Union and Journal*, 25 April 1862.
32.   Samuel Cony, Address delivered to the Maine State Senate and House of Representatives, as reported in the *Union and Journal*, 9 Jan. 1864.
33.   Henry Worcester, "Maine State Agency in Washington," in *Report of the Adjutant General of the State of Maine for the Years 1864 and 1865*, Vol. I (Augusta: Stevens and Sayward, 1866), 105.

United Efforts

1.   James McPherson, "A War that Never Goes Away," *American Heritage,* March 1990, 47.
2.   Kate Wormeley, *The United States Sanitary Commission: A Sketch of its Purposes and its Work* (Boston: Little, Brown, 1863), 2.
3.   The Cooper Union was a great hall in New York City where large events could be held.
4.   *A Report to the Secretary of War of the Operations of the Sanitary Commission, and upon the Sanitary Conditions of the Volunteer Army, its Medical Staff, Hospitals, and Hospital Supplies* (Washington: McGill & Witherow, 1861), 24.
5.   *Ibid.*, 28.
6.   William Howell Reed, *The Heroic Story of the United States Sanitary Commission: 18611865.* Reprinted from the *Christian Register* (Boston: Geo. H. Ellis Co., 1910), 9.
7.   *Ibid.*, 10.
8.   *Ibid.*, 12.
9.   Gregory Coco, *A Vast Sea of Misery: A History and Guide to the Union and Confederate Field Hospitals at Gettysburg, July 1-November 20, 1863* (Gettysburg, PA: Thomas Publications, 1988), 160.
10.   Robert E. Denney, *Civil War Medicine: Care and Comfort of the Wounded* (New York: Sterling Pub. Co., 1994), 350.
11.   Erysipelas is an acutely infectious disease of the skin caused by bacteria characterized by inflammation and fever.
12.   *The Sanitary Commission Bulletin*, #23, 31 July 1861.
13.   *Construction of General Hospitals* [pamphlet], War Department, 20 July 1864.
14.   *Portland Daily Press*, 16 May 1863.
15.   Louise Titcomb to Rebecca Usher, October 17, 1863. Rebecca Usher Collection, Maine Historical Society.
16.   Relief Agencies Collection, Maine State Archives.
17.   Abraham Lincoln, *The Collected Works of Abraham Lincoln*, ed., Roy P. Basler, Vol. VII (New Brunswick, NJ: Rutgers University Press, 1953), 253-254.
18.   *Sanitary Commission Bulletin*, #40, 1 August 1865.

Notes on Nursing

1.   Mary A. Livermore, *My Story of the War: A Woman's Narrative of Four Years Personal Experience* (Hartford: A. D. Worthington and Co. 1889), 487.
2.   Lena Dixon Dietz, *History and Modern Nursing* (Philadelphia: F. A. Davis Co., 1963).
3.   Florence Nightingale, *Notes on Nursing: What it is and What it is Not* (New York: D. Appleton, 1860), 6.
4.   Catherine McAuley High School in Portland, Maine, is named for this woman who founded the Sisters of Mercy.

5. *A Report to the Secretary of War of the Operations of the Sanitary Commission, and upon the Sanitary Conditions of the Volunteer Army, its Medical Staff, Hospitals, and Hospital Supplies* (Washington: McGill & Witherow, 1861).
6. Harold Elk Straubing, ed., *In Hospital and Camp: the Civil War Through the Eyes of its Doctors and Nurses* (Harrisburg: Stackpole Books, 1993), 144-145.
7. Amanda Akin Stearns, *The Lady Nurse of Ward E* (New York: Baker and Taylor, 1909), 17-18.
8. Louisa May Alcott, *Hospital Sketches* (Boston: Redpath, 1863), 26.
9. *In Hospital and Camp*, 102.
10. L. P. Brockett and Mary Vaughn, *Woman's Work in the Civil War: a Record of Heroism, Patriotism and Patience* (Philadelphia: Zeigler, McCurdy & Co., 1867), 175-176.

Heroines All!—Sketches

1. *Maine Bugle: Campaign IV,* July 1897, 199.
2. Pension Records. National Archives and Records Administration.
3. *Maine Bugle*, 199.
4. Elizabeth Akers Allen, *Poems by Elizabeth Akers Allen (Florence Percy)*, (Boston: Ticknor & Fields, 1866), 190.
5. "Elizabeth Akers Allen, a Gifted Maine Writer," *Maine Sunday Telegram*, 3 Sept. 1911, 13+
6. Philip Willis McIntyre, *Elizabeth Akers Allen*. n.d. manuscript. Elizabeth Akers Allen Collection, Maine Historical Society. (Mr. McIntyre was the son-in law of Mrs. Allen.)
7. "Elizabeth Akers Allen, a Gifted Maine Writer."
8. Richard Cary, "The Misted Prism: Paul Akers and Elizabeth Akers Allen," *Colby Library Quarterly*, Series VII, No. 5 (March 1966): 193-227.
9. Florence Percy,"Correspondence," *Portland Transcript*, 18 July 1863.
10. Akers Allen, 201.
11. Cary, 223.
12. Mary Livermore to Elizabeth Akers Allen, 15 Aug. 1897. Special Collections, Colby College Library.
13. The Sorosis Club was founded in 1868 by professional women as a protest to the New York Press Association's refusal to allow admittance to women.
14. "Elizabeth Akers Allen, a Gifted Maine Writer."
15. "Maine's First Woman Soldier: Mrs. Nancy M.A. LaGross, Who Enlisted as a Private Soldier and Served Through the War." Newspaper clipping from unknown source (1893?). M.A. Little scrapbook, Maine Historical Society.
16. Mary A. Gardner Holland, *OurArmy Nurses* (Boston: Lounsbery, Nichols & Worth, 1897), 308-311.
17. "Maine's First Woman Soldier."
18. Pension records.
19. *Bangor Daily News*, 15 Sept. 1904.
20. Pension records.
21. Freeport (Maine) Historical Society records.
22. *Six Town Times*, 30 July 1897.
23. Pension Records.
24. *Ibid.*
25. Mrs. E.A. Bent Cooper to Commissioner, 7 Oct. 1896. Pension Records.
26. Pension Records.
27. *Ibid.*
28. Mary Livermore, *My Story of the War: A Woman's Narrative of Four Years Personal Experience* (Hartford: A. D. Worthington, 1889), 252-253.
29. Diane Cobb Cashman, *Headstrong: the Biography of Amy Morris Bradley, 1823-1904; A Life of Noblest Usefulness* (Wilmington, NC: Broadfoot Publishing Co., 1990), 143-144.
30. *Ibid.*, 144.
31. Frederick N. Knapp, "Fifth Report Concerning the Aid and Comfort Given by the Sanitary Commission to Sick and Invalid Soldiers," *Sanitary Commission Bulletin No. 77*, 1 Oct. 1863, 22-23.
32. Cashman, 161+.
33. "Miss Amy Bradley: A Life of Self-Sacrifice and Great Usefulness," *Wilmington Morning Star*, 16 Jan. 1904.
34. "Mrs. Mary A. Brown, 98, Who fought in Civil War with Husband, Dies," *Portland Press Herald*, 16 March 1936.

35. "Maine's Only Woman to Shoulder a Musket in the Civil War Now Afflicted with Strange Malady," *Portland Sunday Telegram*, 17 Sept. 1930, 12.
36. *Ibid.*
37. Apparently there was some confusion as to Mary Brown's actual age. She was most likely 96 at the time of her death, not 98 as the *Portland Press Herald* reported.
38. *Gettysburg Compiler*, 4 Aug. 1909.
39. "Days of Dread," *Philadelphia Weekly Press*, 16 Nov. 1887.
40. Gregory Coco, *A Vast Sea of Misery* (Gettysburg: Thomas Publications, 1988), 53-54.
41. "Death of Dr. Hunt," *Portland Daily Advertiser*, 24 July 1909, 1-2.
42. Pension Records.
43. Holland, 323-324.
44. Pension Records.
45. *Ibid.*
46. *Ibid.*
47. Holland, 310-311.
48. Frank Moore, *Women of the War: Their Heroism and Self-Sacrifice* (Hartford: S.S. Scranton & Co., 1866), 373-374.
49. Pension Records.
50. Death Records, Maine State Archives,
51. *Dictionary of American Biography*: Vol. IV. (New York: Charles Scribner's Sons, 1937), 323-325. Hereafter cited as *DAB*.
52. Sarah Sampson to Dr. Alonzo Garcelon, 14 June 1861. Relief Agencies collection, Maine State Archives.
53. Livermore, 247.
54. Charles Schlaifer and Lucy Freeman, *Hearts Work: Civil War Heroine and Champion of the Mentally Ill, Dorothea Lynde Dix* (New York: Paragon House, 1991), 151.
55. Circular found in private collection.
56. Mary E. Dupee to Ellen Bacon, 24 April 1865. Rebecca Usher Collection, Maine Historical Society.
57. L. P. Brockett and Mary C. Vaughan, *Woman's Work in the Civil War: a Record of Heroism, Patriotism and Patience* (Philadelphia: Zeigler, McCurdy & Co., 1867), 464.
58. *Ibid.*, 463.
59. National Association of Army Nurses Records. Archives, Fifth Maine Regiment Community Association,
60. Edward B. Warren was a private with Company B of the 10th Maine Infantry.
61. Harriet Eaton, Journals, 28 Oct. 1862. Southern Historical Collection, Wilson Library, University of North Carolina at Chapel Hill.
62. *Ibid.*, 2 Nov. 1862.
63. The colonel of the 17th Maine was Thomas A. Roberts of Portland; Dr. William Westcott of Standish was the assistant surgeon; the adjutant was Charles W. Roberts of Portland. Charles C. Hayes was the representative of the Maine State Agency. George W. Martin of Portland was captain of Company B of the 17th Maine. Joseph Drew, who was 18 when he enlisted in Stowe, Maine, died of disease.
64. Harriet Eaton, 9 Dec. 1862.
65. *Ibid.*, 12 Dec. 1862.
66. *Ibid.*, 13 Dec. 1862.
67. Colonel George Varney of Bangor and Adjutant Lewis P. Mudgett of Stockton, Maine.
68. Harriet Eaton, 14 Dec. 1862.
69. *Ibid.*, 15 Jan. 1863.
70. *Ibid.*, 26 Jan. 1863. Grinell is probably James A. Grinell, Co. E, 20th Maine.
71. *Ibid.*, 4 May 1863.
72. *Ibid.*, 19 Oct. 1864.
73. *Ibid.*, 24 Dec. 1864.
74. Records of the First Baptist Church of Hartford, Connecticut. Connecticut State Library.
75. Jane Thurston, "In Memoriam," *Portland Eastern Argus*, 17 June 1885.
76. Pension Records.
77. *Ibid.*
78. *Ibid.*

79. Maine Camp Hospital Collections. Maine Historical Society.
80. Moore, 115.
81. Isabella Fogg to J.W. Hathaway, 10 Nov. 1862. Relief Agencies Collection.
82. George Knox. Letter. *Portland Daily Press*, 15 Nov. 1862, 2.
83. Moore, 120-121.
84. Harriet Eaton, 18 Mar. 1863.
85. Maine Secretary of State, *Acts and Resolves Passed by the Forty-Third Legislature of the State of Maine, 1864* (Augusta: Stevens and Sayward, 1864), 322.
86. Pension Records.
87. Moore, 124.
88. Isabella Fogg to Frank Moore, 17 Mar. 1866, Frank Moore Papers, William R. Perkins Library, Duke University.
89. *Ibid.*
90. Pension Records.
91. S. S. Reed to Ellen Forbes, 30 Aug. 1863, Tolman/Pottle Family Papers, Maine Historical Society.
92. Abby Libby to Ellen Forbes, 28 Jan. 1863, Tolman/Pottle Family Papers.
93. Pension Records.
94. *Ibid.*
95. *Ibid.*
96. Hannibal Hamlin to President Benjamin Harrison, 30 Jan. 1891, Tolman/Pottle Family Papers.
97. *Portland Eastern Argus*, 31 July 1861.
98. N. P. Willis, "Lookings on at the War," *Home Journal*, 31 Aug. 1861.
99. Pension Records.
100. *Ibid.*
101. *Sarah Jane Foster: Teacher of the Freedmen,*Wayne E. Reilly, ed. (Charlottesville: University Press of Virginia, 1990), 2-8.
102. Sarah Jane Foster, "The Duty of the Hour," *Portland Daily Press*, 30 June 1863, 1.
103. *Sarah Jane Foster: Teacher of the Freedmen*, 23.
104. Harriet L. Fox, "Maine State Agency in Portland: Report for 1864," in *Report of the Adjutant General of the State of Maine. 1864/65,* Vol. I, (Augusta: Stevens & Sayward, 1866), 69-72. (hereafter cited as the *AG's Report*)
105. Housewife: a small sewing kit usually containing needle, thread, extra buttons, possibly small scissors, and other items for making repairs to clothing. Also known as a "comfort bag."
106. Maine Camp Hospital Collections. Maine Historical Society.
107. Cyrus Eaton, *History of Thomaston, Rockland, and South Thomaston*, Maine,Vol. II (Hallowell: Masters, Smith & Co., 1865), 55.
108. Abba A. Rutherford, "Letter from a Late Battlefield," *Portland Daily Press*, 1 Oct. 1863, 1.
109. John M. Gould, *History of the 1st, 10th, and 29th Maine Regiments in the Service of the United States from May 3, 1861, to June 3, 1866* (Portland: 1871), 87.
110. John Mead Gould, *The Civil War Journals of John Mead Gould, 1861-1866*, William B. Jordan, ed. (Baltimore: Butternut and Blue, 1997), 84.
111. *Ibid.*, 96.
112. *Ibid.*, 101.
113. *Portland Daily Press*, 28 June 1862.
114. Abba A. Goddard, "Letter from Mrs. Goddard," *Portland Daily Press*, 29 July 1862, 2.
115. Abba A. Goddard, "Letter from Harper's Ferry," *Portland Daily Press*, 1 Oct. 1862, 1.
116. Abba A. Goddard, "Letter from Harper's Ferry," *Portland Daily Press*, 18 Aug. 1862, 1.
117. Abba A. Goddard, "Letter from Harper's Ferry," *Portland Daily Press*, 23 Aug. 1862, 1.
118. Abba A. Goddard, "Letter from Harper's Ferry," *Portland Daily Press*, 9 Sept. 1862, 1.
119. Abba A. Goddard, "Letter from Harper's Ferry," *Portland Daily Press*, 1 Oct. 1862, 1.
120. *Ibid.*
121. *Ibid.*
122. Abba A. Goddard, "Letter from Mrs. Goddard," *Portland Daily Press*, 24 Jan. 1863, 1.
123. Pension Records.
124. Abba A. Goddard, "Letter from a late Battle-field," *Portland Daily Press*, 1 Oct. 1863, 1.
125. Harriet Eaton, *Journal*, 26 Nov. 1862.
126. Pension Records.

127. Thomas C. Hubka, *Big House, Little House, Back House, Barn: the Connected Farm Buildings of New England* (Hanover: University Press of New England, 1984), 95-97.
128. Records. North Yarmouth (Maine) Historical Society.
129. "Caroline Dana Howe Died Today: One of Maine's Most Brilliant Writers Succumbs to Old Age," *Portland Daily Advertiser*, 30 Oct. 1907, 2.
130. Caroline Dana Howe, *Ashes to Flames and Other Poems* (Portland: Loring, Short, and Harmon, 1885).
131. "Maine Men and Women of the Time," *Lewiston Sun Journal*, 23 June 1892.
132. "Mrs. Howe's Wartime Experience," *Portland Daily Advertiser*, 6 Nov. 1907, 16.
133. *Ibid.*
134. Caroline Dana Howe, "Abraham Lincoln," *Portland Transcript*, 29 April 1865, 1.
135. Simon Percy Crosby, *Two Crosby Families* (St. Paul: H.W. Kingston Co., 1912), 53-55.
136. Amanda Akin Stearns, *The Lady Nurse of Ward E* (New York: Baker and Taylor, 1909), 20-21.
137. *History of Woman Suffrage, Vol. 11, 1861-1876* (New York: Susan B. Anthony, 1881), 53.
138. Stearns, 141.
139. *Bangor Whig and Courier*, 19 Sept. 1893.
140. *Ibid.*, 21 Sept. 1893.
141. "Old Orchard Woman, Civil War Nurse, is Dead: Mrs. Addie J. Parmenter Recently Celebrated 97th Birthday," *Biddeford Daily Journal*, 11 July 1927.
142. *Ibid.*
143. *Ibid.*
144. *Ibid.*
145. Pension Records.
146. U.S. Congress. Private and Special Law: Chapter 468, 50th Congress, 1st Sess., 1888.
147. Hugh McLellan, *History of Gorham, Maine* (Portland: Smith and Sale, 1903), 669.
148. Pension Records.
149. U.S. Congress, House, *Mrs. Abba E. Jackson*, 50th Congress, 1st Sess., 1888. Report No. 1370.
150. "Letter of Presentations," *Portland Daily Press*, 5 Jan. 1864, 2.
151. Abba E. Jackson, "Acknowledgement," *Portland Daily Press*, 15 July 1864, 2.
152. U.S. Congress, House, *Mrs. Abba E. Jackson*, 50th Congress, 1st Sess., 1888. Report No. 1370.
153. McLellan, 669.
154. Pension Records.
155. "A Female Soldier from Maine," *Portland Daily Press*, 5 Jan. 1864, 4.
156. Abner Small, *The 16th Maine in the War of the Rebellion* (Portland: B. Thurston Co., 1886), 89.
157. Bee Middleton, *Hearts of Fire. . . Soldier Women of the Civil War* (Franklin, NC: Genealogy Pub. Co., 1993), 84.
158. F. F. Cavada, *Libby Life: Experiences of a Prisoner of War in Richmond, Va., 18631864* (Philadelphia: J. B. Lippincott and Co., 1865), 145.
159. Holland, 423.
160. Florence Collins Porter, *Maine Men and Women in Southern California* (Los Angles: Kingsley, Mason & Collins, 1913), 53.
161. Pension Records.
162. *Portland Daily Press*, 21 July 1864, 3.
163. *AG's Report: 1864/65*, Vol . I, 81.
164. Clipping from unknown newspaper in private collection.
165. Mary A. Fitch to Col. Arnold Rand, 3 April 1889. Mass-MOLLUS Collection, U.S. Army Military History Institute.
166. L. C. Bateman, "The Heroism of a Maine Woman in the Civil War," *Lewiston Journal: Illustrated Magazine Section*, 16-20 Feb. 1907, 10.
167. John C. Vaughn fought at Vicksburg, the Shenandoah Valley, and at Martinsburg, where he was wounded. Vaughn was repeatedly assigned to command troops in eastern Tennessee throughout the war beginning in the spring of 1862.
168. Bateman, 10.
169. *Ibid.*
170. *Ibid.*
171. Vital Records/Death Records, Maine State Archives.
172. Pension Records.
173. *Ibid.*

174. "Lottie Hartford Reminisces Interesting Family History Observing her 84th Birthday," *Lewiston Evening Journal*, 9 Oct. 1962.
175. Shirley Simmons, personal interview by Lynda L. Sudlow, April 1994.
176. Pension Records, Veterans Administration, Togus, Maine.
177. *Proceedings of the Sixth Annual Convention*. Maine Department, National Alliance, Daughters of Union Veterans, 1918, 44-45
178. Sarah Low Papers, New Hampshire Historical Society.
179. Sarah Low to Lydia Hale, Sept. 1862, Sarah Low Papers.
180. Hannah Ropes, *Civil War Nurse: the Diary and Letters of Hannah Ropes* (Knoxville: University of Tennessee Press, 1980), 77.
181. *Ibid.*, 92.
182. Winifred Stonemetz, *Sarah Low: Dover's Civil War Nurse* (Dover, NH: Northam Colonial Historical Society, 1962), 7.
183. *Ibid.*, 10.
184. Sarah Low to Col. Arnold Rand, 23 Feb. 1886, Mass-MOLLUS Collection.
185. Stephen G. Abbott, *The First New Hampshire Volunteers in the Great Rebellion* (Keene, NH: Sentinel Printing Co., 1890), 269.
186. Ruth Mayhew, "Letter from Mrs. Mayhew," *Portland Daily Press*, 23 July 1864, 2.
187. Ruth Mayhew to (Ellen Bacon)?, 19 July 1863 in *Daily Press*, 5 Aug. 1863, 2.
188. Ruth Mayhew to Harriet Fox in *Portland Daily Press*, 16 Feb. 1864, 1.
189. Ruth Mayhew to Harriet Fox, 26 Feb. 1865, Relief Agencies Collection.
190. Joan Pratt, "Daughters of Union Veterans of the Civil War, 1861-1865: Ruth Mayhew Tent #14." (Rockland, ME), n.d., unpublished manuscript.
191. Moore, 279.
192. *The History of Waterford, Oxford County, Maine* (Portland: Hoyt, Fogg & Dunham, 1879), 264.
193. C. E. McKay, *Stories of Hospital and Camp* (Philadelphia: Claxton Remsen & Haffelfinger, 1876).
194. McKay, 20.
195. *Ibid.*
196. *Ibid.*, 40.
197. *Ibid.*, 51-52.
198. *Ibid.*, 67-78.
199. Mary Elizabeth Massey, *Women in the Civil War* (Lincoln, NB: University of Nebraska Press, 1994), 128.
200. Moore, 296.
201. E.E . McLellan to Mr. Watson, 27 Oct. 1863, Relief Agencies Collection.
202. *Ibid.*
203. *Ibid.*
204. *Ibid.*
205. Myrtle Lovejoy, *This was Stroudwater: 1727-1860* (Portland: National Society of Colonial Dames of America, 1985), 155.
206. Brockett and Vaughan, 456-457.
207. Gould, *History of the 1st, 10th, and 29th Maine Regiments*, 87.
208. Carded Record Service. National Archives and Records Administration.
209. Fox, 71.
210. "George F. Shepley," *Portland Daily Press*, 22 July 1878, 3.
211. Helen Shepley to Col. Arnold Rand, Mass-MOLLUS Collection.
212. Holland, 171.
213. *Ibid.*
214. *Ibid.*, 172.
215. *Ibid.*
216. Pension Records.
217. *Ibid.*
218. Vital Records, Lynn Historical Society, Lynn, Massachusetts.
219. Brockett and Vaughan, 461,462.
220. Carded Record Service.
221. John T. Hull, *Centennial Celebration: an Account of the Municipal Celebration of the One Hundredth Anniversary of the Incorporation of the Town of Portland* (Portland: Owen Strout & Co., 1886), 63.
222. Sarah Palmer to Mr. Arnold [Rand], 19 Feb. 1897, Mass-MOLLUS Collection.

223. Pension Records.
224. Helen Coffin Beedy, *Mothers of Maine* (Portland: Thurston Press, 1895), 370.
225. Thirty-Ninth Congress, United States Congress, Sess. I, Res. No. 103, 23 July 1866.
226. Oliver Seymour Phelps & Andrew Servin, *The Phelps Family in America, Vol. I* (Pittsfield, MA: Eagle Pub. Co., 1899), 621-622.
227. *DAB*, 435.
228. James Peckham, *Nathaniel Lyon, and Missouri in 1861* (New York: American News Company, 1866), 339.
229. *Ibid.*
230. Paul Fleury Mottelay, *The Soldier in our Civil War* (New York: J. H. Brown, 1884), 117.
231. Frank Moore, *Anecdotes, Poetry, and Incidents of the War: North and South.* (New York, 1866), 458.
232. Christopher Phillips, *Damned Yankee: the Life of General Nathaniel Lyon* (Baton Rouge: Louisiana State University Press, 1990), 258-261.
233. Mark M. Boatner, *The Civil War Dictionary* (New York: Vintage Books, 1987), 935.
234. Jerena East Giffen, *First Ladies of Missouri: Their Homes and Their Families* (Von Hoffman Press, 1970), 114.
235. "Personal," *Portland Daily Press*, 24 March 1863, 3.
236. "An Appeal to the Citizens of this City," *Portland Daily Press*, 13 Jan. 1865, 3.
237. *DAB*, Vol VII, 530.
238. Giffen, 114.
239. "Death of Mrs. Mary Phelps," *Patriot-Advertiser* (Springfield, Mo.), 21 Jan. 1878, 3.
240. Frances B. Greene, *History of Boothbay, Southport and Boothbay Harbor, Maine* (Portland: Loring Short and Harmon, 1906), 606.
241. Pension Records.
242. Edward Wiggin, *History of Aroostook, Vol. I* (Presque Isle: Star Herald Press, 1922), 266-267.
243. Pension Records.
244. *Ibid.*
245. *Ibid.*
246. Bangor *Daily News*, 20 May 1896, 3.
247. "Mrs. Arbella F. Pollister, Union Army Telegrapher, Dies at Fort Myers, Fla.," *Portland Press Herald*, 23 Dec. 1932, 1+.
248. "Mrs. G.A. Pollister Dies at Daughter's Home, Aged 86 Years," News-Press (Fort Myers, FL), 23 Dec. 1932.
249. "Mrs. Arbella F. Pollister, Union Army Telegrapher," 1+.
250. Pension Records.
251. Harriet Eaton, 12 Oct. 1862.
252. John Goddard to Israel Washburn, 6 June 1862. Regimental Correspondence Files, Maine State Archives .
253. *Kennebec Journal*, 28 Oct. 1864.
254. Corelli C.W. Simpson, *Leaflets of Artists* (Bangor: John H. Bacon, 1893), 22
255. Sarah Jane Prentiss, "A Few Words about Mrs. Fales," *Kennebec Journal*, 28 Oct. 1864.
256. Sarah J. Prentiss to (Bell)?, 21 April 1865. Livermore Falls Historical Society.
257. *Oxford Democrat*, 6 Nov. 1877, 2.
258. William B. Lapham and Silas P. Maxim, *History of Paris, Maine* (Paris, ME: 1884), 438.
259. Rebecca Usher Collection. Mr. Nichols is Reverend John Taylor Gilman Nichols of the 2nd Parish Church in Saco.
260. Brockett and Vaughan, 455.
261. Almira Quinby to Thomas Quinby printed in the *Union and Journal* (Biddeford), 8 May 1863, 2.
262. Brockett and Vaughan, 455.
263. Skinner-Ropes Manuscript Collection. Special Collection Division, General Library, University of California, Riverside.
264. John R. Brumgardt, ed., *Civil War Nurse: the Diary and Letters of Hannah Ropes* (Knoxville: University of Tennessee Press, 1980), 7.
265. *Ibid.*, 8-9.
266. *Ibid.*, 12.
267. *Ibid.*, 17- 19.
268. *Ibid.*, 46.

269. Hannah Ropes to Alice Ropes, Nov. 1862, in *Ropes*, 105.
270. Hannah Ropes to Alice, 6 July 1862 in *Ropes*, 53.
271. *Ibid.*, 6 Oct. 1862, 69.
272. *Ropes*, 82-83.
273. Hannah Ropes to Alice, Dec. 1862, in *Ropes*, 116.
274. *Ibid.*, 11 Jan. 1863, 121-122.
275. Charles Sumner to "My dear Chandler," 21 Jan. 1863, 125.
276. M. M. Boyce to Mrs. Sumner, 23 Jan. 1863, 127.
277. Emma T. Bennett, *Emeline B. Rose, Civil War Nurse* (unpublished manuscript, 1965).
278. *Ibid.*
279. Emeline Rose, *Journal*, 23 April 1861. Private collection.
280. *Ibid.*, 28 Oct. 1861.
281. Uriah Proctor to Emeline Rose, 21 Nov. 1861. Private collection.
282. Rose, 13 June 1863.
283. *Ibid.*, 20 June 1863.
284. *Ibid.*, 28 June 1863.
285. *Ibid.*, 6 July 1863.
286. Pension Records.
287. *Ibid.*, 1 Jan. 1864.
288. Pension Records.
289. Bennett.
290. Dr. Horton to Emeline Rose. Private Collection.
291. Rebecca Usher, *Journal*, 23 Jan. 1865. Rebecca Usher Collection,
292. Sarah Sampson to Alonzo Garcelon, 14 June 1861. Relief Agencies Files.
293. *Ibid.*
294. *Ibid.*
295. Sarah Sampson, "Mrs. Sampson's Report," in *AG's Report: 1864/65*. Vol. 1, 108-110.
296. *Ibid.*, 111.
297. *Ibid.*, 116- 119.
298. Gordon Struble, "Sarah Sampson, Moving Force Behind the Bath Children's Home," *Bath Historical Society Newsletter*, Oct. 1990, 2.
299. Ted Cohen, "Children' s Home Shut Down After 132 Years," *Portland Press Herald*, 30 Sept. 1996, A1+.
300. Pension Records.
301. "A Bath Woman in Civil War," *The Bath Independent*, 18 Aug. 1906.
302. Pension Records.
303. *The Story of One Regiment: The Eleventh Maine Infantry Volunteers in the War of the Rebellion: 1861-1865* (New York: J.J. Little Co., 1896), 435.
304. Holland, 191.
305. "Mrs. Hillman Smith: Death on Sunday Night of Prominent Auburn Woman," *Lewiston Evening Journal*, 16 Feb. 1914, 7.
306. *Ibid.*
307. *Ibid.*
308. *Ibid.*
309. "Loss to Augusta Me: Mrs. Williamson dies at age 80 Years," Clipping from unknown newspaper. Archives, 8th Maine Regiment Association, Peaks Island, Maine.
310. "Mrs. Hillman Smith."
311. *Ibid.*
312. Cyrus Eaton, 424.
313. Emily Souder, *Leaves from the Battle-Field of Gettysburg* (Philadelphia: Caxton Press, 1864), 17.
314. *Ibid.*, 13-14.
315. *Ibid.*, 23.
316. *Ibid.*, 23-24.
317. Charles W. Roberts was the adjutant of the 17th Maine Regiment at that time.
318. Captain Young was Milton M. Young of Co. K of the 17th Maine Regiment, who died from his wounds.
319. Souder, 40.
320. *Ibid.*, 133- 134.

321. *Ibid.*, 138.
322. *Ibid.*, 139.
323. *Ibid.*, 139- 140.
324. Sylvia Dannett, *Noble Women of the North* (New York: Thomas Yoseloff, 1959), 249.
325. McKay, 96.
326. Noel B. Gerson, *Harriet Beecher Stowe* (New York: Popular Library, 1976), 77-79.
327. Charles Edward Stowe, *The Life of Harriet Beecher Stowe* (Boston: Houghton Mifflin, 1891), 156.
328. *Ibid.*
329. Gerson, 94-95.
330. *Ibid.*, 194
331. William David Barry, "Mrs. Jane P. Thurston, the Woman who Owned the State of Maine," unpublished manuscript, n.d., 3.
332. *Ibid.*, 4.
333. "Mrs. Thurston's Plan to End the War," *Portland Daily Press*, 26 Mar. 1863, 2.
334. Jane Thurston, *The Plan to Close the Rebellion and Unite the States in Six Months* (Portland: March 1863), 29-30.
335. Shelby Foote, *The Civil War: a Narrative: Red River to Appomattox* (New York: Vintage Books, 1986), 551-552.
336. "Unfortunate Occurrence in the Representatives' Hall," Portland *Eastern Argus*, 6 Jan. 1870, 2.
337. Barry, 6.
338. *DAB*, Vol. XVIII, 560.
339. *The National Cyclopaedia of American Biography*, Vol . VIII (New York: James T. White, 1898), 413.
340. *DAB*, Vol. XVIII, 560.
341. Lovejoy, 186.
342. Brockett and Vaughan, 453, 456.
343. Louise Titcomb to Rebecca Usher, 1 Oct. 1863, Rebecca Usher Collection.
344. *Ibid.*, 27 April 1864.
345. *Ibid.*, S June 1864.
346. Pension Records.
347. *Portland Evening Express*, 15 July 1905.
348. Carded Record Service.
349. Rebecca Usher to Martha Osgood, 20 Feb. 1865, Rebecca Usher Collection.
350. Carded Record Service.
351. Martin H. Jewett and Olive Hannaford, *The History of Hollis, Maine* (Farmington, ME: Knowlton & McLeary, 1976), 112, 139.
352. Martha Osgood to Annie, 19 Oct. 1862, Rebecca Usher Collection.
353. *Ibid.*
354. Rebecca Usher to Ellen Bacon, 23 Nov. 1862, Rebecca Usher collection.
355. Rebecca Usher to Martha Osgood, 22 Nov. 1862, Rebecca Usher collection.
356. Rebecca Usher to Ellen Bacon, 5 Dec. 1862, Rebecca Usher collection.
357. Martha Osgood, "Buxton and Hollis Report," in *Reports of the Aid Societies Tributary to the Sanitary Commission in Maine*, 82. U.S.S.C Collection, New York Public Library.
358. *Ibid.*
359. Maine Camp Hospital Collections.
360. Rebecca Usher to Ellen Bacon, n.d..
361. Rebecca Usher, Diary, Rebecca Usher Collection.
362. Rebecca Usher to ?, n.d., Rebecca Usher Collection.
363. Rebecca Usher, Diary, 19? Jan. 1865.
364. "Card," *Portland Daily Press*, 4 Jan. 1865, 3.
365. Rebecca Usher to Martha Osgood, 2 Feb. 1865.
366. *Portland Daily Advertiser*, 23 Mar. 1865, 3.
367. Rebecca Usher to Ellen Bacon, 4 Feb. 1865.
368. Rebecca Usher to Martha Osgood, 20 Feb. 1865.
369. Ellen Bacon to Rebecca Usher, 12 April 1865.
370. Ellen Bacon to Rebecca Usher, 12 April 1865.
371. Rebecca Usher to Martha Osgood, 1 May 1865.
372. Jewett, 112.
373. Brockett and Vaughan, 458.

374. *Ibid.*
375. "An Appeal in Behalf of Sick Soldiers," *Union & Journal,* 11 Oct. 1861.
376. Cashman, 99-100.
377. "Mrs. Francis G. Warren: Death of a Biddeford Lady After Illness Lasting Over Twenty Years," *Biddeford Daily Journal,* 24 Jan. 1898.
378. Henry Burrage Collection, Maine Historical Society.
379. Pension Records.
380. Death records, Maine State Archives.
381. Pension Records.
382. *Ibid.*
383. *Walt Whitman's Memoranda During the War & Death of Abraham Lincoln,* reproduced in facsimile (Bloomington, IN: Indiana University Press, 1962), 40.
384. Harriet Wright to Charles Coleman, 10 Dec. 1865, Private collection.
385. Pension Records.
386. "Mrs. Harriet J. Wright: Former Saco Woman Was Nurse at Washington During Civil War," *Biddeford Weekly Journal,* 26 Mar. 1915, 8.
387. *AG's Report,* 1862 & 1863.
388. Private family records.

The Unfinished Battle

1. Sylvia Dannett, *Noble Woman of the North* (New York: Thomas Yoseloff, 1959) 343.
2. *Sangamo Journal,* 13 June 1836, in *The Collected Works of Abraham Lincoln,* Vol. VI, ed. Roy P. Basler (New Brunswick, NJ: Rutgers University Press, 1953), 48.
3. Elizabeth Cady Stanton, Susan B. Anthony, and Matilda Joslyn Gage, eds., *History of Woman Suffrage, Vol. II* (Rochester, NY: Susan B. Anthony, 1881), 3. Hereafter cited as *HWS.*
4. Samuel Langhorne Clemens and Charles Dudley Warner, *The Gilded Age,* Vol. 1 (New York: Harper & Bros., 1865), 200-201.
5. Josiah H. Benton, *What Women Did for the War, and What the War Did for Women* (Boston: 1894), 8.
6. "An Interview with a Yankee School-Mistress," *Portland Daily Press,* 9 Sept. 1867), 2.
7. Catherine Clinton, *The Other Civil War: American Women in the Nineteenth Century* (New York: Hill and Wang, 1992), 88.
8. Augustus Freedom Moulton, ed., *Memorials of Maine: A Life Record of Men and Women of the Past* (New York: American Historical Society, 1916), 168-169.
9. *HWS,* Vol. II, 50-79.
10. Moore, *Women of the War,* 469.
11. Livermore, 436.
12. Cary, 196-197.
13. Mary Livermore to Elizabeth Akers Allen, 15 Aug. 1897, Special Collections, Colby College Library.
14. Giffen, 114.
15. Anne Firor Scott, *Natural Allies: Women's Associations in American History* (Urbana, IL: University of Illinois Press, 1991), 74.
16. "Petition for pay to volunteer nurses," 30 Jan. 1866, Congressional Records, National Archives.
17. Frederick Douglass, *Frederick Douglass on Women's Rights* (New York: Da Capo Press, 1992), 14.
18. Samuel Cony, *Address of Governor Cony to the Legislature of the State of Maine, January 1866* (Augusta: Stevens & Sayward, 1866), 10-11.
19. *HWS,* Vol. II, 884-885.
20. *Ibid.,* 418.
21. Elizabeth Frost and Kathryn Culen-DuPont, *An Eyewitness History: Women's Suffrage in America* (New York: Facts on File, 1992), 214.

Bibliography

Abbott, Stephen G. *The First Regiment New Hampshire Volunteers in the Great Rebellion*. Keene, NH: Sentinel Printing Co., 1890.

Adams, George Worthington. *Doctors in Blue: the Medical History of the Union Army in the Civil War*. New York: H. Schuman, 1952.

Alcott, Louisa May. *Hospital Sketches*. Boston: J. Redpath, 1863.

Allen, Elizabeth Akers. *Poems by Elizabeth Akers Allen* (Florence Percy). Boston: Ticknor and Fields, 1866.

Allen, Elizabeth Akers. Special Collections. Colby College Library, Waterville, Maine.

"An Auburn Woman at the Front ." Date and paper unknown. 8th Maine Regiment Memorial Society Archives, Peaks Island, Maine.

Baltimore American (Baltimore, Maryland).

Bangor Daily News (Bangor, Maine).

Bangor Whig & Courier (Bangor, Maine).

Barry, William David. "Mrs. Jane P. Thurston, the Woman Who Owned the State of Maine." n.d.

Bath Historical Society Newsletter (Bath, Maine).

Bath Independent. (Bath, Maine).

Beattie, Donald W., Rodney M. Cole, and Charles G. Waugh, eds., *A Distant War Comes Home: Maine in the Civil War Era*. Camden, ME: Downeast Books, 1996.

Beedy, Helen Coffin. *Mothers of Maine*. Portland: Thurston Press, 1895.

Bennett, Emma. "Emeline P. Rose, Civil War Nurse," 1965.

Benton, Josiah H. *What Women did for the War, and What the War did for Women*. Boston: n.p., 1894.

Biddeford Daily Journal (Biddeford, Maine).

Boatner, Mark M. *The Civil War Dictionary*. New York: Vintage Books, 1987.

Brockett, L. P., and Mary C. Vaughan. *Woman's Work in the Civil War: A Record of Heroism, Patriotism and Patience*. Philadelphia: Zeigler, McCurdy and Co., 1867.

Brunswick Telegraph. (Brunswick, Maine).

Burrage, Henry. Papers. Maine Historical Society. Portland, Maine.

Burgess, Lauren Cook. *An Uncommon Soldier: The Civil War Letters of Sarah Rosetta Wakeman, alias Private Lyons Wakeman, 153rd Regiment, New York State Volunteers*. Pasadena, MD: Minerva Center, 1994.

Carded Record Service, National Archives and Records Administration. Washington, D.C.

Cary, Richard. "The Misted Prism: Paul Akers and Elizabeth Akers Allen ." *Colby Library Quarterly*. Series VII, March 1966. No. 5. 196-197.

Cashman, Diane Cobb. *Headstrong, the Biography of Amy Morris Bradley, 1823-1904: A Life of Noblest Usefulness*. Wilmington, NC: Broadfoot Press, 1990.

Cavada, F. F. *Libby Life: Experiences of a Prisoner of War in Richmond, VA, 1863-1864*. Philadelphia: J.B. Lippincott and Co., 1865.

Clemens, Samuel Langhorne and Charles Dudley Warner. *The Gilded Age*. New York: Harper and Bros., 1901.

Clinton, Catherine. *The Other Civil War: American Women in the Nineteenth Century*. New York: Hill and Wang, 1984.

Coburn, Louise Helen. *Skowhegan on the Kennebec*. Vol 2. Skowhegan, 1941.

Coco, Gregory. *Vast Sea of Misery: A History and Guide to the Union and Confederate Field Hospitals at Gettysburg, July I - November 20, 1863*. Gettysburg, PA: Thomas Publications, 1988.

Coleman Letters. Private collection.

Conklin, Eileen F. *Women at Gettysburg, 1863*. Gettysburg, PA: Thomas Publications, 1993.

Cony, Samuel. *Address of Governor Cony to the Legislature of the State of Maine, January, 1866*. Augusta: Stevens and Sayward, 1866.

Crosby, Simon Percy. *Two Crosby Families*. St. Paul, MN: H. W. Kingston Co., 1912.

Dannett, Sylvia G. L. *Noble Women of the North*. New York: Thomas Yoseloff, 1959.

Denney, Robert E. *Civil War Medicine: Care and Comfort of the Wounded*. New York: Sterling Publishing Co., 1994.

Dictionary of American Biography. New York: Charles Scribner's Sons, 1937.

Dietz, Lena Dixon. *History and Modern Nursing*. Philadelphia: F. A. Davis Co., 1963.

Dore Family Letters. Private collection.

Douglass, Frederick. *Frederick Douglass on Women's Rights*. Philip S. Foner, ed. New York: DaCapo Press, 1976.

Eastern Argus (Portland, Maine).

Eaton, Cyrus. *History of Thomaston, Rockland, and South Thomaston, Maine*. Vols. 1 & 2. Hallowell: Masters, Smith and Co., 1865.

Eaton, Harriet. Diaries. Southern Historical Collection, Wilson Library, University of North Carolina at Chapel Hill.

Foote, Shelby. *The Civil War: a Narrative: Red River to Appomattox*. New York: Vintage Books, 1986.

Foster, Sarah Jane. *Sarah Jane Foster, Teacher of the Freedmen: A Diary and Letters*. Wayne E. Reilly, ed. Charlottesville, VA: University of Virginia Press, 1990.

Frost, Elizabeth and Kathryn Culen Dupont. *An Eyewitness History: Women's Suffrage in America*. New York: Facts on File, 1992.

Gardner, Ira. *The Recollections of a Boy Soldier in the 14th Maine Volunteers*. Lewiston: Lewiston Journal Company, 1902.

Gerson, Noel B. *Harriet Beecher Stowe*. New York: Praeger, 1976.

Gettysburg Compiler (Gettysburg, Pennsylvania).

Giffen, Jerena East. *First Ladies of Missouri: Their Homes and Their Families*. Von Hoffman Press, 1970.

Gould, John M. *History of the Ist, 10th, and 29th Maine Regiments in the Service of the United States from May 3, 1861, to June 3, 1866*. Portland: 1871.

Gould, John M. *The Civil War Journals of John Mead Gould, 1861-1866*. William B. Jordan, ed. Baltimore: Butternut and Blue, 1997.

Greenbie, Marjorie. *Lincoln's Daughters of Mercy*. NewYork: Dutton, 1944.

Greene, Frances B. *History of Boothbay, Southport and Boothbay Harbor, Maine.* Portland: Loring Short and Harmon, 1906.

Hamilton, Gail. "A Call to my Country-Women." *Atlantic Monthly.* March, 1863, 345-349.

Hatch, Elizabeth W. *Report of the Kennebunk Soldier's Aid Society.* Kennebunk, 1866. Special Collections. Kennebunk Free Library, Kennebunk, Maine.

History of Waterford, Oxford County, Maine. Portland: Hoyt, Fogg and Denham, 1879.

Holland, Mary A. Gardner. *Our Army Nurses.* Boston: Lounsbery, Nichols and Worth, 1897.

Howe, Caroline Dana. *Ashes to Flame and Other Poems.* Portland: Loring, Short and Harmon, 1885.

Hubka, Thomas C. *Big House, Little House, Back House, Barn: the Connected Farm Buildings of New England.* Hanover: University Press of New England, 1984.

Hull, John T. *Centennial Celebration: an Account of the Municipal Celebration of the One Hundredth Anniversary of the Incorporation of the Town of Portland.* Portland: Owen Strout and Co., 1886.

Jewett, Martin H. and Olive Hannaford. *A History of Hollis, Maine.* Farmington, ME: Knowlton and McLeary, 1976.

Jones, Herbert. *Old Portland Town.* Portland: Machigonne Press, 1938.

Jordan, William B. *Maine in the Civil War: a Bibliographic Guide.* Portland: Maine Historical Society, 1976.

Kennebec Journal (Augusta, Maine).

Knowlton, Evelyn H. *Pepperell's Progress: History of a Cotton Textile Company.* Boston: Harvard University Press, 1948.

Lapham, Wm. B. and Silas P. Maxim. *History of Paris, Maine.* Paris, ME: n.p., 1884.

Leisch, Juanita. *An Introduction to Civil War Civilians.* Gettysburg: Thomas Publications, 1994.

Lewiston *Evening Journal* (Lewiston, Maine).

Lincoln, Abraham. *The Collected Works of Abraham Lincoln.* Roy P. Basler, ed. New Brunswick, NJ: Rutgers University Press, 1953.

Livermore, Mary A. *My Story of the War: A Woman's Narrative of Four Years Personal Experience.* Hartford, CT: A. D. Worthington and Co., 1889.

Lovejoy, Myrtle Kittridge. *This was Stroudwater, 1727-1860.* Portland, ME: National Society of Colonial Dames of America, 1985.

Low, Sarah. Papers. New Hampshire Historical Society Manuscript Division, Concord, New Hampshire.

Maine Bugle: Campaign IV (Rockland, Maine).

Maine Camp Hospital Collections. Maine Historical Society. Portland, Maine.

Maine Farmer (Augusta, Maine).

Maine Secretary of State. *Acts and Resolves Passed by the Forty Third Legislature of the State of Maine, 1864.* Augusta, ME: Stevens and Sayward, 1864.

Maine State Agency of the Sanitary Commission. Letters and Correspondence. Collection. Maine Historical Society.

Maine Sunday Telegram. (Portland, Maine).

"Maine's first woman soldier: Mrs. Nancy M. A. LaGross, who enlisted as a private soldier and served through the war." Scrapbook clipping from unknown source. Maine Historical Society.

Mass-MOLLUS Collection. U. S. Army Military History Institute, Carlisle, Pennsylvania.

Massey, Mary Elizabeth. *Women in the Civil War*. Lincoln, NE: University of Nebraska Press, 1966. (Originally published as *Bonnet Brigades*)

McIntyre, Philip Willis. "Elizabeth Akers Allen." n.d. Elizabeth Akers Allen Collection, Maine Historical Society.

McLellan, Hugh. *History of Gorham, Maine*. Portland, ME: Smith and Sale, 1903.

McKay, Charlotte. *Stories of Hospital and Camp*. Philadelphia: Claxton, Remsen and Haffelfinger, 1876.

McPherson, James. "A War that Never Goes Away." *American Heritage*. Mar., 1990, 41-50.

Medical and Surgical History of the War of the Rebellion. Washington, D.C.: Government Printing Office, 1888.

Middleton, Lee. *Hearts of Fire... Soldier Women of the Civil War*. Franklin, NC: Genealogy Publishing Service, 1993.

Military Service Records. Maine State Archives. Augusta, Maine.

Moore, Frank. *Anecdotes, Poetry and Incidents of the War: North and South, 1860-1865*. New York: Printed for the Subscriber, 1866.

Moore, Frank. Papers. William R. Perkins Libary, Duke University, Durham, North Carolina.

Moore, Frank. *Women of the War: Their Heroism and Self-Sacrifice*. Hartford: S.S. Scranton and Co., 1866.

Mottelay, Paul Fleury. *The Soldier in Our Civil War*. New York: J. H. Brown, 1884.

Moulton, Augustus Freedom, ed. *Memorials of Maine: a Life Record of Men and Women of the Past*. New York: American Historical Society, 1916.

National Association of Army Nurses. Records. Fifth Maine Regiment Community Association Archives. Peaks Island, Maine.

National Cyclopaedia of American Biography. New York: James T. White, 1898.

News-Press. (Fort Myers, Florida).

Nightingale, Florence. *Notes on Nursing: What it is and What it is not*. New York: D. Appleton, 1860.

Olmsted, Frederick Law. *Hospital Transports: a Memoir of the Embarcation of the Sick and Wounded from the Peninsula of Virginia in the Summer of 1862*. Boston: Ticknor and Fields, 1863.

Oxford Democrat (Norway, Maine).

Patriot-Advertiser (Springfield, Missouri).

Peckham, James. *General Nathaniel Lyon, and Missouri in 1861*. New York: American News Company, 1866.

Pension Records. National Archives and Records Administration, Washington, D.C.

Petition for Pay to Volunteer Nurses. National Archives and Records Administration, Washington, D.C.

Phelps, Oliver Seymour and Andrew Servin. *The Phelps Family in America.*. Vol. 1, Pittsfield, MA: Eagle Pub. Co., 1899.

Phillips, Christopher. *Damned Yankee: the Life of General Nathaniel Lyon.* Baton Rouge: Louisiana State University, 1990.

Porter, Florence Collins and Helen Brown Trask. *Maine Men and Women in Southern California.* Los Angeles: Kingsley, Mason, and Collins, 1913.

Portland Daily Advertiser (Portland, Maine).

Portland Daily Press (Portland, Maine).

Portland Evening Express (Portland, Maine).

Portland Freedmen's Aid Society. Pamphlet. Maine Historical Society.

Portland Press Herald (Portland, Maine).

Portland Sunday Telegram (Portland, Maine).

Portland Transcript (Portland, Maine).

Pratt, Joan D. Untitled manuscript, n.d. Ruth Mayhew Tent #14, Rockland, Maine.

Reed, William Howell. *The Heroic Story of the United States Sanitary Commission: 1861-1865.* Reprinted from the Christian Register. Boston: Geo. H. Ellis Co., 1910.

Regimental Correspondence Files. Maine State Archives, Augusta, Maine.

Relief Agencies Collection. Maine State Archives, Augusta, Maine.

Report of the Adjutant General of the State of Maine, for the Year 1863. Augusta: Stevens and Sayward, 1864.

Report of the Adjutant General of the State of Maine, for the Years 1864 and 1865. Augusta: Stevens and Sayward, 1866.

Rockland Free Press (Rockland, Maine).

Ropes, Hannah. *Civil War Nurse: The Diary and Letters of Hannah Ropes.* John R. Brumgardt, ed. Knoxville: University of Tennessee Press, 1980.

Rose, Emeline Proctor. Journals. Private collection.

Ross, Kristie. "Arranging a Doll's House, Refined Women as Union Nurses." *Divided Houses: Gender and the Civil War.* New York: Oxford University Press, 1992.

Sanitary Commission. *A Report to the Secretary of War of the Operations of the Sanitary Commission, and upon the Sanitary Condition of the Volunteer Army, its Medical Staff, Hospitals, and Hospital Supplies.* Washington, D.C.: Magill and Witherow, 1861.

The Sanitary Commission Bulletin (Philadelphia, PA). Various issues.

Schlaifer, Charles and Lucy Freeman. *Heart's Work: Civil War Heroine and Champion of the Mentally Ill.* New York: Paragon House, 1991.

Semi-Annual Report of the Maine Camp Hospital Association of Portland with Letters and Journals of Nurses. Portland: N. A. Foster and Co., 1863.

Simpson, Corelli C. W. *Leaflets of Artists.* Bangor: John H. Bacon, 1893.

Six Town Times (Freeport, Maine).

Skinner-Ropes Manuscript Collection. Special Collection Division, General Library, University of California, Riverside, California.

Small, Abner. *The 16th Maine in the War of the Rebellion.* Portland: B. Thurston Co., 1886.

Smith, Adelaide. *Reminiscences of an Army Nurse during the Civil War.* New York: Greaves Pub. Co., 1911.

Souder, Emily Bliss. *Leaves from the Battle-field of Gettysburg.* Philadelphia: Caxton Press, 1864.

Stanley, R. H. and G. O. Hall. *Eastern Maine and the Rebellion.* Bangor: 1887.

Stanton, Elizabeth Cady, Susan B. Anthony, and Matilda Joslyn Gage, eds., *History of Woman Suffrage, 1861-1876.* New York: Susan B. Anthony, 1881.

Stonemetz, Winifred. *Sarah Low: Dover's Civil War Nurse.* Dover, NH: Northern Colonist Historical Society, 1962.

The Story of One Regiment: The Eleventh Maine Infantry Volunteers in the War of the Rebellion: 1861-1865. New York: J. J. Little Co., 1896.

Stowe, Charles Edward. *The Life of Harriet Beecher Stowe.* Boston: Houghton Mifflin Co., 1891.

Straubing, Harold Elk, ed. *In Hospital and Camp: the Civil War through the Eyes of its Doctors and Nurses.* Harrisburg, PA: Stackpole Books, 1993.

Sturtevant, Lawrence M., ed. *Sarah Sampson and the Third Maine Regiment of Volunteers in the Civil War 1861-1865.* Privately bound collection of transcribed letters.

Teg, William. *History of Brownfield, Maine.* Cornish, ME: Carbrook Press, 1966.

Tolman/Pottle Family Papers. Maine Historical Society Library. Portland, Maine.

Union and Journal (Biddeford, Maine).

United State Sanitary Commission Reports. (Philadelphia, Pennsylvania).

U. S. Sanitary Commission Collection. Special Collections. New York Public Library.

Usher, Rebecca. Collection. Maine Historical Society. Portland, Maine.

War Department. *Construction of General Hospitals.* 20 July 1864.

Weekly Press (Philadelphia, Pennsylvania).

Werthheimer, Barbara Mayer. *We Were There: The Story of Working Women in America.* Pantheon, 1977.

Whitman, Walt. *Walt Whitman's Memoranda During the War & Death of Abraham Lincoln.* Facsimile. Bloomington: Indiana University Press, 1962.

Wiggin, Edward. *History of Aroostook County.* Presque Isle, ME: Star Herald Press, 1922.

Wiggin, Kate Douglas. *Rebecca of Sunnybrook Farm.* New York: Grosset and Dunlap, 1903.

Willis, N. P. "Lookings on at the War." *Home Journal.* Saturday, Aug. 31, 1861.

Wilmington Morning Star (Wilmington, N.C.).

Wittenmeyer, Annie. *A Collection of Recipes for the Use of Special Diet Kitchens in Military Hospitals.* U. S. Christian Commission, [1864?].

Wormeley, Kate. *The United States Sanitary Commission: A Sketch of its Purposes and its Work.* Boston: Little, Brown, 1863.

Yorke, Dane. *Men and Times of Pepperell.* Boston: Pepperell Manufacturing Co., 1945.

Young, Agatha. *The Women and the Crisis.* New York: McDowell, Oboensky, 1959.

Index

About the Author

Lynda L. Sudlow, who is, by profession, a librarian, currently resides in North Yarmouth, Maine. She has been an ardent student of history for many years and first became interested in the Civil War during the years she lived on Peaks Island, off the coast of Portland, Maine. Peaks Island boasts not one, but two large Victorian "cottages" which served as reunion halls and summer retreats for veterans of the 5th Maine Volunteer Infantry and the 8th Maine Volunteer Infantry in years past. Researching the history of the 5th Maine building prompted her interest in the war and in Civil War reenacting. Author of various articles for newspapers and magazines, plus two smaller books, *A Vast Army of Women* is her first "real" book.

THOMAS PUBLICATIONS publishes books about the American Colonial era, the Revolutionary War, the Civil War, and other important topics. For a complete list of titles, please visit our website at www.thomaspublications.com, or write to:

THOMAS PUBLICATIONS
P.O. Box 3031
Gettysburg, PA 17325